MISSION 101

The Untold Story of the SOE and the Second World War in Ethiopia

DUNCAN MCNAB

The
History
Press

Also by Duncan McNab

The Usual Suspect: The Life of Abe Saffron
The Dodger: Inside the World of Roger Rogerson
Dead Man Running (with Ross Coulthart)
Above the Law (with Ross Coulthart)

Cover image: Ken Burke (reclining) with old friends, Ted Body (behind) and Bill
Howell (right), and patriot troops resting on a riverbank in Ethiopia. *(Australian
War Memorial)*

First published in the UK 2012
First published by Pan Macmillan Australia 2011

The History Press
The Mill, Brimscombe Port
Stroud, Gloucestershire, GL5 2QG
www.thehistorypress.co.uk

British Library Cataloguing in Publication Data.
A catalogue record for this book is available from the British Library.

ISBN 978 0 7524 8269 9

Typesetting and origination by The History Press
Printed in Great Britain

CONTENTS

To the late Ken and Grace Burke, my thanks for adding lashings of zest to what would otherwise have been a fairly normal childhood

1

IT HITS THE FAN

On 1 September 1939, Hitler's forces invaded Poland. Two days later, at 11.15 a.m., Britain's Prime Minister Neville Chamberlain made an unprecedented live broadcast on the BBC from the Cabinet Room at Number 10 Downing Street. He told the British people, and those tuning in around the globe:

> This morning the British Ambassador in Berlin handed the German government a final note stating that, unless we hear from them by eleven o'clock that they were prepared at once to withdraw their troops from Poland, a state of war would exist between us. I have to tell you now that no such undertaking has been received, and that consequently this country is at war with Germany.

He finished the broadcast saying, 'It is evil things we will be fighting against – brute force, bad faith, injustice, oppression and persecution – and against them I am certain that right will prevail.'

Chamberlain's broadcast was followed by a broadcast from Buckingham Palace, in which King George VI told his people:

> In this grave hour, perhaps the most fateful in our history, I send to every household of my peoples, both at home and overseas, this message, spoken with the same depths of feeling for each one of you as if I were able to cross your threshold and speak to you myself. For the second time in the lives of most of us, we are at war. Over and over again we have tried to find a peaceful way out of the differences between ourselves and those who are now our enemies, but it has been in vain. We have been forced into a conflict, for we are called, with our allies, to meet the challenge of a principle which, if it were to prevail, would be fatal to any civilised order in the world.

Within minutes of the declaration of war, the first air-raid sirens were heard over England. The BBC fell briefly silent. During the silence, with many Britons believing a German air raid was imminent, a BBC journalist phoned New York, telling the expectant media pack that, 'Forty-five minutes ago, air-raid sirens broke the Sabbath morning. We are now sitting comfortably underground. The all-clear signal has been sounded and we will emerge into the sunlight to see what has happened.' Luckily, the plane that prompted the sirens was a friendly one, a French aircraft whose pilot had failed to file a flight plan.

In Australia, the arrival of another war just over two decades after the alleged 'war to end all wars' was not unexpected. Churches around Australia, then enjoying a far greater patronage than they do these days, were reporting record attendances, with prayers for peace being at the forefront of the day's religious pursuits.

The Sunday papers were reporting the growing tensions surrounding the deadline of Chamberlain's ultimatum to Hitler. French Prime Minister Edouard Daladier was quoted as observing dramatically, and with an accurate glimpse of the near future, that it was a 'question of saving the world'. On a lighter note, the father of Sydneysider and soon-to-be opera sensation Joan Hammond told the *Telegraph* that his daughter was about to hit the big-time in Vienna. He said:

> I am not at all worried. Joan has just signed a 12-month contract to sing at the Grand Opera House [in] Vienna. Part of her contract is free passage through Germany at any time. She could get to London if trouble started.

Luckily for Joan she was still in London, having just appeared at the Proms with Sir Thomas Beecham. Her Vienna career would be on hold for a few years. Japan, the papers assured us, had declared it would stay neutral.

On the soap boxes in Sydney's Domain – Australia's answer to London's Hyde Park Speakers' Corner – Mrs Adela Pankhurst Walsh was in full flight decrying the impending war and urging peace with Germany. She was the daughter of British suffragette Emmeline Pankhurst and sister of Sylvia Pankhurst, a vocal supporter of Ethiopian independence following its invasion by Italian forces almost four years earlier. Adela had emigrated to Australia in 1914 and married Tom Walsh of the Federated Seamen's Union of

Australasia. That Sunday, she was speaking on behalf of the 'Guild of the Empire', an anti-communist group she had founded, and was doing a fine job offending the sensibilities of Sydneysiders by insisting that Britain and, by association, Australia should not fight in Europe. In her mind, an anti-communist like Hitler and his cohorts was preferable as an ally, not an enemy. The crowd responded by hissing loudly. Mrs Pankhurst Walsh would end up being interned in 1942 for her advocacy of peace with Japan – not a popular move in a post-Pearl Harbor world.

By nightfall on that crisp early-spring day in 1939, most of Australia had settled in for a quiet Sunday night at home. On the menu were sandwiches made from the leftovers of the traditional Sunday roast lunch. Pubs were closed, but for those who hadn't thought to stockpile, the sly groggers that plied their trade out of discreet back doors could always be relied on for supplies. Though television had had its first public outing at that year's New York World's Fair it hadn't made it past shock-and-awe and into production. Radio with its news, serials, quizzes and music was still the Australian family's most popular form of in-home entertainment. It was at 9.15 that Sunday night that the ABC and all commercial networks interrupted their programming for a special broadcast by Prime Minister Robert Menzies.

Australia had been alerted to the declaration of war, not through the usual formal diplomatic channels, but instead by a naval signal that had been passed to Sir Frederick Shedden, then Secretary of the Department of Defence. The signal stated, 'Commence hostilities at once against Germany.' Within the hour, the Executive Council met at the Prime Minister's room in Melbourne's Commonwealth Offices. There was no doubt that the fight was on. Menzies wasted no time in talking to the Australian people.

The Prime Minister, echoing the sentiments of the King and the British Prime Minister Chamberlain – who, allowing for the time zones, had broadcast within the previous hour – told the Australian nation:

> Fellow Australians, it is my melancholy duty to inform you officially that, in consequence of the persistence by Germany in her invasion of Poland, Great Britain has declared war upon her and that, as a result, Australia is also at war. No harder task can fall to the lot of a democratic leader than to make such an announcement.

The broadcast was followed at 10.14 p.m. by a proclamation of war issued in Canberra. At 11.47 p.m., all military districts were formally notified that war had begun.

Within hours special editions of newspapers had hit the late-night newsstands. In Kings Cross paper sellers were mobbed by crowds hell-bent on getting the latest news and analysis. The call to arms was underway with radio announcements recalling naval officers and sailors to their ships. Militia units, made up of civilian volunteers, were mustered for compulsory 16-day training courses.

Pattie Menzies, wife of the Prime Minister, added a woman's perspective to what was about to befall Australian families. She told the *Daily Telegraph*:

> We do not know what the future holds, but I am quite confident the women of Australia will remain calm – will respond to any calls that may be made upon them just as they have responded so nobly before.

In Sydney's working-class inner-city suburb of Newtown, the *Daily Telegraph* reported a weeping Mrs S Childs commenting:

> It's just like the night of the outbreak of the last war. Tonight we were sitting comfortably at home in front of the fire saying that there surely could not be another war, when the broadcast was made and Bob had to go back to his ship.

World War I was still fresh in the minds of Australians, but these raw memories did little to deter the crowds that queued outside army barracks in the cities and major towns. There was a war on and the men of Australia didn't want to be spectators.

In the lead-up to the declaration, Australia had already been on high alert. The Defence Committee had met on 24 August and, anticipating the bad news, had put forward a range of recommendations including sending a mere 44 more troops to Darwin and enlisting a local militia to keep our northern border safe, installing guns at the Port Kembla steelworks, and placing guards at infrastructure installations important to the war effort such as railway yards, wireless stations and factories. Rifles and ammunition were sent to the far-flung outposts in Port Moresby and Rabaul in Papua New Guinea. Tensions ratcheted up a notch on 1 September when a telegram was sent from London stating, 'Precautionary stage awaited against Germany and Italy.'

The following day, the citizen militia forces were on high alert, and all military districts were ordered to man the coastal defences. With no Germans in sight, or any intelligence that they were en route to our island, it would be a long wait on the beaches. If nothing else, the public could rest a little easier for the preparations. The Japanese added further drama to the outbreak of war by changing their tune, announcing they would remain 'independent' rather than a more comforting 'neutral'. Thus our traditional enemy, Germany, was foremost in the fears of the Australian people. Nearly nine months later, Italy would join Germany, and become a fierce opponent of British, Australian and Allied forces.

Behind the bravado was a disturbing problem – Australia was not well equipped for a war either on the home front or on a far-flung battlefield. As historian Gavin Long observed:

> Britain lacked military equipment, and knew that the Dominions could not fully arm their own expeditionary forces; indeed that Australia for example, was still awaiting delivery of modest orders from Britain that had been lodged four years before . . . An additional curb on plans for a possible expeditionary force was provided by the fact that army staff were acutely aware of their lack of equipment and the time it would take to acquire it.

The first Allied casualty of World War II was thought to have been British Pilot Officer John Isaac of the RAF's 600 Squadron whose Bristol Blenheim light bomber crashed into Heading Street, Hendon in North London a little under two hours after Chamberlain declared war. Unfortunately, Australia's RAAF managed a similar landmark two days later when a Wirraway – a single-engine training aircraft that was adapted to light-bomber and ground-attack work for the war – crashed while landing at Darwin at 10.30 a.m. on 5 September 1939. The plane was one of five Wirraways and an Anson being ferried to 12 Squadron in Darwin for coastal patrols. On board were Flying Officer AV Dolphin and Corporal HW Johnson. Both were killed in the crash.

It wasn't until 28 September 1939 that the first Australian serviceman died in action against Germany. At the controls of his Bristol Blenheim, and over Germany on a reconnaissance mission, was RAF

Wing Commander Ivan Cameron, at the time on loan to Britain's 1010 Squadron. Though swift and manoeuvrable, the Blenheim was no match for the Luftwaffe fighter piloted by Feldwebel Klaus Faber, who sent the Allied bomber crashing to the ground just near Kiel, a city that was home to one of the Reich's largest naval bases and key shipyards. In the years that followed, around 39 000 Australians would join Wing Commander Cameron on the roll of the dead in what Winston Churchill called 'the unnecessary war'.

For the Australians who would soon join the war, many would have their first taste of action not in Europe against Germany, but in North Africa and the Middle East, against both the Germans and the Italians. A handful of those men would fight in a critical yet little known operation in Italian–dominated Ethiopia, spearheading the first operation of what became famous later in the war as the Special Operations Executive.

2

ITCHING FOR A FIGHT

On 9 September 1939 our comrades across the Tasman upped the stakes in the race to arms by announcing the formation of a special military force of 6600 volunteers for service at home or abroad. This put enormous pressure on Robert Menzies and his government to follow suit. The *Sydney Morning Herald* on Thursday, 14 September declared, 'The outward complacency of the Federal Government actually engaged in carrying on a war is beginning to arouse more than astonishment among the Australian public.' Menzies did not appear keen to rush headlong into war despite the urging of a bloodthirsty press. He chose to remain what these days might be called 'alert not alarmed' and to keep his ill-prepared forces closer to home, particularly with the disturbing behaviour of Japan, which was flexing its muscles in China, seizing coastal territories and valuable resources that would be handy in the prosecution of a broader war.

Menzies was still hedging his bets as he responded to the media clamour the following day on his regular Friday night radio broadcast, saying:

We are at war as part of the British Empire. Our strategic position may very well change from time to time according to the alignment of the combatant nations. At present time, the prime necessity is to ensure the defence of Australia itself. But it would be wrong to assume that throughout the duration of the war our duty would be circumscribed as that ... It may be that under some circumstances, Australian forces might be used to garrison some of the Pacific Islands, to cooperate with New Zealand, to release British troops at Singapore, or other posts around the Indian Ocean. Under other circumstances it may be practicable to send Australian forces to Europe.

He also used the broadcast to announce the creation of the 2nd AIF (Australian Imperial Force), following in the footsteps of World War I's 1st AIF – a division and auxiliary units comprising 20 000 men, made up of a brigade-strength group of around five thousand or more men from New South Wales, one from Victoria, and one from a compilation of the rest of the country. Privates and non-commissioned officers were required to be aged between 20 and 35, subalterns (officers below the rank of captain) under 30, captains under 35, majors under 40 and lieutenant colonels under 45. The volunteers would preferably be single men not in 'essential civil jobs', like those in manufacturing and transport industries.

In those early days of the war, the only problem facing the recruiters for the nation's armed services was too many volunteers. Finding 20 000 men to volunteer didn't seem a hard task; equipping them properly was another matter. It was something of a blessing for the government, many members of which recalled how the issue of conscription had divided Australia during World War I, and had been one of the motivations for Labor Prime Minister Billy Hughes swapping sides and becoming prime minister in a conservative Nationalist government. Taking a softer and more politically astute route this time, unmarried men over the age of 21 who hadn't already volunteered for service were called up for three months of training with the civilian militias, and could only serve within Australia and its territories. Unlike years later in the Vietnam war era, few publicly objected to their compulsory training.

Gavin Long wrote that:

> . . . the War Cabinet decided to inform the Dominions Office that the period needed to train the Second AIF even up to the stage where it might be possible to send units abroad for garrison duty and further training would afford a further opportunity for the international situation to clarify itself as to the possibility of the dispatch of an expeditionary force from Australia.

Menzies was slowly moving toward engagement.

The organisation responsible for the 2nd AIF was formed and called the 6th Division. Command was given to 52-year-old Major-General Thomas Blamey, a man with a distinguished military career and a penchant for scandal. During his term as Victoria's Police

Commissioner, he was almost arrested in a Melbourne brothel by his own police, who hadn't recognised their leader. The American general, Douglas MacArthur, later the Supreme Commander of the Allied Forces in the South West Pacific, said of his Australian colleague that he was 'sensual, slothful and of doubtful moral character but a tough commander likely to shine like a power-light in an emergency. The "best of the local bunch."'

Despite early predictions of a rush to join, by mid October 1940, only 3400 men had joined up in New South Wales; disappointingly, only 1200 were from a State-wide militia that numbered 25 000. Part of the problem, according to a Mr LM Long of Goodooga in the north-west corner of New South Wales who had driven into Coonamble to enlist, was Menzies and his fence-sitting. Long said:

> By this time there was a general atmosphere of unconcern, the Prime Minister's speeches telling everyone to carry on, and the decidedly 'carry-on' attitude of most people I met had its effect on me. At Walgett, when I announced I was going to enlist, the response was such that I began to imagine people looking at me with a surprised air. In Coonamble, Bob's girl had raised her eyes and said, 'But why?' I was beginning to feel half-hearted about it.

Despite the inauspicious beginning, Mr Long did enlist, and finished the war as Captain Long.

Gavin Long, the author not the aspiring soldier, wrote:

> Indeed, only the most resolute or the most carefree were likely to surmount official barriers and public indifference; yet those obstructions had the effect not only of selecting a force of splendid soldiers in the making, but, when reinforced by a conviction (which seems to have been fairly general) that the people as a whole were not greatly interested in their fate, of deeply influencing the character of the force and, by accident, breeding a sense of superiority which it never lost.

Long reported one recruit as saying:

> There was, I believe, a large body of men, perhaps the majority, who were adventurers at heart but common citizens by force of circumstance, how many of us are not who saw in this call a

glorious combination – the life of an adventurer with the duties of a citizen.

They certainly weren't in it for the money, with the average unmarried private receiving 5 shillings (50 cents) per day, which is a little under $A70 per day these days. Oddly, the volunteer militia men were on 8 shillings per day.

Many of the adventurers and aspiring soldiers, both young and old, who had queued outside Victoria Barracks in Sydney's Paddington, and at other recruiting hubs around New South Wales, would become founding members of a new regiment, the 2/1st Field Regiment, Royal Australian Army. In his history of the regiment, *Six Years in Support*, the author Eric Haywood, who joined up on 30 October 1939 and went on to win the Military Cross, observed of the early members of the regiment:

> The few among them who had fought in the First World War considered themselves to be the lucky ones who, among the thousands of veterans who tried to enlist, succeeded in convincing recruiting officers that ten years or so of their lives had never existed, instead of conveniently having been mislaid.

Haywood also observed:

> They were Australians. Whatever their civilian occupation, the plans they had laid for that spring of 1939 suddenly became insignificant. They came from behind a plough, a shop counter, a factory bench, a steering-wheel, an office desk or a lectern . . . The majority, however, knew nothing of war.

All would soon become 'gunners', and sport an in-depth knowledge of field guns – and later, the bitter knowledge of half a decade of war.

Volunteering for service early in October 1939 were four men who would be posted to the 2/1st Field Regiment. A little over a year later, however, they would find themselves not with their regiment on the battlefields of North Africa, but on a secret mission behind enemy lines in Ethiopia. Each of the four were in the last flush of youth. The oldest, at 33, was Sergeant Ronald Charles Wood, born on 28 April 1906 in Goulburn, New South Wales, the son of a well-to-do auctioneer. Wood had attended Sydney's prestigious King's School, the favoured haunt of country people desiring a good education for their sons. Wood was an experienced bushman with a love of adventure that had taken him to New Guinea as a rubber planter. At the outbreak of war he was between jobs, and staying with his parents who had by then moved to the Sydney beachside suburb of Manly. He was the only man involved in a committed relationship, and had, at the time war broke out, been planning to marry, something that was put on hold by his enlistment.

Next up was John Kenneth Burke, 33 years old, born on 26 June 1906, in Newcastle, and a man who had a number of claims to fame, including a developing reputation as one of the regiment's bad boys. He preferred to be called Ken because he didn't want to be confused with his father John, with whom he didn't get on. Ken was a gifted sportsman who had been sent to St Joseph's College in Sydney, then one of Australia's most influential private Catholic schools. Though not the most committed student, he was a fine athlete, excelling in tennis, swimming and rugby. On finishing school, he slipped into the family business, then one of the largest produce merchants in Australia. Thanks to his family's wealth and his sporting prowess, he was a well-known face in the New South Wales social scene. When in Sydney, it was a day at the Randwick races, drinks at the Long Bar of the Hotel Australia in Rowe Street and then dinner, dancing and perhaps a few more drinks at those classy Martin Place society establishments, Prince's or Romano's.

Ken became well known to the broader public as a very capable rugby full-back for Newcastle's Wanderers, and later the NSW Waratahs. In 1929 he stepped into the national spotlight as fullback for the Newcastle side when they played the New Zealand All Blacks. Ken was reported as 'the hero' and his 'handling throughout was delightful, and his kicks never failed for length and hardly ever for direction. His tackling was not, perhaps, the most distinguished feature of his play, but he usually had to deal with overwhelming numbers.' His talent for dealing with overwhelming numbers would come in very handy during his army career.

He met the All Blacks again that year, this time playing for Australia. 'Burke's Great Game' was the headline, with the journalist enthusing, 'the outstanding player for Australia was certainly Burke, the fullback. He gave a flawless display right through the piece, and capped his effort with a snap field goal.' Though of average height, he was solidly built and fitted the description of the classic Australian 'brick shithouse'.

William Rowland Howell, 30 years old, was born on 30 August 1909 into a family that could trace its roots back to the early days of the colony. Though born in Queensland, Bill's family had spent a chunk of his childhood in New South Wales where his father was a bank manager and a man devoted to the bush and understanding the culture of indigenous Australia. The family finally settled in genteel Bowral in the southern highlands not far from Sydney. Like Ron Wood, Bill attended The King's School, but in his case as a boarder. The school noted with faint praise, 'he achieved no outstanding distinctions at the school, but belonged to that majority who play their part *fortiter* and *fideliter* [bravely and faithfully] and uphold the good name of the school when they leave it'.

After King's, Bill, though not a keen student at school, proved himself to be a very keen student of the bush, helped along by his father's insights. In the lead-up to the war, he was the overseer of Summerland Hill Station at Ilfracombe in central Queensland. His employer, Mr P Sale, said of him:

> . . . he had wanted to join the air force. When he was rejected because he was too old, he picked the artillery as offering the most excitement. It was his first experience of the army but he was keen on anything he put his hand to, and I have no doubt he would be a first-class soldier in no time. He is a splendid bushman. Only a slightly built chap, he is all wire, and can travel all day without looking troubled. He has been knocking around the Queensland outback ever since he left [The] King's School, Parramatta.

Mr Sale, singing Bill's praises, went on:

> He was a jackaroo for several years and had been overseer of other stations before he came here. He told me that he once broke his arm when he was tossed from a horse he was galloping wildly across a paddock. But since I have known him I don't think any horse could throw him. He was always the first to undertake any sport or games and was always in the thick of things. He had a responsible job here, overseeing 62 000 acres and he did it well. He was a real man and always popular.

Like Ken Burke, Bill didn't mind a good time either, and was, like most bushmen, utterly practical. His then very young nephew David remembers finding his uncle, who had just travelled from Longreach to Point Piper in Sydney's well-to-do east, asleep in an empty bathtub – Bill reckoned it looked like the best place for him to catch a few hours sleep, and did so.

The youngest of the sergeants was Edmund Maxwell Body, 24 years old, born in Sydney on 15 September 1915. Ted's family were major players in the sheep industry, and were also reputed to be 'the best sheep men in Australia'. Ted came from the family property Bundemar near Trangie in the central west of New South Wales. He too was a King's School old boy, following in his father's footsteps. Unlike Bill Howell, the dashing, sociable and charismatic Ted ended up as school vice-captain, and excelled at shooting, tennis and rugby. In 1936 he toured England with the school's rugby team, rubbing shoulders and banging heads with lads from 'many of Britain's leading schools' as one paper noted of the tour. Though he listed his occupation as grazier, like Ken Burke he was a man about town, and a well-known face on the Sydney social scene. Ted had travelled to Sydney with close friend and cousin Malcolm Irving. Though the pair intended to serve together in the 2/1st, according to the family history, 'on 9 January 1940, one day before they were to sail, Mal was given the devastating news that he had tuberculosis and consequently was classified unfit for further service'. Though a small mercy, Mal had marched with his cousin and fellow soldiers through the Sydney streets the week before the bad news.

Body had enlisted in Marrickville in Sydney's inner west, Burke had enlisted at Hamilton, a Newcastle suburb, and both Howell and Wood had enlisted at Victoria Barracks. They were the adventurers Major Hayward had talked about. All were single – though Wood was poised to marry a local northern beaches girl at the time he volunteered – and all shared a physical nature and what family members described as a very strong larrikin streak. The epitome of the early volunteers.

In the first days of their training, Howell, Body, Wood, Burke and their fellow new recruits slipped the drab and shapeless khaki outfit of jacket and trousers unkindly nicknamed a 'giggle suit' and began a round of tiresome and occasionally invasive medical examinations at the Holsworthy Army Base on Sydney's south-western fringe. Their feet were assessed for their capacity to march long distances, their throats were checked, eye charts were recited, ears were inspected, and inevitably the new recruit would feel the chilly hand of the Army Medical Officer clasping a spot that he'd rather they didn't – and then be told to cough. With all medical boxes ticked, the other pressing task was to sign on the dotted line on the 'Attestation Form for special forces raised for service in Australia and abroad'.

The form covered a thumbnail of the recruit's past such as address, next of kin, religion and date and place of birth – the latter was problematic for some who recalled their families interned during World War I because they had a German name or ancestry. On the second page was the result of the medical examination, which for those about to enter service was '1. Fit for Class 1'. Underneath was the 'Oath of Enlistment' in which the aspiring soldier swore allegiance to serve:

> . . . our Sovereign Lord, the King, in the Military Forces of the Commonwealth of Australia until the cessation of the present time of war and twelve months thereafter or until sooner lawfully discharged, dismissed or removed, and I will resist His Majesty's enemies and cause His Majesty's peace to be kept and maintained, and that I will in all matters appertaining to my service faithfully discharge my duty according to law.

The oath was then either sworn, or, in what was a rather contemporary touch, affirmed, in the presence of an officer.

The wave of recruits into the army overwhelmed its infrastructure. Barracks and beds were in desperately short supply, so it was during their induction at Holsworthy that the freshly minted soldiers of the 2/1st AIF learned that they would be heading to nearby Ingleburn. The town was described rather colourfully by Major Haywood as, 'a quiet little country town sucking at the teat of its railway station. In the still air of those early spring mornings the locomotives laid a white feathery trail that hung like a canopy over the rails long after the train had gone.' He added, 'then the ground rose in steep grassy slopes that resembled the banks of a river to the undulating grazing-land sweeping away to the Nepean River at the foot of the Blue Mountains.'

Though Haywood may have been slightly moved by Ingleburn in the early morning, it could in part have been the after-effects of a long and chilly night of sleeping in a tent. With demand far exceeding expectations, the recruits were sent into what had recently been paddocks and scrubland. Building of rectangular prefabricated barracks was proceeding apace, and by the end of October 1939, 60 per cent of huts were completed. Men could now sleep on a straw mattress with blankets in a hut that offered each man a meagre 12 feet of floor space for recreation. (The space recommended for prison cells by the American Public Health Association was 'a minimum 60 square feet per person'.) All part of the training. But the bad news didn't end there. The place had no electricity, the roads were dirt and the grass and scrub had been trodden into dust, which, with the coming of a long, hot and dry summer would go on to be the cause of a unique local ailment, 'Ingleburn throat'. To add to their misery, the food was dreadful. The cooks weren't regular army, but volunteers who had made the mistake of bragging about kitchen expertise and swiftly found themselves 'volunteered' for cooking duties. Their bragging didn't translate into reality. Primitive kitchens didn't help the problem, and the supplies of 'fresh' meat were of dubious quality, and often had to be condemned. Good food was well down the Australian Army's list of priorities. The eclectic selection of men who had volunteered presented something of a challenge to the officers tasked to induct them into army life and train them to be effective soldiers and gunners. As Major Haywood wrote, 'The men themselves were not angels. At the beginning they were raw and untrained.' He also spoke volumes for the lot of an officer when he offered:

To them, the embodiment of an Australian solider was a man who regarded, with equal contempt, the enemy and superior officer. Their idea of a trained soldier was one who was ready and willing to fight, had been taught the rudimentary handling of an individual weapon, and then was told where to find and kill the enemy. There was no regimental tradition. The only peg they hung a mantle of pride on was their own individuality.

The army's traditional response to individuality was discipline, training and routine, all in generous measures – this was also born of the need to hone an effective fighting force. By 7 November the home of the 2/1st Field Regiment was inhabited by its commanding officer, Lieutenant Colonel LC Kelly, 21 officers and 577 enlisted men, including Wood, Body, Howell and Burke. The three King's men had known each other before the war, and each had taken quickly to Ken Burke, the fellow private-school man and rugby player. In a letter to his fiancée, Ron said his three mates had described Ken as a 'very fine chap indeed'.

The daily routine at Ingleburn began at 6 a.m. with reveille, the traditional military wake up call by bugle, and then morning ablutions. Those feeling a little under the weather could present themselves for sick parade at 6.30 a.m. Breakfast followed at 8 for an hour. At 9 a.m., things got serious, and it was time to learn the art of soldiering. For the 2/1st Field Regiment this was primarily about keeping themselves alive and becoming effective gunners. Most of the morning, through to a half-hour break for lunch at 1.30 p.m., was taken up training on 18-pounder guns and 4.5-inch howitzers. Training was regularly interrupted out on the dusty ranges with a necessary salt-water gargle in an attempt to keep the Ingleburn throat under control.

After lunch, it was back to work on the big guns, or to exercise in the paddocks, or to learn how to use smaller weapons, a task made a little tricky because these weapons were still in short supply. Training was not just for the enlisted men, with all from the commanding officer down to the youngest and newest of soldiers participating. There was not much point heading into battle if everyone didn't have the same baseline of knowledge – weapons weren't much good if you didn't know how to use them. The soldiers called the day over at 5.30 p.m. and went to dinner. The officers dined an hour later at 6.30 p.m. Lights out at 10.15 p.m. However, as their proficiency improved, night exercises were introduced. As Major Haywood noted, 'training did progress and the unit reached a stage where that most difficult, and most essential task, the occupation of gun positions during darkness, could be carried out with reasonable success.'

What the new soldiers learned from all this was that their task, as gunners, was to work as a team. As the Major also said, 'the drivers, technical assistants, medical orderlies and even the much maligned cooks were all essential, if not spectacular, components of a regiment of field artillery.' While only one man pulled the firing lever, it was the culmination of the well-rehearsed process of a team, and a process that recommenced as the firing lever was pulled. The team combined the skills of the men who kept the ammunition supplied, the 'observers' who directed fire to the target and changed the direction of fire as the shells hit the ground. And then there were the signallers who maintained contact with other gunners, and their commanders. It was this training that formed the strong bonds of trust and respect between men, which would stand the four in good stead when they were operating behind enemy lines in Ethiopia a year later.

The only note of disquiet during the training period was the grumpiness of the recruits who, quite reasonably as it turned out, thought they were being rorted by the private contractors operating the canteen where they could pick up a few luxuries to make life easier. In mid November they did something that was unusual for a disciplined force – they held a demonstration to protest their case. Someone was a little savvier than average, and as the demonstration got underway, reporters from the Sydney press arrived to record the moment. What was described as a 'blot on the good name of the Second AIF' was in fact effective, with the private contractor being removed, the army installed to operate the canteen, and the prices dropping dramatically. Peace, at least in Ingleburn, was returned.

On 23 November the rumour mill was in full swing, speculating that a long sea voyage for the regiment was looming. In Europe, Poland had surrendered to Germany, and around one hundred and sixty thousand troops from the British Expeditionary Force had been sent to France and were stationed along the borders of Belgium and Germany. Rumours had been spurred on by the announcement three days before by New Zealand, committing the first of their expeditionary force to service overseas. What the recruits didn't know was that Australia would respond again to the Kiwi lead, with the Cabinet deciding that the 6th Division could be committed overseas when they had reached a satisfactory level of training.

When a round of vaccinations for all troops began on 4 December at the Ingleburn camp, the men knew their departure was at hand. Confirmation of their impending deployment arrived two days before Christmas, when the regiment was given a few days' pre-embarkation leave. Though their destination remained unconfirmed, the vaccinations, combined with the latest news, made the Middle East a good bet. It would have been an even better bet if the men had known that on 15 December, Colonel George Vasey, a World War I veteran, along with 50 officers and 60 other ranks from the Australian Army, joined a similarly sized group of New Zealanders and sailed to Palestine on board the nearly new P&O liner SS *Strathallan*. Their task was to find a suitable training area for the 2nd AIF. Their departure was kept a well-guarded secret.

Back at Ingleburn, Christmas passed and on the men's return from leave after the New Year hangovers, a flurry of activity began, starting with practical medical matters like X-rays and blood grouping. Guns were taken out to the range and tested to make sure they were ready for battle. Entertainment came courtesy of films, newsreels and lectures which were – much to the amusement of the troops – on the risks of venereal disease in foreign lands. Major-General John Northcott, a Gallipoli veteran and the recently appointed Deputy Chief of General Staff, popped by to bring the officers up to speed on their destination, and to provide a little motivation. His arrival also confirmed their destination (though not to the enlisted men) as he delivered a lecture with the rather uninspiring title of 'Palestine Generally'.

On Thursday, 4 January 1940, minus those who were out on the Green Hills Artillery Range working the guns, the regiment joined their fellow soldiers who formed the new 2nd AIF and marched through the streets of Sydney's central business district. The 6000-strong contingent stopped at the Cenotaph in Martin Place to salute their forebears from World War I's 1st AIF. Taking their salute was the Governor-General, Lord Gowrie, holder of the Victoria Cross for his bravery in the Sudan War in 1898. The regiment marched to Central Station at 3 p.m. for transport back to Ingleburn. Beleaguered Sydney commuters these days might be surprised to hear that the regiment's war diary recorded 'arrangements for this march were excellent and the cooperation given by NSW Government Railways deserves special mention and praise'. The *Sydney Morning Herald*, now much happier to see plenty of men in uniform, enthused:

> The long khaki columns thrilled the heart of Sydney as it had not been thrilled for a quarter of a century, since that still spring day in 1914 when the First AIF marched through the same streets on its way to Anzac and imperishable glory . . . the marching was magnificent.

For the families of those marching, there was the fervent hope that not all of the Anzac history would be repeated.

After their very successful march through the city, it was back to the reality of preparation for war, and time was very short. The night of 5 January was taken up with tactical exercises and shooting practice for all the troops. This exercise marked the end of their formal training on Australian soil and it was then the troops were told of their destination. The next time their guns would fire would be in the Middle East. Originally, the Government had planned for the troops to receive further training in the Middle East followed by deployment to France, but with the capitulation of the French in the middle of 1940, coinciding with Italy's declaration of war, these plans would change dramatically.

The following morning the business of moving and loading their transport to Palestine got underway. From 7 to 9 January the regiment loaded their guns and equipment aboard a ship designated as HMT U5, better known to the travelling public as the Orient Lines RMS *Orford*, a well-loved passenger liner and a familiar sight in Sydney Harbour.

At 6.45 a.m. on 10 January 1940, the new and rather tired soldiers of the 2/1st Field Regiment AIF marched out of their barracks at Ingleburn, joining their compatriots in the 2nd AIF from other parts of the camp, and headed to the nearby Ingleburn railway station. Rather than Major Haywood's 'occasional train' stopping at the little station, this morning there were special trains waiting to speed them toward the docks at Pyrmont where the *Orford* waited. The operation went smoothly, with the war diary noting, 'the administration and transport arrangements for this move were very commendable and the organisation for same reduced confusion to a minimum'.

Though their departure had not been reported in the Australian media, word had spread quickly, and the foreshores of Sydney Harbour were packed with people waving farewell to the first Australian troops to leave for World War II. The *Orford* slipped her berth at Pyrmont at 12.42 p.m. and made her way up the harbour. Major Haywood captured the moment, writing:

> ... there were few men who were not moved by the enthusiasm of that send-off. Most of them had never sailed out of Sydney Harbour before and the sparkling expanse of water looked at its

midsummer-time best. They knew that war must take its toll, and it was natural they should wonder whether or not this might be their last glimpse of a real scene equal to any in the world.

Among the thousands that sailed that morning were Burke, Howell, Body and Wood. They would be joined by their new commanding officer and the five Australians who would soon be part of what historians now believe to be the first mission of the Special Operations Executive. The five would play a pivotal role in the ousting of Italian forces that had invaded and colonised Ethiopia five years before. What they didn't know was that another Australian, Arnold Wienholt – a politician, big game hunter, pastoralist, spy, and, like Burke, a 'household name' in the early decades of 20th century Australia – would be there a little before.

3

THE GANG OF FIVE
GO CRUISING

On board the *Orford* that morning were Burke, Howell, Wood and Body, now sergeants. It was here they met the officer who had been assigned to control the four individualists. He was Allan Hooper Brown: lean and handsome, six foot two, 25 years old and born on 3 April 1914. Allan was born in the Melbourne suburb of Caulfield, the son of a builder. The family moved to Sydney when Allan was still a child, and settled on the north shore around Mosman. Unlike his mates, Allan was a public school boy who had finished his education and joined the Commonwealth Bank as a bank officer like one of his brothers.

Another brother was an army staff sergeant. At the declaration of war, Allan was a member of the militia, and he enlisted on 21 December 1939 in Sydney. Allan missed the Ingleburn barracks sojourn of the new recruits. With his militia background, his training was brief, and he was quickly kitted up and shown aboard the RMS *Orford* with the rest of 2/1st Field Regiment – just over two weeks from bank officer to military officer and on the way to war.

Over their few short months of training at Ingleburn, Body, Burke, Howell and Wood had become fast friends. Upon Brown's arrival, the four sized up their newly minted lieutenant; they had met quite a few officers in their short service history, ranging from the uninspiring through to martinets, and in their new officer they found a man who wasn't 'in awe of himself' as Ken Burke noted, and was someone they respected for the man he was rather than his rank. The army had got it right. It was a working relationship, and ultimately a friendship, that despite the inconvenience of rank would grow during the long voyage, and later on in the arduous months of training before the five headed off on their hazardous mission into Ethiopia.

After slipping her mooring, the *Orford* was joined by her fellow Orient Liners *Otranto*, *Orcades*, the P&O liner *Strathnaver*, all laden with troops, and one of their escorts, the British battleship HMS *Ramillies*, which were all moored further up the harbour.

What the men didn't know until they passed through the Heads and into the Tasman Sea was that there were more ships to come. Waiting for them out of sight of land – and the prying eyes of any German spy – was the rest of the convoy, designated as US1, carrying soldiers from New Zealand and including some other ships well known to Sydneysiders. Leading the convoy was another Orient Liner pressed into service as a troop carrier, the *Orion*, and *Strathnaver*'s sister ship, *Strathaird*. Less known to the locals were the Canadian Pacific Steamships' *Empress of Canada*, the New Zealand Shipping Company's *Rangitata*, the Poland–South America Line's *Sobieski* and the British troop ship *Dunera*.

Even though there were no reports of German raiders in the area, the convoy was heavily protected. The Revenge class British battleship HMS *Ramillies* led the escort. She had come into service near the end of World War I and was both slow and obsolete when compared to the newer battleships in the British fleet. However, with a main armament of eight 15-inch guns that could lob a shell weighing 870 kilograms some 26 or so kilometres, she still had sufficient firepower to make an enemy vessel think twice about engaging her. With the *Ramillies* was the slightly more modern HMAS *Australia*, a County Class heavy cruiser launched in 1928 and another County Class cruiser of similar vintage, HMAS *Canberra* and the Town Class light cruiser HMAS *Adelaide*. Like the *Ramillies*, the *Adelaide* was well past her prime but could still pack a punch. She was nicknamed HMAS *Long Delayed* because her construction had started in 1915, and although she was launched in 1918 she was not completed until 1922. Early delays were caused by lack of materials due to World War I, and then later by the need for modifications based on the experiences of similar ships during the war.

HMAS *Australia* would make it through the war with a dazzling record of achievement. The *Canberra* was lost at the Battle of Savo Island on 9 August 1942, with 193 of her company killed. The *Adelaide*, given her age, spent most of the war on convoy and patrol duty in the Pacific and Indian Oceans.

An army diarist, Corporal Roland Hoffman, flushed with excitement by his departure toward the war, recorded the moment:

It was an unforgettable sight to see these ships, flanked by war-ships of the British and Australian navies. They kept in perfect formation – it seemed as if their engines might be throbbing in unison. Here were approximately 13 000 troops on their way. Here was the spearhead of Australia and New Zealand's challenge to Nazism, or any other 'ism' that might menace the Empire and democracy at large.

The convoy headed south along the coast of New South Wales, and on 12 January 1940 was joined by the troop carrier *Empress of Japan* sailing out of Melbourne. She was carrying men from the 6th Division Headquarters, which, along with its leader General Blamey, had been based in Melbourne.

The problem with convoys was that their progress was dictated not by the needs of military and political masters but by the maximum speed of the slowest ship, and so the convoy cruised along at 12 knots (twenty two kilometres per hour), thanks to the tortoise-like pace of the *Dunera*. The *Dunera*'s speed wasn't the only concern she caused: as a coal-burning ship, she occasionally coughed a large cloud of highly visible black smoke, thus making the convoy even more obvious to any enemy vessel in the vicinity. With the scenes on Sydney Harbour to mark the convoy's departure and *Dunera*'s bad habits, the convoy's voyage did not get off to a discreet start.

Morale on board the *Orford* was high for the 2/1st Field Regiment and their fellow shipmates from the 2/1st Australian General Hospital. There was adventure in front of them, and the voyage, thanks to the comforts of a passenger liner pressed into service as a troop carrier, looked to be a comfortable one. As Major Haywood noted in *Six Years in Support*, soldiers found:

> . . . hot baths (including the choice of fresh or sea water) in massive tubs gushing through the wide gauge taps. Swimming in the ship's pool was permitted and the crew kept it clean. After the hot summer weeks at Ingleburn, it was a pleasure to walk along the well-scrubbed decks, a brisk wind blowing in one's face, watching the antics of the porpoises following the ship's wake.

The food was also up to the standards of a liner, with the men enjoying a menu normally reserved for paying passengers. The war diary, a diary of daily occurrences kept by the regiment's administrators, reported:

... living and messing conditions aboard are admirable, but owing to the increase of personnel on board over a normal passenger run the training and recreational space is very limited. Food is excellent, well prepared, the menus offering a big variety and the men are very contented in this regard. A typical dinner for the troops comprises soup, roast beef, cabbage, lima beans, potatoes and stewed fruit for dessert.

There was also a 'wet canteen', which came in very handy for after-dinner drinks on balmy summer nights. The onboard medical officers noted the canteen was almost therapeutic, giving the men 'an outlet for their abundant energy and a pleasant means of spending the evening after their duties had been performed'. For the men, it was the opposite of the dust, huts and poor food of the Ingleburn barracks.

The virgin sailors had their first taste of true ocean adventure when the convoy entered the Great Australian Bight and encountered the customary large and rough seas. The troops were made of stern stuff, however, and their enjoyment of the food and canteen was not hampered by lousy weather and seasickness. Australian troops, it seemed, came equipped with fine sea legs.

Their first port of call on the voyage was Fremantle, which was reached on the afternoon of 18 January 1940. The *Orford* waited offshore for the night, and then made her way to a berth the next morning. Everyone, except those for whom duty called, was given leave from 2 p.m. until midnight. The troops were welcomed into homes within the cities of Perth and Fremantle, and into the hotels and other establishments where a little fine company could be found. As Major Haywood reported:

... they found themselves guests at exclusive clubs or had great difficulty in paying for their own drinks at any corner pub. Perth was handed to them during their stay, and its rightful owners felt relief when they got it back, slightly the worse for wear, on 20th January.

The major also noted, 'there were incidents in plenty – most of them humorous, but some boisterous to a degree where they ceased to be funny. The hospitality and tolerance of those citizens of Fremantle and Perth were tested to the limit.'

'Sticky' Wilson, one of the troops, recalled, 'one day's leave, and bless them, they gave us 10 shillings pay for our day out.' One hospitable local dropped Sticky and his mates at the Perth RSL where, he said:

All First War diggers, fighting for our company. We were first in the club of the convoy. Stayed for a couple of hours, then went for a walk around. The police were very good natured, allowing our fellows to direct traffic and making allowance for the fact that the hotels were providing free beer. What a sight it was to see at the end of the day. Aussie soldiers and sailors, Kiwis, French sailors, English sailors, all making their way to Fremantle, mostly by tram and pretty merry.

For those less alcoholically inclined there was an outdoor screening of the hit film *Goodbye Mr. Chips* starring Robert Donat and Greer Garson.

Historian and author Craig Stockings, writing in *Bardia: Myth, Reality and the Heirs of Anzac*, offered a slightly more entertaining view:

In company with the New Zealanders, the soldiers of the first convoy took the opportunity to wreak considerable havoc in the town, drinking heavily, commandeering fire engines and trams, and even depositing a car on the steps of the general post office.

However, both Perth and the 2/1st AIF got through the experience relatively unscathed. When the convoy departed, they had a total strength of 34 officers and 583 other ranks, a reduction of 12 soldiers from their number on arrival. Seven had been discharged, or as Major Haywood kindly put it, 'it was considered that the war was more likely to be won without the aid of seven of the regiment's other ranks' and five came to the same conclusion on their own and didn't bother heading back to the ships.

Many of the men on board that morning, as the convoy sailed from Fremantle, would be among the nearly 40 000 Australian servicemen who would never see their families or Australia again. For men like Allan Brown, Ken Burke, Ron Wood, Bill Howell and Ted Body it was the first step in what would be years of continuous fighting, relieved by only brief periods back at home, either on leave or in hospital recovering from wounds or the litany of diseases that are part of war in Africa or the tropics. Many of these men would still be in the fight as the war drew to a close in Europe and then later in the Pacific.

News of the convoy's departure from the Australian mainland was broadcast around the world by German radio, which provided a bit of humour for those on board not suffering too badly from a hangover. As they left Fremantle, they were joined by the French heavy cruiser *Suffren*. Later in her career, as Germany swarmed through France, the *Suffren* was surrendered to the British rather than be allowed to fall into German hands or the control of the Vichy Government. She was then put into service with the British navy, and ended her career after the war in the bombardment of the Vietnamese port of Haiphong, one of the triggers for the war in Indochina that ended up with another generation of Australians heading overseas to fight. In addition to the *Suffren* was the Royal Navy's HMS *Kent*, and both she and the *Suffren*, along with the elderly Australian destroyers *Vampire* and *Voyager*, had been on the hunt around Java and Sumatra for any German ships heading home, or for German raiders keen to prey on Allied shipping.

With the arrival of the two new cruisers, the ships of the Australian Squadron left the convoy around 5.30 p.m. on 20 January. Now in the Indian Ocean, the convoy was more attuned to the risk of attack by submarine, so lookouts were posted on all ships from 4.30 a.m. to 8 p.m. In addition to increased vigilance, the troops were required to wear gas masks around their necks during the morning parade, and in the 'gas alert' position from 10.30 a.m. to 11.30 a.m., when they wore the mask over their faces, thus making conversation rather tricky, but as with their weapons, familiarity was the key to survival. The only other notable occurrence on this first leg of the journey was an instruction to all troops advising of the danger of sitting on a ship's railing. The warning was a little late for one soldier on the *Otranto* who took an accidental dive backward into the Indian Ocean; luckily the ship's propellers missed him, and he was picked up by the *Rangitata*. When not muttering into gas masks, watching for submarines or avoiding falling overboard, the men trained, honing their weapons and their tactical and leadership skills.

The naval ships joined the training regime by exercising their guns, and the transports had a spot of practice laying smoke screens in the event of needing to hide from the enemy. As they came into radio range, the occasional broadcast of Nazi propaganda by the

Third Reich's plummy-toned Lord Haw-Haw added some amusement for the bored soldiers, particularly when the men on the *Orford* found that their ship had been sunk, along with the *Orcades*. According to Lord Haw-Haw, everyone on board both ships had perished. Lord Haw-Haw was toasted in the wet canteen as both vessels sailed on.

Boxing was the perfect sport for the limited deck space: it provided exercise, entertainment and spectacle as well as the opportunity for a spot of gentlemanly gambling. Ken Burke, a fine sportsman, acquitted himself well in the ring, while his three fellow sergeants, Body, Howell and Wood provided enthusiastic support from ringside. Burke also reckoned they made a little bit of money thanks to his prowess. The four sergeants and the rest of the enlisted men also threw themselves into mock horse races, reliving the great racing triumphs at Royal Randwick and the Melbourne Cup racing carnival. Thoroughbreds were replaced by finely bred wooden horses, and bookmakers prowled the decks, tending to the needs of the happy and the luckless punters.

In keeping with maritime tradition, the crossing of the equator was marked by the traditional ceremony featuring King Neptune and the induction into the King's court of those who hadn't crossed before. The large number of inductees made the usual ceremony, in which the inductees were subjected to creative, embarrassing and often messy tasks like being forced to crawl through garbage, put into stocks or body painting, a little tricky, so all officers and 40 other ranks were selected for initiation into 'The Solemn Mysteries of the Ancient Order of the Deep' – a good opportunity for a little fun at the expense of the officers if nothing else, and it certainly put a little zest into a long sea voyage.

As January drew to an end, the men got their first whiff of a different world, when the unmistakable blend of charcoal smoke, perfume and decay was on the wind. Land was not far away.

On 30 January the convoy arrived at the port of Colombo in what was the British colony of Ceylon. In *The First at War*, EC Giveny described the harbour:

> What a crowded scene! Merchant ships, naval ships, local small craft, and frenzied activities were everywhere. Anchored nearby were a French troop ship and, to our surprise, because Japan, though not at war, was decidedly 'in the other camp', a Japanese

merchantman, brightly painted and bedecked with flags. Bumboats closed in and small boys, high in their rigging, called, 'I di, I di,' meaning they were offering to dive for any pennies thrown into the water.

They were joined by some of the Australians who couldn't resist the chance to show off.

The ships moored inside the breakwater midmorning, and immediately began refuelling and restocking. All troops were ferried ashore, and then marched through the Ceylonese capital's streets to 'B' Echelon Barracks. For the young Australians it was a dramatic change from the bush or the neat suburban streets of home. Major Haywood said of his first taste of a very foreign port:

> For all aboard, landfall was a welcome relief from the tedious voyaging and a sharp reminder that home was behind them. A busy port contrasted with the quiet unhurried life of the hinterland; modern hotels with the native bazaars; limousines with rickshaws, and the ostentatious splendour of temples with the squalor of a native mother lying amid the rubbish on the pavement while a naked baby fought with the flies for possession of an equally naked breast. The clean, well-ordered life of equality in Australia seemed a long, long way off.

Armed with wide-eyed wonder, a sense of adventure and pockets full of money they had converted into the local currency at the barracks, the young Australians grasped the chance to experience as much as possible in Colombo in the day and a half allotted to them. Colombo was at their mercy. For those who preferred pursuits other than a 'pleasant walk through the colonnaded shopping centre near the sea front, shaded by the palm trees to sample the local refreshments', as Major Haywood reported, the thoughtful and experienced medical staff had made sure each soldier was equipped with a 'rubber sheath' – though they weren't boy scouts, the army wisely thought that in the days before effective antibiotics it was best to always be prepared.

All over Colombo the troops and sailors sweated in their woollen uniforms bargaining with local vendors for must-have souvenirs. Local entertainers coaxed cobras out of baskets and coins out of the visitors' pockets.

At the end of their brief freedom, they returned to the barracks and marched back to the jetty. After the long slog across the Indian Ocean, they'd seized the opportunity for a bit of fun on dry land, and not all were on their best behaviour. Of their leave in Colombo, Craig Stockings wrote that although:

> ... strict lectures were given on bearing and behaviour, such efforts had little effect. As senior Australian officers were entertained at Government House, powerful arak liquor flowed liberally in the city. The Australians again ran amuck with, among other incidents, soldier-drawn rickshaw races adding to the chaos.

The convoy departed Colombo on the morning of 1 February, minus the *Empress of Japan*, *Orcades*, *Otranto* and *Orion*, which were still taking on supplies and would catch up. The French troop ship *Athos* joined the convoy, along with HMS *Sussex* and the Royal Navy's aircraft carrier, HMS *Eagle*. The *Eagle* was one of the first aircraft carriers in the Royal Navy, and had started life in 1911 as a superdreadnought battleship destined for the Chilean Navy. She made it through until 11 October 1942 when she was sunk by torpedoes fired from the German submarine *U73*. Her arrival on the convoy brought with it a little excitement, when during exercises one of her planes crashed into the sea, but luckily there were no casualties.

On 5 February the *Ramillies* provided another break in the monotony of the voyage, when the old battleship departed, signalling the convoy, 'God speed. Good luck. Safe return.' The Australians would hear from her again when she bombarded the Italian-occupied Libyan port of Bardia in August 1940. As the group moved toward the Suez Canal, its numbers further reduced with the departure of *Athos* heading toward Djibouti and the *Strathaird*, *Empress of Japan*, *Orion*, *Rangitata* and *Orcades* heading toward Aden on 8 February. The next day, the comforting sights of HMS *Sussex* and HMS *Eagle* slipped from view as they left the convoy just near the colourfully named Hell's Gate, a narrow strip of water marked by a lighthouse, surrounded by utterly desolate land and quite a few wrecks. It also meant that the Suez Canal and their destination were close at hand.

As the convoy motored toward the Canal, the onboard training regime came to an end and preparations for landing began. With the area comfortably in Allied control, anti-submarine lookouts ceased, as did the decidedly unpopular gas-mask drills. The jokes about how they had improved the soldiers' looks had worn off a long time before. Though they had had some bumps on their way across the Bight, the journey across the Indian Ocean had been day after day of strong sun, flat blue seas and an empty horizon. The medical officers on board noted of the men, 'they appeared to be content, but signs of boredom appeared towards the end of the trip'. By the time they caught their first sight of Suez, the men were ready for dry land.

In their report of the journey, the doctors also noted that while the ship's medical facilities were more than satisfactory, the regiment's medical equipment was 'totally inadequate', which is not a promising prospect for men heading into battle. The 'rubber sheaths' had obviously done their work well, or the lads had just been very well behaved, with only 12 cases of venereal disease reported. State-of-the-art treatment in 1940 involved putting them into an isolation ward and deploying some rather unpleasant remedies. The doctors were also proud of their 'solely prophylactic' treatment for those who thought they might be at risk – as the Senior Medical Officer reported:

> On return to the ship, those exposed to infection received urethral irrigation with 1/4000 potassium permanganate solution. This combination prevented many cases of V.D. I am sure the issuing of calomel ointment would be an additional safeguard.

The punishment may well have exceeded the crime.

4

FOLLOWING THE LIGHT HORSE

On 8 February 1940 the convoy entered the Red Sea, passing the Twelve Apostles of the Island of Perim. The soldiers' view was of sand stretching toward distant peaks and plateaus and a bare red and unforgiving landscape – the exact opposite of their home. At 8.30 a.m. on 12 February, the *Orford* entered the Suez Canal and by 1 p.m. it was at Ismailia, the control centre for the Canal and about halfway between Port Said and Suez, around 120 kilometres by road to Cairo.

The soldiers' arrival in Egypt was marked by Britain's Secretary of State for the Dominions, the Right Honourable Anthony Eden, who boarded the *Otranto* and met with the 16th Brigades commander, Brigadier Allen, and his staff. Eden was no stranger to war, having been commissioned into the King's First Rifle Corps in World War I, and finding himself in the midst of the Battle of the Somme. At the age of 19, the young officer saved the life of a fellow officer and was later awarded the Military Cross for his bravery. Many of the Australians on board the *Orford* also remembered the Somme. Nearly 5000 Australians were killed or wounded in the battle, which was described by the ABC's Kerry O'Brien as, 'the single bloodiest day in this nation's history. Barely a household in Australia remained untouched by the terrible toll of fighting on the Western Front.' It was Eden's solemn task to welcome the Australian troops into the new war on what by then was close to dawn on a wet and cold day. In response Eden was given a glimpse of the Australian sense of humour – and the lack of respect for hierarchy – when he told the men that King George VI had said how appreciated the new arrivals were. One wit in the crowd yelled, 'Did he say anything about us getting any bloody pay?' Eden politely laughed along with the crowd.

With Eden was General Archibald Wavell, who commanded all the British forces in the Middle East. Wavell confirmed the dim

view the troops had of officers – and British officers in particular – when he told them they were 'under my command and will
carry out my orders'. It wasn't a fine diplomatic moment and did
little to support the authority of the Australian officers, who had
their hands full controlling their free-spirited troops.

The *Orford* then made her way through the Bitter Lakes and
at 3.30 a.m. the next day arrived at the huge military camp of
El Kantara.

The men disembarked the *Orford* at the brisk pace of 35 men to
the minute. Forty-five minutes later they had boarded their train,
and at 6 a.m. the train pulled out of El Kantara station and headed
into the gathering day. Allan Brown, Ken Burke, Ted Body, Ron
Wood and Bill Howell and their fellow soldiers from the 2/1st
Field Regiment had their first glimpse of the Mediterranean as
their train swept through the Sinai toward Gaza and their last stop,
Al Majdal on the shores of the Sea of Galilee. Of the trip, Major
Haywood said:

> ... here and there little oases in the desert appeared and were
> rapidly left behind. For most of the journey all that could be
> seen were rolling sand-dunes and all of those in the comparative
> comfort of the train thought of the last generation of Australians,
> so many of whom had sweated and fought their way over the
> same country. Various wayside stations bore the names of battles
> famous during the Sinai Campaign, fought a quarter of a century
> earlier. El Arish, Romani and Gaza were typical of these.

The major neatly caught the thoughts of many of the young travellers moved by their new environment when he wrote somewhat
poetically:

> To many on the train these first glimpses of Palestine must have
> brought similar thoughts to those travellers of long ago, who
> were guided to Canaan, a land 'flowing with milk and honey'.
> Palestine in its early morning garb had a clean, fresh look. The
> young wheat was just showing through the brown earth while
> the fringes of the rail track and land not under cultivation
> bedecked itself with innumerable Flanders poppies, their bright
> red in vivid contrast to the predomination of brown and green.

From the station it was a short trip to the regiment's new home at Qastina, a village and army camp on an elevated site on the coastal plain between Jerusalem and Al Majdal.

Beating the Australians to Qastina was the Machine Gun Battalion 2nd AIF, which had erected enough tents for all the new arrivals. Officers and sergeants fared slightly better, having huts for their messes and the administrative offices. In the first days there was running water, but no sides or roofs on the showers and toilets. The Australians got to know each other better than they had anticipated, or wanted to.

Down in the important part of the camp – the kitchen – cooks from the British Army's 1st Battalion Argyle and Sutherland Highlanders, the Blackwatch and the Royal Horse Artillery Regiment were busy preparing a warm welcome for the newcomers. Australian beer, an important commodity carried on the convoy from Sydney, was in good supply. The war diary reported that 'their work was excellent', a surprising comment considering the state of British cookery at the time – or maybe just reflective of Australia's equally indifferent food scene.

On 14 February they rested, got used to walking around on dry land, and did mundane tasks such as laundry and straightening out their kit. The villagers nearby busied themselves growing citrus and bananas, and tending their flocks; surrounding them were undulating fields, orchards under irrigation, Arab villages and the occasional kibbutz surrounded by high barbed-wire fences. Sheep, cattle and mules, usually tended by local boys, grazed indolently on the fringe of the camp. With the domestic duties done, many of the men settled down to write their first letters home to their families, who were keenly awaiting news from this exotic and foreign land. Highlights from the letters sent home by Burke, Wood, Howell and Body would later be collated by their mothers and then circulated between them and their families – a habit that would continue until the men finally returned to Australia.

At 10.15 the next morning, after ablutions and a shaking of their boots to make sure a scorpion hadn't taken up residence overnight, the men were lined up on the roads of Qastina Camp to be inspected by the Right Honourable Anthony Eden. His inspection coincided with the arrival of their guns, most of which had made the journey intact. The regiment then marched to nearby Julis Camp where other parts of the 2nd AIF were camped and General

Wavell addressed them for an hour and 45 minutes. As Craig Stockings reported, Wavell's visit was another defining moment in the Australian–British relationship: '[Wavell] again made reference to their reputation for lax discipline and explained to them that he expected them to disprove existing notions of Australians as rough, wild undisciplined people given to strong drink.'

Two days later it was time for some recreation, and 500 of all the ranks from the 2/1st were bussed into Jerusalem and Tel Aviv, a bumpy and dusty ride of just under 100 kilometres. Though The war diary for the regiment stated that 'very favourable reports were received regarding the conduct of all ranks and their behaviour augurs well for future leave', according to Stockings, troops (presumably from the other camps in the area) didn't hold the same high standards. He wrote, 'On the first weekend after their arrival 500 Australians were reported absent without permission in nearby Tel Aviv, many to "scrutinize the fleshpots".' He also noted that Colonel Vasey of Australia's 6th Division at Julis told his wife that the lads' behaviour made him 'ashamed to wear the uniform'. Bill Howell, an avid photographer, went wandering with his mates Ted Body, Ken Burke and Ron Wood, snapping photos at the historical sites they had all read of at school.

Ken's reputation for being wild was consolidated over these periods of leave because he just couldn't resist a good time, but unlike his fellow sergeants, he could resist the need to be back on base in time for the morning parade. He found himself in trouble for being absent without leave five times in his first year of service. While alcohol and a good time played a decent-sized part in his absences, Ken was also deeply inquisitive – why hurry back when there were intriguing sights to be seen and interesting people to meet? Luckily for Ken his combination of charm and ability, and perhaps a shortage of men, saw him receive a rap over the knuckles rather than a sojourn in a military prison or dismissal from the army.

Allan Brown, as ever the quiet and thoughtful man, allowed his sergeants their fun without the burden of their senior officer hanging around. Brown, instead, wandered on his own, getting a feel for their new home and for the locals. His inquisitive nature would, a few months later, lead him into a friendship with a man who would alter the course of his life and that of his four sergeants.

While the Australians enjoyed the historical and less-historical sights of Tel Aviv and Jerusalem, Field Marshal Lord Birdwood extended the Australians a 'hearty welcome and good wishes to all new and old comrades'. Birdwood was no stranger to Australian troops, having commanded them during World War I, most notably at Gallipoli. He went on to be Commander of the Australian Imperial Force until the end of World War I. Reports of the recreational exploits of the new batch of Australian soldiers probably hadn't reached his Lordship by that time, or perhaps he had a slightly softer view of the colonial forces than did General Wavell. The AIF historians noted that Birdwood accepted the Australian troops the way they were, and didn't make the mistake of trying to turn them into soldiers of the British army. Unfortunately for his Lordship, the same historians also noted that while he was a fine leader who led from the front, he 'was not a great intellect'. However, the problems offered by Australians on leave were soon cast aside by what is still a commonplace problem in the region – terrorism.

On 27 February leave was cancelled in Jerusalem and Tel Aviv owing to 'an outcome of certain terroristic activities in these places'. The activities weren't directed at the soldiers, but were civilian disagreements that were unpredictable and often violent. Officers carried their revolvers, and armed escorts were required for soldiers and supply convoys leaving the camps, just in case trouble was encountered.

Camp life in those early days was focused on making conditions as comfortable as possible. Sanitation was at best dubious, so with skills often learned in the Australian bush, the men set about making more peaceful and private facilities. Tents were personalised with reminders from home, packing cases were turned into tables, and white stones and occasionally flower beds added a few welcoming touches. Roads and the living quarters were given Australian names with a touch of humour such as 'Kings Cross'. Their attempts at normality helped divert thoughts away from the grim prospect of their first battle.

In their down time, the men amused themselves with rugby (with Ken Burke firmly in the limelight), boxing tournaments and establishing a surf club along Australian lines, complete with patrols featuring lads in bathing costumes and caps. The sight of the lifesavers in their outfits provided shock and amusement in equal measure to the local population. For the more sedately minded, there was correspondence to and from home to catch up with, regular movies and newsreels, and the high point of any Australian military base, the wet canteen in the evening. All these pursuits were duly recorded in the camp newspaper, *Artilleryman*, a racy little publication sporting a gossip column, news items picked up from radio broadcasts, stories of various happenings on the base, and that great Australian tradition, slabs of sporting news from both the base and home (Australia and England).

Along with domestic issues, training was well underway, with the soldiers and their officers heading off to the nearby British army schools to learn skills such as the ins and outs of motoring in a Bren gun carrier, which was a vehicle that had tracks like a tank rather than wheels, weapons training and the use of ciphers. They familiarised themselves with new weapons including light machine guns like the Bren gun, anti-tank rifles which fired a bullet capable of piercing a tank's armour and mortars. The mortar was little more than a tube into which a bomb was dropped; when it hit the base of the tube, propellant in the bomb was detonated and hurled the bomb back up the tube and then around 500 metres in the desired direction. All of this training would come in very handy when they faced an organised and well-entrenched enemy. It was practice, practice and more practice to remove any doubt that could prove fatal under fire.

Just after Anzac Day 1940, for many, a day that brought back stories told by their fathers, older brothers and uncles of the adventures of the Light Horse in the nearby desert during World War I, the men set out for their own taste of desert operations at Bir Asluj. The location was just south of Beersheba and was well out of the way of any form of civilisation – perfect for artillery practice. Beersheba was a name that resonated strongly with them. At sunset on 31 October 1917, the Australian 4th Light Horse Brigade was tasked to attack and seize the town, then in Turkish hands. They were successful, and the battle went on to be famous as the only great mounted infantry charge in history, and it is also claimed to be the last great cavalry charge.

While the Australians were marking Anzac Day, German troops were sweeping through Norway and Denmark, and Italy and Japan were quiet on the subject of their intention to join the fray. On the French border, there had only been minor skirmishes between the Allied forces and the Germans. The lack of any major battle between Allied and German forces had led to the war being described as the 'Phony War' and by Churchill as the 'Twilight War'. That would

change on 10 May 1940 when the Germans began their invasion of
the Netherlands, Belgium, Luxembourg and finally France.

When the 2/1st arrived at Bir Asluj, the only mark on the barren
landscape was the remnants of a railway bridge, blown up by TE
Lawrence in 1917. Major Haywood described their two-week
sojourn in the desert:

> The men of the regiment worked, ate and slept with sand; sand
> that was soft when the tractors and guns ploughed through it,
> and hard when slit trenches and gun-pits had to be dug – sand
> that belonged nowhere and everywhere and respected no barrier
> of tents, clothing or utensil lids . . . Starting with simple troop
> shots, the programme built up to engagement of regimental
> targets, with air cooperation shoots interposed. The regiment
> showed directing staff what it could do and had learned, but with
> something of a shock, what it could not do.

The wave of terror that had put a temporary halt to the Australians'
tourism quickly passed, training was well advanced, and soon the
Australians were allowed back into Tel Aviv and Jerusalem. The men
were somewhat better behaved this time, and the locals were very
happy to see them. Aside from the business the adventurous and
thirsty young men brought with them, the Australian reputation
in the region was a fine one. Both Jewish and Arab newspapers
hailed their arrival. One Jewish-owned newspaper marked the
AIF's return with an enthusiastically headlined article, 'Pride of the
British Army', and went on to say, 'If you ask a British general who
are the best soldiers in the British Empire he will answer without
hesitation: "The Anzacs".' It's a fair bet the paper had not sought a
comment from General Wavell.

The newspapers, unlike their associates back in Sydney, did not
record a few of the more colourful activities of the Anzacs. A popular local form of transport was the gharry, a horsedrawn cart that
could be hired to get from A to B. Inevitably this novel mode of
transport provided an opportunity for sport and perhaps the occasional bet among the soldiers. Brigadier Allen was moved to instruct
his men to cease organising gharry races, and competitions to see
how many soldiers could pile onto one. Nor was he impressed by
the robustness with which his troops enjoyed the outdoor dining
and drinking opportunities – something foreign in Australian cities,

where eating and drinking were conducted behind closed doors within strict trading hours. He was also less than enthused when uniformed troops, not necessarily sober, helped local police direct traffic or wandered about the streets with their uniforms not up to parade-ground standards, and used language he thought inappropriate for Australian soldiers in uniform. The brigadier was keen to avoid reinforcing the prejudices of General Wavell and his British colleagues against the rowdy Australians.

Just like contemporary Australian youth, the Anzacs were inveterate and inquisitive travellers. Armed with cameras, groups of soldiers would head off on trips arranged by the YMCA, or just with their mates, exploring places they had only heard of in the obligatory history and scripture classes of their school days. Arab children were always willing to pose for a photo, colourful caravans and camels were snapped, and Solomon's Pools and the Wailing Wall were inspected and recorded in grainy black and white. On these adventures, the bonds formed in training were broadened and strengthened as the young men from the new world gave the old world a thorough going over.

5

THE SANDS SHIFT

In late May 1940, after their time spent in the sands near Beersheba, the regiment moved camps to nearby Julis, where they joined the 2/2nd Field Regiment, which had recently arrived from Australia. The problem facing the new arrivals was that they were unarmed, which for a regiment of gunners is a very tricky situation. The army's solution was simply to give the new regiment half the equipment of the 2/1st and hope that more weapons would eventually arrive. Gunnery practice was taken in turns. Luckily there wasn't an enemy in sight, although that was about to change.

On 10 June 1940 the world of the Australian troops changed dramatically when Benito Mussolini declared war on Britain. It was the culmination of a terrible few weeks. A month earlier the Germans had swept into the Netherlands, Belgium and Luxembourg and were heading toward France, succeeding in a brief but effective campaign. With Europe falling rapidly under German control, the British Expeditionary Force was evacuated from the beaches of Dunkirk beginning on 27 May. The German army was only weeks away from marching along the Champs-Élysées. In the Middle East the British were outnumbered by Italian troops, with British intelligence estimating that the Italians fielded around 215 000 men in the coastal areas of North Africa alone, compared to around 50 000 British troops in Egypt. The Italians could also boast modern and significant airpower compared to a few British squadrons of obsolete aircraft.

With Italy's declaration of war and the German conquest of a large slice of Europe, the Australians of the 2nd AIF were now in a location that was poised to become the next hub of the war. The Italians were perfectly placed to invade Egypt from their stronghold in Libya, and to the south and west of Egypt was what Mussolini and his cohorts liked to call 'Italian East Africa', consisting of Ethiopia (conquered in a bloody war nearly five years before), Eritrea and parts of Somalia – all tantalisingly close to essential British oil supply lines and the Suez Canal. Winston Churchill, who became Britain's Prime Minister just a month before Mussolini declared war, noted:

> ... during July and August [1940] the Italians became active at many points. There was a threat from Kassala [north-east Sudan] westwards towards Khartoum. Alarm was spread in Kenya by the fear of an Italian expedition marching four hundred miles south from Abyssinia toward the Tana River and Nairobi. Considerable Italian Forces advanced into British Somaliland.

Back in Palestine, the enormity of the problem was becoming obvious. As Major Haywood wrote:

> Its meagre forces and still more meagre equipment and ammunition were totally inadequate to meet the onslaught of a determined aggressor, and it seemed too much to hope that Italy would not correctly appreciate the position and seize the initiative.

In between hoping, praying, crossing fingers and wondering what the first taste of real battle would be like, the Australians were busy protecting themselves, as best they could, from where the first attacks would come: by sea and by air. Guns were sited with a clear line of fire to roads and beaches. Slit trenches, narrow, shallow trenches designed to provide some meagre cover during battle, were dug. The men practised with their weapons, though not firing the precious live rounds that would be needed when the enemy finally showed up. One gunner, slightly the worse for wear after a night of leave, returned to the camp with a camel that he, with black humour, introduced as the 2/1st secret weapon. Day after day on high alert passed by as June slipped into July and nothing happened.

In early July the gunners found they had to learn another new skill, when they were instructed to join their fellow Australians in the 2/4th Infantry Battalion to form two anti-aircraft regiments. Their task was to protect the oil refinery and port city of Haifa. On 6 July Brown, Burke, Body, Howell and Wood, along with their colleagues, moved to their new headquarters at the Haifa Military Hospital, and were introduced to the 3.7-inch anti-aircraft gun and its supporting equipment such as predictors, a rudimentary fire control system and range-finders. Their equipment was all borrowed from a British regiment. For the gunners, the move to smaller and more agile weapons was not met with enthusiasm. Ted Body observed, 'the transfer was not wholeheartedly welcomed as the field gunners were always somewhat disdainful of their AA [anti-aircraft] colleagues'. The old question of size, apparently.

The only break from the tension was the occasional excursion to the Turkish baths at nearby Acre, for a truly Middle Eastern experience. Major Haywood went to the baths and reported that a 'huge stone slab, heated by a wooden furnace below, filled the centre of the room at the head of a flight of stone stairs'. He said, 'Batches of about twenty naked troops were sealed in, to stroll round through steam or to test their endurance and the heat of the slab by sitting on it. Ancient, possibly unhygienic, but very, very efficient.' Fortunately for the Australians, their bathing wasn't interrupted by an Italian attack.

There was no time for recreation on 15 July, however, when air-raid sirens announced the arrival of the first enemy engagement of their war. Slipping overhead with the sun glinting from the fuselage were 10 Italian bombers, arranged to two flights of five, and in sight were their targets: the Haifa oil depot and nearby railway yards. Around 90 bombs rained down, hitting their targets and coming close to the Australian camp. In the wake of the attack, the Allies' anti-aircraft guns were moved to locations near Mount Carmel and Acre which gave them a better field of fire.

Every Italian aircraft returned to base unscathed, and headed back for a return visit on 24 July. *Time* magazine reported the second attack saying:

> . . . on the other side of Alexandria, at Haifa in Palestine, where the British oil pipeline from Mosul reaches tide water, the Italians claimed a success last week which the British do not deny. Ten big Italian bombers, flying at great altitude from the Dodecanese Islands, giving the British bases at Cyprus a wide berth, dumped 50 bombs on the Haifa oil terminal and refinery, started fires which burned for days afterward.

The same edition of *Time* also made mention of a (comparatively) minor piece of unfolding history that would soon impact Brown,

Body, Burke, Howell and Wood and shape their experience of the war. The magazine reported:

> Little brown Haile Selassie, whom Britain recognises as Ethiopia's rightful Emperor, passed by plane through Khartoum on his way to join his warriors somewhere on his former country's border. Said he: 'Italy has set the seal of her own doom and has provided my people with the moment to strike . . . We shall fight with the utmost tenacity. God's time is now at hand!'

Well, not quite. Selassie would spend some time plotting with the British in Khartoum, and wouldn't return to the homeland from which he was exiled in 1936, until early the following year.

Around this time, Lieutenant Allan Brown was spending his down time getting to know the ancient port city on the slopes of Mount Carmel. Haifa dates back to the late Bronze Age, around 1550 to 1200 BC, and at the time of Brown's wandering was primarily Muslim, with Christians and Jews trailing well behind in numbers. Over recent decades, this has been reversed, with Haifa now predominately Jewish, followed by Christians, with Muslims coming a distant third. Among the many displaced people in Haifa was a small gathering of Ethiopian Coptic clergy, a Christian faith that dates back to the fourth century in Ethiopia, who, like their Emperor Haile Selassie, had fled their homeland following the Italian invasion and subsequent colonisation. The Coptic Church is a dominant force in Ethiopia and for the clergy, as for their Emperor, ousting the Italians from Ethiopia was high on the agenda. One of the priests encountered Lieutenant Brown, and their mutual inquisitiveness soon moved into a friendship. They met regularly in the coffee houses and the smattering of Coptic churches in Haifa and Jerusalem, where there was a small Ethiopian community.

The story the priest told Brown was a romantic tale of life in Ethiopia before the brutality of the Italian invasion. Brown was truly hooked when he heard of the battles between the ill-equipped Ethiopians against the weapons, soldiers and aircraft of the modern Italian military. With World War I and the appalling gas attacks and their aftermath on a generation firmly in his mind, Brown was horrified to hear the Italians had used gas as part of their arsenal in Ethiopia. A sense of fair play is part of the Australian character, and that sense had driven many of the young men to enlist to fight in yet another foreign war. The plight of the Ethiopians touched Allan Brown deeply.

The priest told him of the passion of the Ethiopian patriots, who had been fighting a guerilla campaign against the Italians since their invasion of Ethiopia in October 1935. What they lacked was modern weapons, tactics and leadership to fight the contemporary Italian army. Ancient rifles and military tactics dating back hundreds of years were not effective against a modern army with a ready supply of explosives, machine-guns and aircraft. A different type of warfare was called for.

Brown realised that, with the dismal state of British forces in the region, perhaps the only way to dislodge the Italians from Ethiopia was through guerilla warfare using irregular forces – forces for which the Ethiopian patriots would certainly qualify. Australian troops had first-hand experience of these techniques when fighting against the Boers in South Africa at the turn of the century. The Boers, though greatly outnumbered by British forces, had been brutally effective, blowing up trains, bridges and railway infrastructure, and using their bushcraft to ambush troops and then escape. The Germans, led by Colonel Paul Emil von Lettow-Vorbeck, had then used similar techniques against the British in East Africa during World War I to great effect against his much larger enemy. Although he finally surrendered to the British two weeks after the Armistice of 11 November 1918, he made it through without once suffering a defeat. The British also had their own experiences from World War I to consider, primarily the adventures of TE Lawrence in the Middle East. They had learned some lessons that could be very handy in a war against Germany and Italy.

In 1939 the British had added three interesting titles to their library of Field Service Regulations. They were, according to William Mackenzie's *Secret History of the SOE* [Special Operations Executive]:

> ... three slender pamphlets printed on rice paper and bound in brown cardboard covers without indication of their contents. The original intention was to have them translated into various languages, but it is not clear what use was eventually made of them. They were entitled, 'The Art of Guerrilla Warfare', 'Partisan Leader's Handbook', 'How to use High Explosives'.

Mackenzie noted of two of the publications:

> The Handbook was designed as a handy collection of practical
> tips for the aspiring guerrilla leader on the lower levels; the notes
> on explosives were equally technical and practical.

Ted Body recalled of the priest and Brown:

> This priest had long talks with Brown and convinced him that
> a small force with arms, ammunition and explosives etc could
> play hell behind the Italian lines and win many locals over from
> the Italians if they could get there. The speed and ferocity of the
> Italian invasion of Ethiopia had left a large chunk of the popula-
> tion feeling either supportive of the Italians because they were
> too frightened not to be, or powerless to oppose them. A show
> of strength by the Patriots, supported by other nations, might just
> be the catalyst to foster an uprising.

Thanks to the priest's network, the enthusiastic young officer later
met with Ras Kassa, military adviser to Haile Selassie, when he
passed through Jerusalem. Ras Kassa had a particular hatred for the
Italians, because three of his sons were murdered by them in the
purges in Addis Ababa. In conversations with Brown, Ras Kassa
spoke widely of the hopes of the patriots, potential allies and enemies and the realities of fighting in a country utterly foreign to the
young Australian officer and his sergeants. Brown put it concisely,
saying, 'He told us much about Abyssinia that was to prove useful
to us later.' Their conversation consolidated in Brown's mind the
notion that 'the job that lay ahead of us was chiefly one of sabotaging the enemy resources and destroying communications, blowing
up forts, ammunition dumps and inflicting damage wherever we
could'. Back at the camp, Brown shared his story of Ethiopia, and
a fledgling plan for an Australian-led guerilla force, with his four
sergeants, knowing well that if the plight of Ethiopia didn't quite
grab them, the prospect of high adventure in a place they had only
read of certainly would. An additional temptation was the chance
to operate outside the normal disciplines of army life, something
Brown knew would appeal to their maverick natures.

Body recalled:

He asked us four, Bill Howell, Ron Wood, Ken Burke and I, if we would like to go with him if he could get permission. We were all plain gunners in 2/1st Field Regiment, three of us from The King's School and Ken Burke from Joeys.

The lads jumped at the chance to take what would soon become their style of war into what Bill Howell described in a letter to his mother as, 'Gosh knows where in the middle of Africa!'

The problem confronting Brown was the layers of both British and Australian army bureaucracy that would need to be shifted to get the mission underway. For Brown and his men it was a frustrating experience. What he didn't know, and what was also probably not known by his superiors in Palestine, was that the plotting of a similar mission was well advanced; a mission that would become one of the earliest missions of the Special Operations Executive (known also as the 'Baker Street Irregulars', thanks to their London address and a few men with a fondness for Sherlock Holmes). The SOE was Britain's wartime secret service, established to arrange and execute acts of subversion and sabotage overseas, particularly throughout Nazi-occupied Europe. One of their most famous operatives was the New Zealand-born and Australian-raised Nancy Wake, who joined the SOE's French section in June 1943. In the European winter of 1940, Allan Brown and his sergeants would spearhead one of the SOE's first missions.

Brown was relentless in pestering his superiors in the AIF about his plan, and when that proved unsuccessful, any senior British officer he could find. He frequented the administrative offices, messes and clubs, telling of his plans for fostering insurrection in Ethiopia to anyone polite enough to listen, or cornered so they couldn't escape. A press release for the American market dramatically entitled 'They came by stealth' said of Brown, 'Authority at first denied him the right to wage such unorthodox warfare. But his persistence defeated authority as it defeated the Italians.' However, it was a combination of determination and sheer good luck that saw a less starchy superior pass along Brown's ideas and contacts in the Ethiopian community to British military intelligence.

September came around, and the regiment moved to Cairo, where the men gave up anti-aircraft work to return to their beloved big guns. In the months that followed they would find themselves fighting a long campaign in the Western Desert. Before that happened, however, the troops all managed to find a good time in the Egyptian capital. During the war, Cairo was a melting pot of cultures. The night air carried jazz music; dance tunes mingled with the exotic sounds of North Africa as the men lounged around the pool at the Mena House. Hollywood classics were played in a huge outdoor cinema at Helwan, where the service bordered on the decadent: the troops, cosy in wicker armchairs, smoked contentedly while 'tall coal black Nubians in white gowns reaching to the ground' and highlighted with red sashes and the ubiquitous north African fez, again in red, maintained a constant supply of cigarettes, beer and peanuts. More fun than a melting ice-cream and a bag of sticky sweets at the local cinema back home.

For Brown and his four sergeants, lingering in Cairo and then the Western Desert was not in their immediate future; they would head in the opposite direction. On 15 October 1940 the five were detached from their regiment for the wonderfully broad reason of 'special duties' with the British army. Ted Body commented, 'No-one knows how he [Brown] wangled it but we got seconded to the British Army.' Brown also had no idea who actually approved their secondment, but by that time they were looking forward to the adventure rather than pondering how it all came about.

Their first stop was Geneifa, a nondescript base in a remote piece of countryside near the Suez Canal that was home to a British commando unit; here the guerilla-training manuals came in handy, particularly the manual on explosives. For men who had grown up celebrating Empire Day (Queen Victoria's birthday) with fireworks and bonfires, the chance to move up from small explosions to something much larger was irresistible. They took to their training with gusto and a natural talent for war. Their pre-war physical prowess came in handy when learning deadly hand-to-hand combat skills, and as well-drilled gunners they adapted to machine-guns and mortars as second nature. Among the tricks they learned, as Xan Fielding noted in *One Man in His Time*, were to:

> . . . blow up trains in the approved manner of Lawrence of Arabia [and to make] booby traps and 'surprise packets' of explosives, which their instructor facetiously told them to address to a suitable recipient. Most of them chose someone obvious, like Hitler or Mussolini.

Allan Brown was fortunate his men were mates, as Fielding later observed that some soldiers were fond of addressing the packets to their commanding officer. Just a joke. Probably. Reports surfaced of outdoor toilets exploding at inappropriate – at least for those occupied in the toilet – moments, much to the amusement of an audience of four sergeants. Their officer was, wisely, scarce. Brown was a steady hand and a blind eye rolled into one.

Their training was brief, and at the end they were still none the wiser about what the next step would be, only that the destination was Ethiopia, a country they had read about a few years before during the Italian invasion, and a place they needed an atlas to find. Ted Body recalled them speculating, 'It was thought that we, along with our equipment, would be parachuted in somewhere behind the Italians.' However, the prospect of jumping out of a perfectly good aircraft was not in their future, and instead they were soon on a leisurely journey by steamer and rail to Khartoum, the starting point of their venture into Ethiopia. What they didn't know, and in an oddity of history would never know, was that Arnold Wienholt, grazier, journalist, soldier, big-game hunter, member of the Queensland parliament, member of the House of Representatives and a spy for the British, had beaten them to it. While Brown was still pestering the British hierarchy to take guerilla warfare to Ethiopia, Wienholt was poised to enter Ethiopia with the same purpose in mind – and it wasn't the first time he had operated there. Wienholt was no stranger to guerilla warfare courtesy of his service in the Boer War, and later against Colonel von Lettow-Vorbeck in the East Africa campaign during World War I.

6

LAND OF THE LION KING

Ethiopia, the destination of Arnold Wienholt, and a few months later of Allan Brown, Ken Burke, Ted Body, Ron Wood and Bill Howell, is an ancient land, and for most of its people the day-to-day existence had been virtually unchanged for generations. The country has, however, punched above its weight in world affairs over the last century; its emergence courtesy of Haile Selassie. Selassie, sometimes known as 'The Lion', became the Regent of the country in 1916 and Emperor in 1930. Selassie, who reportedly could trace his ancestry back to King Solomon and the Queen of Sheba, was a leader who didn't mind stepping onto the world stage.

Haile Selassie was educated at a French Catholic mission in Harar, a provincial city in the highlands where his father was Governor. Though somewhat slight of stature at a shade over five feet, he had a powerful personality, a fine intellect and, as David Shirreff noted in *Bare Feet and Bandoliers*, '... was serious, deeply religious, at times simple to the point of naiveté'. Selassie read voraciously and developed an insight into international affairs. He knew where the threats and opportunities for his nation could be found. British diplomat Sir Edwin Chapman-Andrews said of Selassie:

> I distinctly recall his features, serene, something of a mystical quality about them. His eyes, in particular, I remember; they seemed at the time to be purple but, of course, were in fact dark brown. He seemed a majestic figure; there was a certain divinity about him that doth hedge a king. He seemed to be with, but not of, us.

In 1916, the reigning monarch, Lij Iyasu, had been deposed, mainly owing to his ongoing flirtation with Islam. He was replaced by his aunt, Zewditu, who promptly appointed Haile Selassie as Regent.

Selassie was a popular choice for the progressives in Ethiopia, and was thought to be the best choice to carry on the work of King Menelik II, who had died in 1913, to modernise the country. In 1923, after travelling extensively in Europe to establish his country's credentials as a leading African nation, he entered the world stage as his country became the continent's only member of the League of Nations. He also kept a firm hand on affairs at home. Many of the nobles and tribal leaders were conservative and resistant to his outward thinking – including his insistence that the country be known as Ethiopia rather than the Arabic name Abyssinia – which, combined with their various disputes and intrigues made for an uncomfortable level of disquiet on occasion. Chapman-Andrews recalled seeing the Minister of War return from the north of the country in Ethiopia's only aircraft: the Minister's carry-on luggage included the head of Ras Gugsa, a challenger to Haile Selassie.

In 1930 Selassie moved from Regent to Emperor after the death of Zewditu. His coronation guests were a flattering array of Europe's soon-to-decline nobility. Britain was represented by King George V's third son, the Duke of Gloucester, who would take an even longer trip in 1944 to Canberra as the Governor-General of Australia. Joining the Duke were the governors of all Britain's nearby colonies of Sudan, British Somaliland and Aden. Italy was competitive, sending a large delegation that included Prince Udine representing his cousin, King Victor Emmanuel III. Less showy delegations were sent from France, Germany, Sweden, Belgium, the Netherlands, Turkey, Egypt, the United States and Japan. Representing *The Times* was Evelyn Waugh, whose travels in Ethiopia resulted in his novel *Black Mischief*.

To commemorate the coronation, Addis Ababa was given a spruce-up, the electricity was turned on, and the poor were fenced off for the duration. The RAF performed a fly-past with four aircraft and the celebration ran for 10 days. The coronation put Ethiopia and its new monarch on the world map.

What Haile Selassie didn't know was that Benito Mussolini and his government were taking the opportunity to have a close look at the real estate. Italy had colonised adjoining Eritrea in 1882, and had been eyeing Ethiopia as a potential addition to their African colonies. However, their plans didn't quite work out as intended. The Ethiopians proved to be a formidable enemy, using their superior numbers to rout the Italian force of around 16000 troops (comprising 10 600 Italians and the rest local Eritrean troops) on 1–2 March 1896 at the Battle of Adwa. *The Spectator* described the Italian loss as a 'great disaster, greater than has ever occurred in modern times to white men in Africa. Adwa was the bloodiest of all colonial battles.' Nearly 6000 were killed, 1500 were wounded and over 3000 were taken prisoner; around 1500 of those prisoners had both hands amputated, a traditional punishment for those who fought against the Ethiopians, and some were castrated.

The defeat had rankled the Italians for years, and with Mussolini and his grand plan for a colony to be known as 'Italian East Africa', with Italian-occupied Eritrea above and Italian Somaliland to the east, Ethiopia was a prime target. What also stirred him on was the fact that Ethiopia and Liberia were the only two independent countries in Africa, so the chance of these relatively poor countries successfully defending themselves against an invasion was remote. To oppose the Italians, the Ethiopians could muster an air force of 13 antiquated planes, four pilots and an army of around 500 000 with weapons ranging from ancient rifles to spears, bows and shields.

By mid 1935 the Italians had over a million well-armed and trained troops in Eritrea, 595 tanks and 390 aircraft with a sufficient number of pilots. They also brought with them a nasty little surprise: mustard gas. The Italians began by testing the Ethiopian defences and abilities with repeated incursions across the border from Eritrea. These events went unremarked upon by the League of Nations, which emboldened Mussolini. The Consul General and Resident Minister at the American Legation in Addis Ababa, Cornelius Van Hemert Engert, wrote:

> The Italian preparations were so obvious that nobody who was there could doubt that the invasion was imminent. Only intervention by the great powers could have stopped it. The United States could perhaps have brought enough pressure on Mussolini to force him to abandon his plans, but we weren't willing to get involved. I even sent a personal cable to President Roosevelt, shortly before the storm broke. I stressed that the great powers must put united pressure on Mussolini, if war was to be avoided.

The great powers remained silent.

At 5 a.m. on 3 October 1935, Italian forces under the command of General Emilio De Bono crossed the border from Eritrea into

Ethiopia. Mussolini had made it clear what he expected of De Bono, writing to him:

> It is my profound conviction that, we being obliged to take the initiative of operations at the end of October or September, you ought to have a combined force of 300 000 men (including about 100 000 black troops in the two colonies, plus 300–500 aeroplanes and 500 rapid vehicles) for without these forces to feed the offensive penetration the operation will not have the vigorous rhythm which we desire.

As for local resistance after the anticipated fait accompli, the dictator offered:

> Five formations of Blackshirts [Mussolini's loyal Fascist troops], who will be carefully selected and trained. These Divisions of Blackshirts will be the guarantee that the undertaking will obtain popular approbation. Even in view of possible international controversies (League of Nations, etc.) it is as well to hasten our tempo. For the lack of a few thousand men we lost the day at Adwa! We shall never make that mistake. I am willing to commit a sin of excess but never a sin of deficiency.

Numbered among the invaders in that sin of excess were Mussolini's sons Bruno and Vittorio, who flew bombers. One of the sons said:

> I noted with regret that my bombs did not create any sensational effects. Perhaps I was disappointed because I had expected the huge explosions and flames I had seen in American war movies. Unfortunately the mud and grass Ethiopian houses were just not designed to provide a satisfactory target to a bomber.

Three days after crossing the border, the Italians swept into Adwa, the scene of their defeat nearly 40 years earlier. This time the situation was reversed, and the Italians moved on.

Finally, in November, the League of Nations rattled its sabre and imposed economic sanctions against Italy. In response, Mussolini surprised quite a few with his measured response, rather than bravado. He said, 'Italy will meet them [the sanctions] with discipline, with frugality and with sacrifice.' Mussolini could afford to be sanguine about the sanctions. The unfettered supply of oil to Italy was critical to his country's future, but its main supplier was the United States, which was not a member of the League and thus not a party to the sanctions.

The sanctions also prevented League of Nations member countries to export aluminium – a major component in military production and particularly of aircraft – to Italy. This sounded fine in theory, but Italy was a major supplier of aluminium to the world market, and in reality the sanctions were little more than posturing. As Churchill observed, 'Thus the measures pressed with so great a parade were not real sanctions to paralyse the aggressor, but merely such half-hearted sanctions as the aggressor would tolerate, because in fact, though onerous, they stimulated Italian war spirit.'

Haile Selassie called all Ethiopians to arms, which, as Van Hemert Engert observed, was probably more a call to mind over matter. He wrote that Haile Selassie was:

> ... elegant, reflective, a lover of neatness, order and tenue – calling all males to bear arms when honestly there weren't any arms to be had. And even when a soldier did manage to score a rifle, chances were the ammunition pack he carried wasn't a proper match; such was the range of guns in use, some which dated back to the Franco-Prussian war.

It was, according to Australian journalist Noel Monks, 'the greatest collection of antiquated rifles I have seen outside a museum.'

To attempt a peace, the Hoare–Laval pact conjured up in secret talks by the British Foreign Secretary Samuel Hoare and French Prime Minister Pierre Laval and designed to appease Mussolini and not push him closer to an alliance with Hitler – came into play, but only behind closed diplomatic doors. (Laval had earlier ceded parts of French Somaliland to Mussolini, making Ethiopia even more vulnerable to the Italian dictator's plan.)

The pact effectively sliced up Ethiopia, with areas already under Italian control ceded to the Italians, and most of the south part of the country available for economic expansion if suitable opportunities arose. In return, the Ethiopians would be given access, via Eritrea, to the sea. Mussolini was keen to sign on the dotted line, and Ethiopia was unaware of the plan being hatched. However, Ethiopia was saved from this fate thanks to a leak to a French newspaper.

Though the plan had been approved by the British Cabinet on 9 December, the Cabinet did a quick about-face and abandoned it nine days later. The ensuing public furore claimed the scalps of Hoare and Laval – and so the battle continued. King George V, during his first audience with Hoare's successor, Anthony Eden, quipped about the debacle of the pact, 'No more coals to Newcastle, no more Hoares to Paris.'

On 26 December the Italians brought a miserable festive season to the Ethiopians, confirming their earlier rumoured use of chemical weapons by unleashing mustard gas by bombs dropped from aircraft and canisters fired from their artillery, primarily in the Harar province in the east of the country. The use of gas, 'the terrible rain that burned and killed' as Haile Selassie later observed, was denied by the Italians. Their denials were thwarted, however, thanks to the intervention of British Military Attaché RJR Firkin, who obtained samples and sent them to Britain for investigation. Based on the findings, the League of Nations again did very little. However, the use of chemical weapons brought reminders of their devastating use in World War I; they also brought a media pack. Evelyn Waugh returned, this time writing for the *Daily Mail*, along with representatives from Associated Press, London's *Daily Telegraph* and America's Hearst Press. Ethiopia was very much on the world stage but for all the wrong reasons.

The Italians, by this time under the command of the more aggressive Marshal Pietro Badoglio, pushed on, with the use of gas still in their arsenal.

The Italians had not only the Ethiopian people in their sights; they targeted buildings and hospitals used or operated by Europeans – the plan was to minimise witnesses to the final stages of the war, and to mop up troublesome locals after the inevitable defeat. On 2 April the British Foreign Secretary told the House of Commons in London:

Eighteen aircraft flying at 1800 feet bombed the town [Harar] between 8.45 and 9.30 last Sunday. The machines circled wide three times and nearly 300 bombs fell on the town. Three fell on the Swedish Mission, 50 on that of the Egyptian Red Cross, 14 on the Roman Catholic Mission, four on the French Hospital and four on the Harar Red Cross which was showing a ground sign five yards square.

The war was close to an end and the Italians were closing on Addis Ababa where Haile Selassie was now locked in discussions with his advisers. Opinions varied widely: some argued Selassie should remain in Ethiopia and continue the fight to the last man, others counselled Selassie to leave the country and take the fight to the League of Nations. The rail line from Addis Ababa to Djibouti – Ethiopia's only piece of rail infrastructure – was still open, and this was the option the Emperor selected. On 1 May, with the Italians only 160 kilometres from the capital, Selassie handed over control of Ethiopia to his Council of State. The Council had concurred with his decision to leave, voting 21 to 3 in favour. The decision was a public-relations coup for the Italians and a weapon they could use later to denigrate the Emperor in the eyes of his people, many of whom had hoped he would stay on and fight.

At 4.20 a.m. on 2 May, the royal family and retinue, minus the Emperor, boarded the train at Addis Ababa's railway station, an elegant French-designed building Selassie had inaugurated in December 1929. Loaded on board with them were 10 tons of personal baggage, 100 steel-bound boxes of gold bars and silver Maria Theresa thalers (a coin that replaced bars of salt as the regularly used currency in Ethiopia) and dozens of boxes of liquor. The Emperor's family fled in style.

Selassie remained at the station and farewelled his family as they began the 784-kilometre journey to the port of Djibouti in French Somaliland. What the Ethiopian people didn't know was that the train stopped around sixteen kilometres out of the city, where he discreetly joined his family. If nothing else, it avoided the sight of the Emperor fleeing his beleaguered nation. The train then stopped at Dire Dawa, still under Ethiopian control, where it seemed the Emperor was having second thoughts about departing. In response to a phone call from Selassie, Chapman-Andrews made his way to Dire Dawa to meet with the Emperor.

He said, 'As a result of that night's consultation the Emperor reluctantly decided to proceed by train to Djibouti and leave the country rather than fulfil his original intention of raising his standard with a view to resisting the Italians between Harar and Jijiga. The military situation in this locality at that time was quite hopeless. If the Emperor had attempted to continue his fight I do not think he could have escaped death or capture.' On 4 May, Haile Selassie and his entourage boarded the British light cruiser

HMS *Enterprise*, which had been despatched to Djibouti to collect him and other fleeing notables. The Italians marched into Addis Ababa the following day.

In the wake of his departure, Addis Ababa was in an uproar. John Spencer, an American and adviser to Haile Selassie, and still in the capital, said:

> The entire asphalted pavement down to the station itself was an unbroken stretch of white. I soon discovered that the incredible appearance of the avenue was caused by the feathers of hundreds of pillows and mattresses that had been disembowelled onto the street by looters who had gone methodically from house to house; what they could not carry away, they scattered onto the road . . . Armed bands were roaming around firing at random. The chief of police, whom I knew, came up to me in a frenzy declaring that a revolution had broken out after the departure of the Emperor and that even the police were killing each other. As though to emphasize his remarks, a machine-gun chattered nearby.

With the Ethiopians turning on each other in the capital, the task of the conquering Italians was much easier.

British Foreign Secretary Anthony Eden marked the moment in a speech to his Leamington constituents:

> Many of you tonight, like myself, have your thoughts in Africa. I have only one observation to make about the events of the last seven months in connection with that dispute. We had an obligation, a signed covenant obligation, to play our part. We have sought to play that part to the full, and so far as we have done this, we have nothing to reproach ourselves with, nothing to apologise for.

Politics and expediency won that day.

At 4 p.m. on 5 May, Marshal Badoglio and his troops marched into Addis Ababa, and by the next morning 25 000 troops occupied the city. Van Hemert Engert observed of the conquerors' arrival:

> There was nothing spectacular about it – no shouting, no excitement, no cheering crowds, not the slightest ceremony. Yet it was

one of the great moments of modern history, and it lacked no genuine element of drama and colour. The setting was an imperial capital in ruins, buildings still burning, the stinking dead still lying on the streets, gutted houses and stores gaping blackly and emptily at us as we drove by.

The same day that the Italians arrived in Addis Ababa, the British High Commissioner in Palestine reported that Haile Selassie had arrived in Jerusalem, 'very frail and under medical supervision'. Despite his condition, he pressed on, leaving his family in Jerusalem, and boarded the light cruiser HMS *Capetown* for a run across the Mediterranean to Gibraltar, and then the liner RMS *Orford* to Southampton. He arrived in London on 3 June to a welcome notably short on high-level officials. Britain was turning a blind eye, giving credit to Churchill's comment that Mussolini 'regarded Britannia as a frightened, flabby old woman'. While Selassie had been on the high seas, the Vatican briefly entered the fray, and not on the side of the conquered Ethiopians or their ancient Coptic Church. Instead, Pope Pius XI – whose successor in 1939, Pope Pius XII, has often been referred to as 'Hitler's Pope' – offered 'the triumphal happiness of great and good people in peace which it hopes and confidentially expects will be a prelude to a new European and world peace'.

After a brief respite in London, Selassie travelled to Geneva, the seat of the League of Nations, and on 30 June he put forward his case for justice in Ethiopia. Speaking in Amharic, with simultaneous translations into French and English, he outlined some of the more grisly points of the invasion:

At the outset, toward the end of 1935, Italian aircraft hurled tear-gas bombs upon my armies. They had but slight effect. The soldiers learned to scatter, waiting until the wind had rapidly dispersed the poisonous gases. The Italian aircraft then resorted to mustard gas. Barrels of liquid were hurled upon armed groups. This means too was ineffective; the liquid affected only a few soldiers, and the barrels upon the ground themselves gave warning of the danger to troops and the population. It was at the time when the operations for encirclement of Mekele were taking place that the Italian command, fearing a rout, applied the procedure which it is now my duty to denounce to the world. Sprayers were installed on the aircraft so that they could vaporize, over vast areas of territory, a fine death-dealing rain. Groups of nine, fifteen, eighteen aircraft followed one another so that the fog issuing from them formed a continuous sheet. It was thus that from the end of January 1936, soldiers, women, children, cattle, rivers, lakes and fields were constantly drenched with the deadly rain.

In order to kill off systematically all living creatures, in order more surely to poison waters and pastures, the Italian command made its aircraft pass over and over again. That was its chief method of warfare. These fearful tactics succeeded. Men and animals succumbed. The deadly rain that fell from the aircraft made all of those whom it touched fly shrieking with pain.

He concluded his address by saying:

It is not merely a question of the settlement. It is the very existence of the League of Nations. It is the confidence that each State is to place in international treaties. It is the value of promises to small States that their integrity and independence shall be respected. In a word it is international morality that is at stake. Representatives of the world, I have come to Geneva to discharge in your midst the most painful of the duties of a Head of State. What reply shall I have to take back to my people?

With that question hanging in the air, Selassie stepped down, but was reported to have quietly and with remarkable prescience said, 'It is us today; it will be you tomorrow.'

The answer from the League of Nations was even worse than Haile Selassie could have contemplated. A week after his address, on 6 July 1936, the League of Nations voted to suspend all sanctions against Italy. Mussolini's invasion and the use of chemical weapons was rubber stamped.

The attitude of Britain and the failure of the League of Nations greatly upset Winston Churchill. He had, from the outset of the Italian aggression, wanted to meet them head-on. He was fully aware that Italian dominance in the region left the Suez Canal and its Red Sea approaches vulnerable. He wrote:

The British fleet which was lying at Alexandria had now been reinforced. It could by a gesture have turned back Italian transports from the Suez Canal and would as a consequence have had to offer battle to the Italian navy. We were told that it was not capable of meeting such an antagonist. I had raised the question at the outset, but had been reassured. Our battleships of course were old and it now appeared that we had no aircraft cover and very little anti-aircraft ammunition.

Britain was looking more and more like a flabby old woman.

Churchill believed that Britain should, despite the odds, have tackled the Italians and cut off their supply lines to Ethiopia, and later wrote, 'The fact that the nerve of the British Government was not equal to the occasion can be excused only by their sincere love of peace. Actually it played a part in leading to an infinitely more terrible war.' Of the League of Nations' role in the Ethiopian conquest, he wrote that it was an 'utter fiasco, most damaging if not fatally injurious to its effective life as an institution'. World War II sealed its fate.

Haile Selassie had one final roll of the dice before the League of Nations in 1938 when he pleaded for the League's members not to recognise the Italian occupation of his country. He failed.

Just as the Coptic priest told Allan Brown and his sergeants, the Italian occupation of Ethiopia got off to a brutal start. Badoglio returned to a victor's welcome in Italy, and was replaced by Marshal Graziani, a man with a notable lack of compassion. One of his first actions was to establish a 'Council of Government' with himself at the top of the pile, and a 'Board of Consultors' made up of six friendly local chiefs and six prominent Italian farmers and merchants to advise the Council.

Mussolini gave him carte blanche to bring Ethiopia to heel. He wrote that Graziani was 'authorized to begin conducting systematically the policy of terror and extermination against rebels and accomplice populations. Without the law of tenfold retaliation the wound will not heal quickly enough.' Key dissenters and potential partisan leaders were rounded up and imprisoned or sent into exile. They were the lucky ones. In the town of Ficce two notable locals who had been persuaded to surrender by their respective fathers-in-law were taken into the market square, shot and then beheaded. Graziani was making his position very clear.

To move forward with his grand plan for Italians to 'colonize these depopulated lands with the fecund Italian race', Mussolini sweetened the pot with US$8 million to build roads and bridges to link Addis Ababa to the other key cities in Italy's growing East African empire, particularly to the Italian-controlled port cities of Massawa, the main port of Eritrea, and Mogadishu in Somalia. Around 60 000 Italian workmen were imported to work on these projects, supported by local workers. In Addis Ababa, European-style buildings were built to house government offices, residences, shops, restaurants and cafes. Addis, in particular the Piazza district on one of the high points on the city, took on a distinctly Italian flavour. Pasta slipped into the Ethiopian diet as a staple for the urban dwellers.

At a social level, the occupiers did some good by introducing a program of vaccinations for the Ethiopians, and by building hospitals, though European patients were given preference over Ethiopian natives. Schools were opened, though as Richard Pankhurst, son of Sylvia, the vocal critic of Italy's invasion of Ethiopia, noted, 'Education of the "native" youth was, however, strictly controlled, with the avowed aim of preventing the emergence of a "native intelligentsia".' With more than a whiff of influence of their soon-to-be ally in Germany, marriage and even affairs of the heart – or other body parts – between the Ethiopians and the occupiers was forbidden. Segregation on public transport was also introduced and strictly policed. The *Gazzetta del Popolo* newspaper was very pleased with developments, declaring, 'the fascist empire must not be an empire of half-castes'. Richard Pankhurst later wrote that King Victor Emmanuel III, at the recommendation of Mussolini, 'prohibited conjugal relations between Italians and "natives" (but did not prevent the former from consorting with "native" prostitutes). A number of ordinances establishing urban and other segregation were afterwards issued.' Nature can always be relied upon to trump the bureaucrats, however, and it was no surprise that business in the city's brothels flourished. Many of these establishments were located in the houses built by the Italians for the local population, which had shunned them, preferring their traditional dwellings.

Life for the Ethiopians in Addis Ababa took a turn for the worse in February 1937 when two Eritrean men, Moses Asgadom and Abraha Daboch, tried to assassinate Graziani. Using hand grenades most likely stolen from the occupying force, the Eritreans attacked, killing several Italian officers and seriously wounding Graziani. The reprisals were swift and vicious, and over three days an estimated 6000–9000 Ethiopians were indiscriminately slaughtered.

Dr Ladislav Sava, a Hungarian national in Addis Ababa at the time, recalled:

> The greatest slaughter began after 6 o'clock in the evening ... during that awful night, Ethiopians were thrust into lorries, heavily guarded by armed Blackshirts. Revolvers, truncheons, rifles and daggers were used to murder completely unarmed black people of both sexes and [all] ages. Every black person seen was arrested and bundled into a lorry and killed, either in the lorry or near the Little Ghebbi, sometimes at the moment when he met the Blackshirts. Ethiopian houses and huts were searched and then burnt with their inhabitants. To quicken the flames, benzene and oil were used in great quantities. The shooting never ceased all night, but most of the murders were committed with daggers and blows with a truncheon at the head of the victim.

Specific targets were foreign-educated Ethiopians, particularly those who had studied in the United States and Great Britain. In writing his subsequent history of the events, Robert Cheesman wrote:

> All the educated youth were hunted out, some were stood up in groups without trial and machine-gunned, and those three or four hundred of the more fortunate were deported to Italy.

The Church, the cornerstone of spiritual and social life in Ethiopia, was also targeted. Cheesman noted that the 'wholesale persecution and slaughter of clergy, burning of monasteries and churches, sometimes with priests in them, recalled the barbarous orgies of the Roman Empire'. However, these appalling events put some steel in the backbone of the patriot movement. One unnamed correspondent, reporting from Djibouti, wrote:

> The Abyssinians know there is nothing left for them but to fight, and the world will presently hear that they were everywhere attacking anew. Those who fled from Addis well know what to expect from Italy and they will fight again.

The only problem with this sentiment was that the Italians were as effective at censorship as they were at the murderous suppression of dissent, and so scant news of their actions and the local patriots reached the outside world.

So effective was the clampdown on communications that news to Haile Selassie, by then in exile in Britain, sometimes took months to arrive. Loyalists would send documents by runner across the Ethiopian tableland, down the escarpment and into the Sudan and the safety of its capital, Khartoum; the letters would then reach the more conventional diplomatic mails to London. According to Christine Sandford, wife of Colonel (and later Brigadier) Daniel Sandford – a man who would feature in the liberation of Ethiopia – the letters described:

> ... in detail the conditions in their provinces, gave details of the fighting against the Italians and of arms and ammunitions captured, and usually ended with an appeal for the Emperor to intercede with the League of Nations or the British Government. In some cases, they begged for him to arrange for the dispatch of arms, which of course he was quite unable to do as neither the British nor the French Government would have allowed them to pass through its territory.

Events in Europe were warming up and the fate of Ethiopia moved from the front page.

7

UNREST IN AFRICA

The invasion and colonisation of Ethiopia by the Italians had been whitewashed by the members of the League of Nations, with only four of its members – China, the Soviet Union, Mexico and New Zealand – refusing to recognise Italian sovereignty. They joined the non-member United States of America in supporting Ethiopia's independence. However, with Europe heading toward yet another world war, the troubles in the Horn of Africa were sidelined by more pressing matters. Ethiopia did, however, have a few vocal supporters to pester governments and woo public opinion. In London, perhaps the loudest voice was that of Sylvia Pankhurst, suffragette, former Communist, strident anti-Fascist and bane of the British establishment. (Her sister Adela would soon offend Australian sensibilities with her anti-war sentiments delivered from a soap box in Sydney's Domain.) The 'tiresome Miss Pankhurst' as she was later dubbed by MI-5 was an ardent supporter of Ethiopian independence and the exiled Emperor. Shortly after the invasion she swung into action, publishing the weekly *New Times and Ethiopian News*. The publication proved quite successful. It stirred up some public interest in Ethiopia's situation and also managed to offend the British Government to the extent that in January 1940, Prime Minister Neville Chamberlain, in deciding that a permit to export the paper should be declined, commented, 'Circulation of this publication abroad was calculated to react adversely on relations between the United Kingdom and non-belligerent powers.' One of those non-belligerent powers – Italy – changed hats a few months later.

One of the most colourful supporters of the Ethiopian cause was Arnold Wienholt, who in 1940 would take part in the same secret mission to rally the Ethiopian patriots, terrorise the Italians occupiers and eventually return Haile Selassie to his throne that later involved Allan Brown and his four sergeants.

In one of the oddities of war, however, Wienholt's involvement in the mission was unknown to his fellow Australians, Brown, Burke, Howell, Body and Wood. The name Wienholt and his exploits were familiar to Australians of their generation, and it is likely the five younger men had read tales of his time as a hunter and adventurer in Africa throughout the 1920s, but they never got to meet the man whose aims concerning Ethiopia so closely mirrored their own. His biographer, Rosamond Siemon, called her book *The Eccentric Mr Wienholt*, which is a fair description.

Wienholt was born on 25 November 1877 on Goomburra Station on the rolling pastoral lands of the Darling Downs, south-west of Brisbane. The Wienholts were an adventuring family. An ancestor, Daniel Wienholt, was carrying around £40 000 of family money on board the HMS *Lutine* when it sank on 9 October 1799; his body washed ashore on the Isle of Sylt on 11 November that year.

Arnold's father, Edward, was one of the four Wienholt brothers, originally a well-to-do merchant family in Wales, who arrived in Australia in the mid 1800s and set about acquiring large tracts of prime land in the Darling Downs. Edward and his partners eventually owned 117 346 hectares of some of the State's finest farming and grazing land. When he registered the birth of his son Arnold, named in honour of his elder brother, Edward listed his occupation as 'squatter'. In 1880 he returned to the United Kingdom with his family and settled at Ross-on-Wye, a pretty market town in Herefordshire. Young Arnold, even then a very determined young man, was sent off to boarding school, first at the Dormer School near Brighton, then Wixenford Preparatory School near Reading and finally, at the age of 13, to Eton in 1891.

Eton at the time was a miserable place, rife with bullying, brutality and snobbery – a problem if you were the son of successful merchants and businessmen rather than the landed gentry. The lean and wiry Wienholt kept to himself and found a natural affinity for sport, particularly boxing, which was a handy ability at Eton. A contemporary reckoned, 'He was conspicuous as a straight running, fearless boy of great energy.'

In 1896, rather than remain in England with his rather aloof father and family, 18-year-old Arnold returned to Australia to work on the family properties. He surprised his squattocracy family by preferring to live in a rough worker's cottage on the estate rather than in the homestead. He made a further point, as his biographer wrote that by:

... choosing to be different from the managerial staff, he elected to wear a practical countryman's dress: cabbage tree hat, moleskin trousers and hob-nailed boots – a far cry from the sartorial elegance of his father and most wealthy Downs squatters.

Arnold Wienholt was definitely his own man.

With the outbreak of the Boer War in 1899, Wienholt decided the family business could manage without him while he did his duty – duty was something Wienholt would never shirk – and had an adventure. It was just before Federation, and each of the colonies that would soon become states sent troops to South Africa for the fray. Wienholt enlisted in the Queensland Imperial Bushmen and sailed to war on 18 May 1900. A month later he was promoted to sergeant, and established a reputation for being both fair and firm. Wienholt was reputed to have used some of his family's significant fortune to fund the purchase of horses for his men. After a year in the South African bush, Wienholt returned to Brisbane and genteel life. By 1908 he was manager of Wienholt Estates Company of Australasia, and responsible for all its Queensland properties. He had also evolved into a fine cattleman.

Arnold Wienholt felt that responsibility to his country meant that entering government was both a suitable profession and an obligation. He was elected to the Queensland Legislative Assembly in 1909 as Member for Fassifern, his local area. His campaign had a few quirks that supported the notion of 'the eccentric Mr Wienholt'. For example, at his campaign launch, with the formalities over, he cleared a space and invited all comers to go three rounds with him. The boxing matches were a hit in both senses, and this crowd-pleaser became a feature of his campaign meetings, and kept the fledgling politician in good physical shape. Local papers touted him as, 'straightforward and manly, offering honesty; not to show how smart he could be to prove himself an honest man'. His accent and reserved nature, a legacy of his upbringing in England, endeared him to the local British elite, and his Germanic name didn't do any harm with the many German families in the region. He beat his Labor opponent 1502 votes to 626.

In Parliament he became known as a man for whom the party line was very much second to his own beliefs, and he regularly voted against his own party, particularly on social issues. It was a telltale of his future life that Wienholt would stand up for the underdog, with the fight for the equality of women as one of his early causes. His biographer wrote that as a politician, 'he could be autocratic and didactic and to be against the entire House didn't intimidate him. He remained alone and aloof from political vendettas but was immovable against waste and government perks.'

Ambition was something Arnold Wienholt did not lack, and with the 1913 Federal election looming he resigned his safe state seat of Fassifern in order to tackle the incumbent Labor Prime Minister Andrew Fisher in his Queensland seat of Wide Bay. The Wienholts had large pastoral holdings within the seat and Arnold was well known and respected in the electorate. British to his bootstraps, to paraphrase Robert Menzies, Wienholt was spurred on by what he perceived as Fisher's lack of loyalty to the Empire. Fisher had a rather more modern approach to Queen and country and at the 1911 Imperial Conference in England had said:

> We are not an Empire. We are a very loose association of five nations, each independent and each willing to remain in fraternal and cooperative union with Great Britain and each other, but only on one condition that if, at any time, for any cause, we decide to terminate that connection, no-one can say nay.

In a speech during his campaign, Wienholt took a swing at Fisher and his modern ideas, saying:

> No matter to what part of the British Empire I belong, I belong not only to that part, but to the Empire of which I form a part. I am proud to be an Australian and prouder still to be a Britisher. As a Britisher I should do my duty and will do my best for all who put their trust in me.

Despite the rousing applause from his audience and a strong campaign, Wienholt was beaten by Fisher in the election held on 31 May 1913.

Of the loss, Rosamond Siemon wrote:

> ... the pain of political failure was deep and lasting. With the shattering setback to his ambitions he needed a safety valve and turned to his confidante, his sister in England, Brenda. His many letters to her open a window revealing the private Arnold

Wienholt, the man Australians did not know. 'I hated being beaten,' he confided. 'I will never enter State politics again, it would seem like admitting defeat. Federal politics or nothing.' Though beaten, his ego was still intact, later saying, 'There will, I fancy, be fresh Federal elections next year and I know I would be asked to either contest the same seat again or be the first man chosen to fight the contest as a Liberal senator (which I think would be a win), so that in a way I am a sort of politician star through having given up one's safe seat in the State House.'

Wienholt, however, did not make good his threat and did return to state politics years later, but in between came his African adventures.

In August 1913, with war between Britain and Germany looming, he was bound for Africa on board the Aberdeen Lines SS *Themistocles*. The *Themistocles* berthed in Durban on 22 September and returned Wienholt to Africa, where he wrote again to Brenda, saying, 'I'm beastly ambitious to be someone, and always have been anyhow. I must look ahead and not back, be equal to either fortune, that grand idea of the old Romans.' In another letter from Cape Town, the prospect of heading off into the bush on the hunt had changed his rather introspective mood: 'I am as happy as a boy after his first rabbit. This Big Lone Wolf is going to get lions, lions, lions!' Wienholt was following in the footsteps of his younger cousin, Arnold Hodson, who had left Queensland and made a name for himself as a big-game hunter, African explorer and author of *Trekking the Great Thirst*, a favourite with Wienholt. He headed off on safari into what was German South West Africa – now Namibia – a dicey place to go wandering at any time, and particularly so with war getting closer. At his side was Joe Bennett, an Aboriginal stockman from a Wienholt property in Queensland.

On 18 July 1914 in Angola, and after nearly nine months trekking through jungle and veldt, 'The Big Lone Wolf' was poised to bag his first lion, a big male. Unfortunately for Wienholt, marksmanship wasn't listed among his numerous talents. From a safe distance of just under 400 metres he fired two shots, the first hitting the lion and the second missing. More annoyed than gravely wounded, the lion disappeared into the scrub. The next morning Wienholt and his bushman tracked the injured animal and found it in long grass – around the same time the lion found Wienholt.

Wienholt said:

> With poor generalship I had got into a bad place, since, though
> I could see him plainly, the thorn bush was too high to shoot
> over, and no-one would dare shoot through it. I could neither
> run away nor remain where I was, so I had to step out clear of
> the bush, almost towards the charging beast.

Wienholt fired, unsure whether the bullet had found its mark – and
the lion kept coming. He described his response: 'This certainty
that he had not been stopped brought a nasty tightening up sort of
feeling, which was perhaps the most unpleasant part of the whole
affair.' The lion attacked, slamming Wienholt to the ground and
first biting off the stock of his gun, and then moving on to his arm
and shoulder:

> . . . he seized me and bit me several times through the wrist,
> breaking it badly and splintering some of the small bones. These
> bites hurt like fury at the moment; it was like a nine-inch nail
> being continually driven through one's hand. The lion bit very
> quickly, but with a horribly silent ferocity.

The lion moved toward his chest, inflicting injuries that were not
overly severe, but as he observed, 'the sight of his big, hairy head, so
near that we almost rubbed noses, was unlovely and offensive'.
    Luckily for Wienholt the lion may have felt the same way. He said:

> Suddenly, after biting me on the chest, the lion whipped around
> and cleared out of sight in the bushes. I would like to describe
> him as 'staggering away to die' but as a matter of strict truth he
> appeared to make off fairly briskly. Why he left me in this abrupt
> and unexpected way I do not know.

Wienholt and his quarry called it a draw. Arnold Wienholt was left
with 12 bite wounds and partial loss of the use of his right hand.
On 4 August that year, while he was recovering in his bush camp,
Britain and Australia declared war on Germany.
    When up and about, Wienholt made his way back to civilisation
on the back of a mule and armed with a plan to take the guerilla warfare he had witnessed during the Boer campaign to the

Germans in the region. His idea was rejected by the Commandant General, and later President, of South Africa, Jan Smuts. Decidedly annoyed at the rejection, Wienholt wrote:

> Smuts said all Australians were mad, all hunters were mad and apparently my scheme was also mad. He informed me there was no water, the natives would murder me! The Germans would shoot us! That only scallywags would go. In fact I had a very painful impression that he did not want to see the Germans attacked.

Wienholt then approached the British and met with a similar response. Disheartened, he finally headed back to Australia, saying, 'I am as miserable as a bandicoot having to sneak home like this, though of course I couldn't hold a rifle or anything else.'

He arrived in Sydney in January 1915. His first priority was to get his right hand functioning, at least in part, and then head back to Queensland to run his eye over the family business that had been minus his attention for 16 months. It was to be a short visit. He persuaded his bookkeeper at Widgee Station, Ivan Lewis to head back to Africa with him to conduct their own spot of guerilla warfare as irregular soldiers with any British or South African force that would take them on. Lewis was also a fine boxer and, unlike his mentor, a good shot. On 10 March 1915 the two, along with three handpicked horses, boarded the steamer *Clan Davidson*, bound for Cape Town. Rosamond Siemon described Wienholt at his departure as:

> ... mature, athletically lean, with yellow-green eyes piercing the distance from a face made older by his moustache and the small Vandyke beard. The Vandyke wasn't an affectation but the result of being unable to shave the large area of scarring left by the lion attack.

Back in Africa, Wienholt started knocking on doors. Thanks to his Eton old-boy network, and his knowledge of German South West Africa, he and Lewis were taken on as scouts and sworn in as privates in the British South African Police Force. He wrote to his sister Brenda, saying, 'I am so pleased with myself at having battled along to the end that I wouldn't change jobs with a Field Marshal.'

In various guises he fought in the African campaign until the end of the war, with a chunk of the time spent in the intelligence corps. By the end of hostilities, Wienholt had risen to the rank of captain and for gallantry had been awarded the Military Cross with bar (the bar is added for further acts that would warrant the award of a Military Cross) and a DSO (Distinguished Service Order), and Lewis was commissioned as an officer. Wienholt's abilities were not only recognised by his allies but also by his former enemies. A German officer wrote to one of his peers in March 1918, 'The wrathful Wienholt is prowling around you looking for his prey.'

The master of guerilla warfare, von Lettow-Vorbeck, told his men during the war:

> . . . from former experience it is known that Wienholt makes extended and daring patrols. Camps should be changed at night and postboys instructed to travel through the bush instead of going along a road if there is any sign of the enemy being in the neighbourhood.

The German was in a good position to comment, as Wienholt and his small band had been dodging the German search parties for weeks while gathering intelligence on their troop movements and dispositions, and undertaking guerilla warfare against the German guerillas. Unfortunately for Wienholt, an error in judgement in late 1915 brought him face to face with von Lettow-Vorbeck.

At dusk, he found, 'I had been led, quite unsuspectingly, into a party of enemy waiting for me in ambush right on the track.' He had misjudged the people of the local settlement, who turned out to be friendlier to the Germans, a fact that became apparent as a rifle was poked into his ribs. His next stop was a long journey to Liwale prison in what is now Tanzania, and after a few months there, a 14-day trek to another prison camp deep in the bush at Mangangira. As *Man* magazine in Australia reported, 'Wienholt was no longer a freebooting individualist but a number. Security was such that escape seemed impossible. For six months, he fretted, sweated and fumed in close confinement.'

It was to be his home for the first months of 1916. Food was in short supply and the prisoners lived on rice and beans, supplemented by meat from an occasional hunting success. Dysentery joined hunger as a regular and debilitating companion. One of the few, rare dietary high points was a mug of rendered elephant fat that Weinholt believed improved his weakened state, commenting, 'I felt much stronger for it; in fact it just made all the difference.' The prospect of escape was also a constant companion and one evening, at the peak of a violent tropical storm, he and his men slipped away from their captors and took to the bush. Wienholt said of the flight:

> The country was just a big sea of level bush, with a little really thick thorn bush. We went fast, and though not very strong (our feet got very sore and badly cut), we travelled like madmen; for we were free, and terribly afraid of being recaptured.

Fifteen days later, and in poor condition from disease and lack of food and water, they happened upon a friendly scout who took them to safety. For five weeks Wienholt was critically ill from a nearly lethal combination of malaria, Blackwater fever (a complication of malaria) and dysentery. It took him almost a year to fully recover.

With his exploits well publicised, in February 1919 he returned to Australia as a hero and something of a celebrity. He married a family friend, Enid Jones, returned to Queensland and set up house at Washpool Farm, and promptly announced, 'It has always been my ambition to sit in Federal Parliament. I think it is a laudable ambition so I might make an attempt for a seat.' On 13 December that year he became the National Party member in the House of Representatives for the seat of Moreton. He found fairly early in his Federal career, however, that politics really wasn't for him, writing to his cousin Arthur Clarke, 'I shall never rise high in politics. I detest speeches and functions, my heart is away in Central Africa and I am longing to be back hunting there again. I hate the look and smell of city humanity.' When the time came to nominate for the 1922 elections, Wienholt didn't bother. Instead he went back to Africa lion-hunting. For eight months of every second year during the 1920s Arnold Wienholt, by then a slightly better shot, slipped into the role of big-game hunter.

He also became a regular public speaker and occasional journalist.

As the 1920s drew to a close, Wienholt, now in his early 50s, was beginning to feel his age. Rosamond Siemon wrote:

He had been living on danger's edge for too long, making himself believe he still enjoyed it. He was 53. The fevers, painful abscesses and jagged rheumatism, coupled with an unbalanced diet for eight months of every hunting year, had made inroads into his coveted physical fitness. His eyes, always peaked like a lion's, and as yellow, were jaundiced from a liver damaged by Blackwater fever and quinine. In his constant need to prove that he was the best, the pressure took a higher toll than he would admit. This was the last hunt. He was ready for change.

On the death of the state member for Fassifern in 1930, Wienholt contested the by-election and found himself back in Parliament. Rosemary Siemon observed, 'The handsome, blond, muscular young politician of 1913 was now an erect, alert and sparely built 53 year old.' Journalist Clem Lack took a slightly more entertaining view, writing that Wienholt looked 'more like an artist from the Latin Quarter who had wandered by mistake into the House'.

His return to state politics was not a spectacular success. With a parliament not averse to sliding its collective nose into the trough, the abstemious Wienholt found himself increasingly isolated with few political friends.

He decided not to recontest his seat in 1935 saying:

I think I can do no good in the House so why should I stop there and really mislead my own people if they think I can? Political life for itself without the feeling that one is doing something of definite use and help, has never appealed to me, and I do not know or see where I am being of service.

Exit Arnold Wienholt from political life. Ethiopia in the prelude to World War II would be his next adventure.

8

FIRST TO WAR

Arnold Wienholt's career had been marked by a loyalty to the now fading British Empire and a passion for the underdog. The two came together with Mussolini's invasion of Ethiopia. He was stirred by the fate of the Ethiopians and believed, quite rightly, that the invasion threatened British colonies in Africa. For Wienholt, Mussolini's actions were 'coldly premeditated and blackly treacherous'. Though now nearly 60, he thought it was time for one more run at the enemy.

Again he used the Eton old-boy network, persuading the editor of the Brisbane *Courier Mail* to authorise him as a war correspondent – an effective ruse at a time when battle was raging and the Italians had yet to quash reporting.

Wienholt wrote to his sister Brenda:

> I am rather hankering to see something of the struggle in East Africa between the Italians and the Abyssinians. I fancy the Italians have bitten off more than they can chew, and I have been offered credentials to act as a war correspondent for some associated newspapers. The difficulty is to be sure of being allowed into Abyssinia these days and that's the only side I want to see things from. To my mind any nation believing it can rely on such an absurdity as the League [of Nations] instead of its own patriotism only shows decadence.

He also observed:

> The Ethiopians were cruelly misled, shamefully betrayed and basely abandoned by the so-called League of Nations, the disgrace, dishonour resting not only on the wretched League as a whole but also on individual members in proportion to their

strength and power to protect those for whose security they had pledged their word.

Wienholt's faith in his Empire was sorely tested.

He departed on the Orient liner *Orion* on 22 November 1935, bound for Aden and then on to Djibouti. The *Orion* would later serve as a troop carrier in the convoy that took Allan Brown, Ken Burke, Ron Wood, Ted Body and Bill Howell to the Middle East, and to the beginning of their work in the liberation of Ethiopia.

In Djibouti he boarded the train bound for Addis Ababa and was on his way when news of the debacle of the Hoare–Laval pact broke. By Christmas Eve the new correspondent was rubbing shoulders with more experienced hands such as Evelyn Waugh and a young WF Deedes (the latter becoming a Minister in various Conservative governments, confidante of Margaret Thatcher and editor of London's *Daily Telegraph*). They were at the Hotel Imperial, which boasted its own park full of eucalypts, beds of swaying carnations, and in the bar and dining room on the ground floor, an upright Steinway for musical interludes.

Deedes, who didn't approach his adventure with the same zest as Wienholt but managed to arrive with an estimated 270 kilograms of luggage, apparently did not appreciate the niceties and later wrote, 'I had arrived in a ramshackle town with facilities unequal to the invasion of journalists that was taking place. Most of them were quartered in great discomfort at the Imperial Hotel.'

Many of the correspondents had very little idea about Ethiopia and what to expect, much to the amusement of Cornelius Van Hemert Engert, who commented on those arriving with:

> . . . rifles, telescopes and ant-proof trunks, medicine chests, gas masks, pack saddles and vast wardrobes of costume suitable for every conceivable social or climatic emergency. Gallagher bought a mule train. Laurence Stallings of Fox Movietone took a large red Indian motorcycle and side car.

According to Van Hemert Engert, the media pack encountered an unexpected dash of colour thanks to Haile Selassie's drillmaster, an African American named Hubert Fauntleroy Julian, who had adopted the rank of colonel and called himself 'The Black Eagle of Harlem'.

The 'Colonel', who had a jaded past as a stunt parachutist, arms dealer and military adviser to numerous African despots, and was allegedly one of the first African American pilots to fly solo across the Atlantic two years after Lindbergh's 1927 crossing, woke the journalists each morning as he drilled the Emperor's troops in the field behind the Imperial. Australian journalist Noel Monks reckoned the Colonel 'bawled at the Abyssinians in French, in German, in Norwegian, in English and in gibberish. In anything but their own language, Amharic. With Julian on the job, no-one in the Imperial Hotel got much sleep after 6.30 a.m.'

The camaraderie of a bar full of journalists and a rude awakening each morning wasn't the teetotalling Wienholt's style and he soon moved to a small house, with a touch of Australia courtesy of the surrounding gum trees. His reports were not spectacular, and the *Courier Mail* pitched the stories more at the famous-hunter-turned-reporter than the content, with headlines like 'Captain Wienholt in Addis Ababa' and 'Captain Wienholt gets his gun'.

His career as a war correspondent lasted just two months. He was frustrated by the Italians making it difficult for journalists to travel outside the capital and so in February 1936 he persuaded the Red Cross to take him on as a transport officer, something that could utilise his talents and get him closer to the fighting. Close to the front, Wienholt threw himself into helping the injured as a de facto medic, dealing with wounds from the clashes and the horrendous results of mustard gas. In addition to his humanitarian work, Wienholt was rumoured to have seized the occasional opportunity and engaged Italian military targets. He was also a regular supplier of intelligence to the British Legation in Addis Ababa.

Wienholt's work in the field provided a sharp learning curve on things Ethiopian, evidenced by his later writings. These accounts of his time in the country demonstrate the contrast between his very proper (and now very old-fashioned) imperial and often imperious views with the reality of life in a Third World country enduring a repressive colonial regime. He wrote:

> It should be realized that the Ethiopians are a most difficult people to understand and amongst themselves as against white people, the most secretive imaginable; without knowledge of their language, one's difficulty is immensely increased. Amharic is a very difficult language to get a hold of quickly ... Ethiopia is,

to a European, very much a land of contradictions, contracts and general topsy-turvydom. Riders dismount off-side of their horse or mule. 'Yes' often really means 'no', especially with an Ethiopian official. One might expect buttons would be sewn off rather than sewn on; indeed, the only thing that happens in Ethiopia as expected is that the sun still rises in the east there. For [the] Ethiopian is literally half-civilised (and thus half-barbarous) and amongst the Emperor's subjects were all extremes.

At the end of April, just two months after joining the Red Cross, it was obvious that the war was lost, and Wienholt returned to Addis Ababa. Australian newspapers had reported that he had been killed near the town of Dessie, and Wienholt was pleased to report that rumours of his death were in fact just that. In the *Courier Mail* he reported that he 'was left in Dessie, knowing nothing of the approach of the Italian-paid shiftas [guerillas]. I divided my unarmed caravan into three groups, the first of which was killed in ambush, whereupon I decided to attack and forced the shiftas to flee. I did not see a single Italian.'

Wienholt's time and usefulness in Ethiopia – at this time – were rapidly drawing to a close. He didn't leave willingly, and later wrote in his short 1938 book *The Africans' Last Stronghold*:

So keen had I become on continuing the campaign that for a long time afterward I actually felt that Haile Selassie, King of Kings and Emperor of Ethiopia, had deserted me, his poor transport officer, personally. I think I must have been either half mad, or at least have lost all sense of proportion.

In May, as Haile Selassie headed to Djibouti on his way to exile, Arnold Wienholt found himself on the very next train. He recalled that on boarding the train:

Ashamed of being forced to fly in this disgraceful fashion, I had little inclination to speak, yet within me I felt that this was not the end of Ethiopia's 4000 years of freedom. I believed (and still do) the struggle for national existence of these poor, brave, betrayed people would yet arise in a manner far more formidable than any the apparent victors had yet experienced.

On his return to Australia, Wienholt held a press conference to tell of his time in this exotic, distant country. He wasn't impressed by some of the Ethiopians, and made his point concisely, saying, 'brigands and brainless chiefs were worse than bombs'. He followed up with a barrage of articles submitted to the *Courier Mail*, all decrying the Italian invasion and colonisation by the Italians, and the world's failure to intervene, and all of which were rejected by the editor, who commented, '[As] the Abyssinian campaign has been completely superseded by later events, including the terrible civil war in Spain, it would be hardly worth our while to publish them.' Wienholt and his long, intriguing career were yesterday's news.

Nonetheless, rejection didn't dampen his passion for the Ethiopian cause. As Rosamond Siemon wrote, 'his concern was for oppressed people, but it was danger to the Empire that obsessed him'. In an interview with journalist Alan Mickle, that obsession shone through. Mickle wrote:

> . . . he told me how he hated Chamberlain, 'the cold blooded logical businessman', and that Mussolini, 'the posing theatrical braggart', and of the overwhelming contempt he had for the Italians as soldiers. Once during the conversation he stood up. A defeated man he may have been but he was not a conquered man. Standing there, this tall thin man with the pointed beard and flashing eyes, I saw Don Quixote come to revisit the earth. Here was indeed a knightly seeker of lost causes for which to fight.

Though the daily press wasn't overly keen on his views, he found himself quite successful as a public speaker, taking every opportunity to lecture on matters Ethiopian and the threat to the Empire. In late 1937, just as Allan Brown would do a few years later to get himself and his sergeants into Ethiopia, Wienholt decided to lobby and pester the British personally. Both he and Brown shared the experience of being ignored by the ruling class of the British military establishment. En route to London, he stopped in Aden, then a British colony and port city on the approaches to the Red Sea and something of a hotbed of Ethiopians plotting the removal of the Italians. Wienholt took the opportunity of the long sea voyage to study Arabic, in part to minimise the language barrier that he had found troubling in Ethiopia. In Aden, he cultivated some sources and, armed with recent intelligence, sailed on to Britain and took up residence in a hotel in London's Bayswater.

One of his first trips was to Bath, where he wangled an appointment with Haile Selassie. Rosamond Siemon wrote:

The meeting was [a] half-hour of strict protocol and formality, conducted in French, which Arnold only half understood. The unsmiling Emperor arranged to discuss Arnold's views later at his legation in London. Instinct told him he had wasted his time. His hopes sank to zero. This was his first and last meeting with the Emperor. Wienholt was not as dazzled by the Emperor as he had hoped to be. He wrote, 'He unfortunately does not possess the courage of a fighting spirit. Otherwise he would not have abandoned his army and country. It is not likely that he would ever return to Abyssinia as a ruler.'

However, the dismal meeting did little to dampen Wienholt's zeal for liberating the Ethiopian people. He pestered Whitehall with plans for a patriot-led uprising in Ethiopia. As mentioned earlier, Weinholt ventured into print in 1938 with a brief book about his experiences in Ethiopia, The *Africans' Last Stronghold* and, in a case of very strange bedfellows, he became a regular contributor to Sylvia Pankhurst's *New Times and Ethiopian News*. None of this had any impact on Prime Minister Neville Chamberlain or his Cabinet when, on 16 April 1938, they signed the Anglo–Italian agreement. As Churchill observed, the agreement gave 'Italy a free hand in Abyssinia and Spain in return for the imponderable value of Italian good will in Central Europe'. A thoroughly disheartened Wienholt left Britain bound for Australia, stopping briefly in Aden to share the dismal results of his lobbying with his local contacts.

Wienholt took rejection of his views on Ethiopia as a challenge and when, back in Australia, he resumed his position on the hustings, where he would talk to anyone who would lend an ear about his 'free Ethiopia' cause. On the day Prime Minister Robert Menzies declared war on Germany, Wienholt was back in the role of grazier, inspecting one of the family properties at Ghinghinda in Central Queensland. He wrote to his cousin and friend Arthur Clarke:

As you know I wanted to face the music after Ethiopia. It infuriated me to see us giving legal sanction ... and legal consent to

so-called conquest . . . I will go as soon as I can get transport to
where I can get congenial and suitable service. I know where, for
I am sure Italy is coming in against us.

The 'where' he alluded to was Aden and its many fans of Ethiopian
insurrection. Again, Wienholt readily pushed aside family and
business to head off on another adventure. He was on the cusp
of his 62nd birthday. He left Australia on 27 September on the
Dutch liner SS *Nieuw Zeeland* bound for Singapore – as usual,
he didn't miss a public relations opportunity, and made sure the
Queensland press was aware of his departure. Just two weeks later,
Ted Body and Ken Burke volunteered to serve in the Australian
army, with their three colleagues following suit shortly after. In
the first weeks of 1940, they would head in the same direction as
Arnold Wienholt.

On 10 November 1939, while the four sergeants were learning
the art of gunnery at Ingleburn, Arnold Wienholt arrived in Aden
and quickly got down to business: he rented a flat in a 'crowded,
depressed starkly arid old camp area in Aden's crater' (a reference
to the oldest part of the city that was built on an extinct volcano)
and hired an interpreter fluent in Arabic and Amharic and set about
brushing up on his Arabic. This adventure proved to be more successful than his previous forays into war zones. On his rounds of the
various military and colonial offices in Aden, he came to the notice
of two men who would prove useful in getting him back into the
military and eventually into Ethiopia.

The first man was Major Arthur Bentinck, an old Etonian like
Wienholt, and also very familiar with Ethiopia. He was described
by the adventurer Wilfred Thesiger as a man with a 'gruff manner, a
game leg and a pronounced cast in one eye'. Bentinck was younger
than Wienholt – 52 – and like Wienholt he was troubled by old
injuries, in his case from World War I. Bentinck's job was to keep his
ears attuned to the various plots and counter-plots festering in the
wartime port city.

The second man was an Australian, Colonel Walter 'Bill'
Cawthorn, a tall and dignified man with a dashing military moustache. Cawthorn started his career as a schoolteacher before
volunteering to serve with the Australian army in World War I.
He rose to the rank of regimental sergeant major and was then
commissioned as an officer. After World War II, he served as High

Commissioner to Canada and then as head of ASIO from 1960 until his retirement in 1968.

While continuing to contribute to Sylvia Pankhurst's publications and to Australian journals, Wienholt also sent regular, unsolicited reports to the War Office in London. One of these reports – on the situation in Ethiopia – came to Colonel Cawthorn's attention. At that point, Cawthorn was honing his spying skills as head of the Middle East Intelligence Centre in Cairo. In the report, Wienholt expounded the benefits of guerilla warfare, putting in a plug for his own abilities. He wrote:

Why should we always risk missing the bus when we might recover a lot of ground there? Lord knows there's been enough underground work and influences against GB [Great Britain] from Italian sources for a long time. I should certainly like to see an attempt allowed. I think I could manage it all right and v. quickly. Please don't think this is just a madman's idea. The chance is really there for us to 'stir the possum' for a change and get a little of our own back.

In May 1940 Wienholt received an unexpected letter from Cawthorn, thanking him for some photographs that had been included in one of the earlier missives. Wienholt's enthusiasm gushed in his reply, writing to Cawthorn that:

I would like to do something useful and would gladly serve in any capacity . . . if in the bush, like natives and never mind being on my own. I have already said I would not attempt to enter Ethiopia (though I should like to) without the Government's permission. If this permission to go to Sudan is not procurable can I be advised to that effect (and this advice would be appreciated one way or the other) so that I can push off and seek the chance of doing something more useful elsewhere than I can here.

His enthusiasm to enter Ethiopia would be shared, perhaps with a touch more restraint, by Lieutenant Allan Brown and his four sergeants just a few months later.

What Wienholt didn't know was that Major Bentinck, Colonel Cawthorn and Colonel Daniel Sandford were well advanced in planning an adventure very similar to what Wienholt had been advocating, to make Ethiopia 'too hot for the Italians'. None of them, at that point, had heard of Lieutenant Allan Brown of the 2/1st Field Regiment in Palestine, who had formulated a very similar plan and had just begun his own campaign to persuade his superiors to give him the green light to make it a reality.

Four days after Italy formally entered the war, Arnold Wienholt was back in uniform. At the age of 62, he was commissioned as lieutenant. Three days later, on 17 June, his orders came through to fly to the Sudan. Mission 101 was about to become a reality.

9

A CUNNING PLAN

Unknown to Haile Selassie in exile, and to Ethiopians under Mussolini's jackboot, Britain's War Office had plans regarding the Italian occupation of Ethiopia that were in direct contrast to the spirit of the Anglo–Italian agreement. The War Office and General Archibald Wavell, then Commander in Chief of the Middle East and a little closer to the action in Cairo, disagreed with the diplomatic pandering to the Italians and had started plotting for Britain to oust the Italians from Ethiopia. With the Italians to the west in Libya and strengthening their grip on the horn of Africa, the British forces in Egypt and Sudan were looking more and more like they were stuck between a rock and an unyielding place. Vital oil supply lines, essential to successfully prosecute the war, were under threat. Bravado and rude comments about the abilities of the Italian troops were cold comfort when their numerical superiority on the ground and in the air was taken into consideration. *The Abyssinian Campaigns,* published by the British Government shortly after the end of the war, observed, 'our own forces were ludicrously inferior in numbers. There were three British battalions – the 2nd West Yorkshires, the 1st Worcestershires and the 1st Essex – less than 2500 men in all to defend Khartoum the capital, Port Sudan the harbour and the Atbara railway junctions from any attack based on [forces from] Eritrea.'

Also in great jeopardy was the Suez Canal, a critical link in the supply line to both the British homeland and to the success of the Allies' campaign in the Middle East and Mediterranean. Also relevant was US President Roosevelt's refusal to allow US shipping into the Red Sea and Suez, which meant that US ships carrying supplies to Britain and her bases in North Africa from the Pacific and Indian ocean areas would have to take the longer and more dangerous route, thanks to the U-boats, via the Atlantic. If the Canal's safety could be guaranteed, then Roosevelt may soften his view.

With all these strategic issues percolating, a cunning plan was needed. In the month before the declaration of war against Germany, Wavell sent for Colonel Daniel Sandford, and the two discussed Sandford's plan to encourage the Ethiopian patriots to upset the Italians as deeply and frequently as possible through guerilla warfare. This plan would eventually have a distinctly Australian flavour thanks to the involvement of Arnold Wienholt, and later Allan Brown and his men.

Dan Sandford was an ideal choice for the task. He had served in India and the Middle East for most of his career and after distinguished service in World War I he had headed to Ethiopia with his wife Christine, resigned his commission and taken up the life of a farmer in the lush tablelands to the north of Addis Ababa. He was also well connected to the Ethiopian hierarchy. When the Italians invaded, Sandford and his family packed up and returned to England.

Sandford was an affable man, bespectacled, slightly plump, balding and with a moustache, and could have passed for a pleasant local grocer. Edwin Chapman-Andrews reckoned he was 'well known to the Emperor and to all the foreign visitors to Ethiopia . . . at 58 he was remarkably fit, energetic and self-reliant.'

With his extensive network of contacts, and the respect of many significant Ethiopians, Sandford, despite his advancing years, was considered the best man to spearhead an insurrection. According to *The Abyssinian Campaigns*, the Italians, though well entrenched and superior in numbers and equipment, were very nervous about the potential of a local uprising, with that nervousness being a 'severe drain upon their resources and a severe handicap upon their dispositions'. On 1 September 1939 Sandford arrived in Cairo and was given command of the Ethiopian section of the intelligence command. Wavell gave him a free hand to develop plans to cause as much havoc as possible, saying, 'You are my expert on Ethiopia. I will leave you to get on with it until it comes my way.'

Sandford, harking back to his artillery days, called his plan Mission 101, after a fuse commonly used in Royal Artillery, and hoped the common fuse would ignite a common cause. His first venture was Khartoum, a far larger centre of Ethiopian insurgency than Cairo or Aden, and also where he struck his first hurdle. General Sir William Platt in Khartoum disagreed with Sandford's belief that Haile Selassie was still popular with his people.

Despite the problem in selling his plans to Platt, Sandford made headway with his logistics, preparing arms depots and supply lines to his old friends, the tribal chiefs in Ethiopia, who were keen to lend a hand. To run his local operation he recruited Robert Cheesman, an old friend and a former British Consul in the Ethiopian province of Gojjam, a key location to any successful fight. He was 61 years old, giving the new outfit a 'Dad's Army' feel that would only grow when Arnold Wienholt joined.

Toward the close of 1939, Haile Selassie's confidante, private secretary and sometime spy, the Eritrean-born Lorenzo Taezaz, slipped into Cairo. He had been travelling through Ethiopia for the previous few months in a variety of disguises, including an army officer and a priest. His mission was to tour the key Gojjam region and nearby districts, set up intelligence links, assess the Italian forces, and, as journalist Daniel Kindie observed, 'give the volcano a kick'. In heartening news for Sandford, Taezaz had found that the Italians preferred the comforts of their forts and fortified towns rather than roaming the countryside. The patriots, it seemed, already had them on edge.

Secret reports prepared at this time gave a snapshot of the situation in Ethiopia. One report noted:

> Resistance has been maintained until now without foreign aid. After having all but disappeared totally and ceased to be able to maintain itself except in the form of mere acts of banditry, resistance displayed a new recrudescence at the beginning of the rainy season, and registered some partial successes. These successes have restored confidence in the rebels . . . Any success, however small, begets enthusiasm and draws new adherents, particularly among the newly rallied chiefs.

The report estimated that in the critically important Gojjam province there were 20 000 rebels. Captain George Steer, a former journalist, personal friend of the Emperor and later attached to him as staff officer, had a less than enthusiastic view. He thought the patriots had 'long since ceased to attack Italian forts' and were 'flagging in attacks on Italian communications. The enemy garrisons, by threats of reprisals on villages and property, were gradually extending their area of control and forming Banda [native soldiers] of irregular submitted Ethiopians.'

Another secret report recommended the best course of action to destabilise the Italians to be:

> Attacks on small convoys, non-escorted on certain routes, after making sure of local intelligence in order to obtain necessary information in a manner to impede the revictualling [resupply-ing] of certain posts, and to render these posts, as well as certain regions, insecure. These attacks could be accompanied by the destruction of small bridges, etc which would give the personnel engaged practise for more important sapping operations.

The report also went on to recommend attacks on the major road that linked Addis Ababa to Asmara in Eritrea. This report accorded nicely with the wiser heads of the British military and with Sandford and his cohorts. It would lay the ground rules for the warfare soon to be waged by Allan Brown, Ken Burke, Ron Wood, Bill Howell and Ted Body.

With the arrival of 1940 – prior to Mussolini's declaration of war against Britain – Sandford went touring to drum up support, and found the French in Djibouti to be very friendly but non-committal when it came to committing to fight the Italians. The Governor of British Somaliland was less pleasant and 'entirely unsympathetic to the idea of encouraging the Ethiopian revolt' according to Dan Sandford. Not one to take rejection to heart, he soldiered on meeting friends and colleagues, describing in a letter to his wife Christine how they had 'trotted in from the bush to see me. This afternoon I spent three or four happy hours with the exiles from the land we love.' He returned to Cairo comfortable in the knowledge that with sufficient leadership and equipment, the patriots could deliver the right results. To get those results, he drew up Plan A and Plan B.

Plan A, later accepted by the War Office and retitled Scheme A, was made up of 'notes on the Abyssinian uprising to be brought about in the event of war with Italy'. The suitably retitled Scheme B detailed the propaganda war that would follow. Spin-doctoring was another of Sandford's interesting collection of talents.

Upon the approval of Scheme A, Sandford began recruiting so that in the event of war he would have the officers, men and logistics ready to put Mission 101 into action. When Italy joined the war on 10 June 1940, Sandford swung into action and two days later Mission 101's first group left Cairo for the five-day trip via train and steamer to Khartoum. On 19 June, 'A' Echelon of the mission headed to Gedaref, a town in mountainous eastern Sudan very close to the Ethiopian border, carrying medical personnel and 40 mules laden with two months' worth of provisions. Arnold Wienholt had by then been added to Mission 101 as an intelligence officer and was en route to Khartoum. General Platt was not as swift off the mark as the men of Mission 101 and on 19 June he formally ordered the 'entry into Ethiopia of British Mission 101 under Colonel Sandford who will coordinate the actions of the Abyssinians under my general directions'.

Platt ordered Sandford to be established in Ethiopia before 1 August, a challenging task because it was the height of the wet season and moving about the highlands was often a difficult, dangerous and just plain miserable undertaking. His next task was the 'coordination of rebel activity so as to prevent enemy troop movements north from Gondar [the old imperial capital 500 kilometres north of Addis Ababa] and south and east from Dangila [a former slave-trade hub about 160 kilometres south from Gondar] in Gojjam'. Both towns were key locations on the main road from Addis Ababa through to Eritrea. This phase of the plan is where the five Australians under Allan Brown would enter the fray. The mission would clear the way for British troops advancing from the Sudan and prevent Italian reinforcements.

Shortly before Italy's declaration of war, General Platt had sent letters, written on linen, to the District Commissioner in Gedaref. These letters were to be held until war was declared and then distributed to 11 Ethiopian chiefs of the patriot movement. Though Britain's track record to this point had been poor, these letters promised arms, munitions, money and food if the chiefs would send mules to the border to collect them. When the curtain rose, runners made their way into Ethiopia with the letters. Sandford's first task was to coordinate these disparate forces into an effective guerilla campaign.

A little spice was added to Sandford's preparations with the arrival of Haile Selassie in the Middle East on 26 June. According to Major Cheesman:

It transpired that the Emperor left England in conditions of secrecy on 24th June under pseudonym of 'Mr Strong'.

He brought with him his second son Prince Makonnen who had been whisked out of the classroom at Wellington College to join his father in London. The journey to Plymouth had been made at night by car, finding the way through blacked-out villages and with all signposts removed. The Emperor's staff consisted of his two confidential secretaries Lorenzo Taezaz and Wolde Giorgis Wode Yohannes, and George Steer. From Plymouth they had travelled by Sunderland flying-boat to Malta and Alexandria.

During the stopover in Alexandria, the Emperor and his entourage waited in the recently captured Italian Sailing Club, where the pictures of Mussolini had been swiftly removed from the walls. From there, it was on to Wadi Halfa in the Sudan and then Khartoum, where the secrecy of the trip had been so tight very few knew of the arrival. Cheesman observed, 'The unannounced arrival caused some embarrassment as no suitable accommodation had been arranged, and what was equally important, no precautions had been taken for His Majesty's safety.' His arrival wasn't universally well received, with Wilfred Thesiger commenting:

> [The visit] had not been welcomed by some officials who regarded his presence as an embarrassment. To conceal his identity, he was given the ridiculous and humiliating pseudonym of 'Mr Smith'. The fact is that the Italian conquest of Abyssinia had gratified not a few, both in the Sudan and in Kenya, who hoped it would lead to a civilized administration in that country and mark the end of raids across the frontier. Now we were at war with Italy, they hoped that Britain would eventually take over and administer Abyssinia.

Thesiger, then in Gallabat, a town at the foot of the escarpment that formed the border between the Sudan and Ethiopia, continued by acknowledging that, 'across the border, however, news of the Emperor's arrival in the Sudan was greeted with rapture by the Patriots and dismay by the Italians'.

Selassie was also greeted by his old friend Dan Sandford, who brought him up to speed on the plans for Mission 101 and counselled the Emperor on the reality they both faced, saying later, 'I had to disabuse His Imperial Majesty ... of the belief that a large force was waiting for him with tanks and guns with which to enter his kingdom.' Sandford reported that Haile Selassie had recovered from his trip, 'and takes a very sane view. He is a wonderful little man.'

The British had a similarly sane view about their lack of strength, with General Wavell candidly commenting, 'I am facing an Italian army which could walk right through the Sudan tomorrow if it wanted to. It doesn't want to because I'm bluffing it with all my available forces.'

During the months leading up to Italy's declaration of war on 10 June, relations on the Sudan–Ethiopia border had been almost convivial, with General Platt reporting, 'A good deal of fraternisation between British and Italians on the frontier has been taking place.' The general, while visiting the area over the 1939–40 festive season, had been pleased by Italian hospitality. He commented, 'On New Year's Eve when I was visiting Gallabat I was most hospitably entertained to dinner by the Italians at Metemma on the opposite side of the frontier. There were about 24 Italian officers present, all most friendly.' It seemed that the Italians had superior catering as well as troops and air power.

On the day of the declaration of war, Wilfred Thesiger and his men shattered the pleasant atmosphere on the border by machine-gunning the closest Italian positions. Friendly relations went out the window. He was prevented in following up his handiwork by a signal from his superiors in Khartoum preventing any offensive actions without permission, so it was back to watching and waiting. The Italians did, however, flex some military muscle.

The Duke of Aosta, a far more reasonable man than Marshal Graziani whom he'd replaced, had been told to cool his heels when he proposed a decisive strike across the border into the Sudan. That didn't preclude him poking at nearby British camps.

Thesiger reported that things were hotting up in Gallabat:

On 27th July the Italians launched a full scale attack on the fort at Gallabat, and the platoon, commanded by Yusbashi Abdallah [a Sudanese officer] withdrew after inflicting some casualties and itself suffering two killed and four wounded. On the same day the Italians captured Kassala, further north, after which they made no further attempt to invade Sudan.

The Italians who attacked Gallabat were posted at Metemma just 500 metres away and their sortie gained them control over a part of the Khartoum-to-Port-Sudan rail link (on the Red Sea and the Sudan's only port).

The British Government's official history of this slice of World War II, *The Abyssinian Campaigns*, gave a disturbing account of the tactical situation at this point:

> At the end of August 1940 the enemy was in a strong position. He controlled the southern entrance of the Red Sea. There was nothing to stop him sweeping up through the Sudan. The southern jaw of his pincers was placed too close, and the northern jaw – Graziani's army from Libya – was touching the skin of the Egyptian plum . . . Resolute and coordinated attacks might have closed the jaws altogether, and Italy might have contributed Africa, as Germany was contributing Europe, to the Axis spoils. The British Empire might have been split by a hostile mass stretching from Narvik to Bulawayo.

10

UPHILL INTO ETHIOPIA

When the Italians captured Gallabat, Sandford's plans took a small knock; he had intended Mission 101 to use the town as the staging point for their incursion into Ethiopia. Instead, he decided to cross the border at a nearby village called Limona, about 19 kilometres south of Metemma.

The original plan to have Haile Selassie accompany his old friend into Ethiopia was temporarily shelved. Sandford's superiors were not as enthused as he was, and they observed, 'Colonel Sandford was by nature an optimist. He seemed to think that if he pretended that there were no Italians between the Sudan and Gojjam they would have been reckoned with.' General Platt was not prepared to risk their only ace card, the Emperor, unless:

> ... we could ensure that, if pressed, his line of retreat back to the Sudan would remain secure. We were determined to take no chances of his falling into Italian hands. If he were to go in by any of the Gallabat routes this could not be guaranteed until the Italians had been driven out of Metemma and Kwara.

Kwara was a fort occupied by the Italians and their native troops.

Platt was also concerned about losing Sandford, with Cheesman writing, 'we cannot under any circumstances allow Colonel Sandford to run unnecessary risks. There is absolutely no-one else with the essential understanding of the Ethiopian, knowledge of their language and conditions in the interior that could replace him.' The problem the general faced was that though Sandford was irreplaceable, he was also the only man with the requisite skills to lead the mission and make it work. What tipped the scales was intelligence indicating that despite their successes, the Italians' morale was declining, thanks in part to:

... fear of the Abyssinians. The Italians showed more dread of the small numbers of elusive forces of chiefs than many times larger numbers of regular British troops who stood and fought and could be found the next day. They also feared the effect of the general unrest on the large numbers of their Colonial Battalions and native Banda [soldiers] in whom they depended for their safety and yet could not trust.

For all Mussolini's rhetoric about avenging the Italian defeat at Adwa, his troops may have remembered the Ethiopians' grisly treatment of their prisoners.

Sandford was finally given the green light and he and his four men, all British soldiers, including a doctor and a radio operator, together with a small number of patriots to act as guides, departed their camp near Doka at 4.10 p.m. on 6 August, along with 54 mules and 36 donkeys, six wireless sets, 13 303 rifles, three revolvers and 30 very old rifles that wouldn't have looked out of place in a museum display. Also on the backs of the animals were boxes of Maria Theresa thalers and sufficient rations for 14 days. (The Maria Theresa thalers to fund Mission 101 came courtesy of some deft arm-twisting by the SOE's chief, Sir Frank Nelson. He persuaded the Royal Mint to coin a few hundred thousand pounds' worth of the coins, and despite their recent minting all were dated 1764. The silver for the coins came from the mysterious coffers of the SOE. The 'genuine' coin was accepted without question in Ethiopia.)

In the reverse of most military missions, Sandford's was top-heavy with officers, causing one wit to observe it was 'just a head with no body'. On 12 August Sandford and the advance party of Mission 101 crossed the border near Limona and into Ethiopia, behind Italian lines and bound for the Gojjam province. They faced a long, hard slog, with not only the Italians to worry about, but the wet season, which usually began in mid June and tapered off toward the end of September. Thesiger wrote, 'Now 58 years old, Dan Sandford was setting out during the rainy season on a journey that few younger men would have attempted at that time of year, even in peacetime.' To add to their problems, the region they were entering was host to a few unpleasant surprises such as malaria and yellow fever, both transmitted by mosquitoes.

To lower the risk of being observed by the enemy, Sandford and his men kept clear of the well-worn tracks used by the locals and their mules, and instead blazed their own trail through the scrub, bamboo and low forest. On their trek they crossed eight rivers and scaled an escarpment. Progress was slow, but aside from the safety of a road less travelled, Sandford believed, quite rightly, that it would make them harder to spot from patrolling aircraft. With the wet season in full cry, the going was hard and, as the reports noted, 'there were several rivers to cross, now in spate, and the patriot escorts were of great assistance in getting the animals through the flood'.

On 20 August, after a gruelling trek through virgin bush, they arrived at their first scheduled major resting place, the village of Sarako. The first leg of the trip had taken its toll, with the loss of four mules and three donkeys from the horse sickness that was common in the area, and in some cases just plain exhaustion. As for the men, malaria had affected a few, both British and locals.

Sandford marked his arrival at Sarako by reading to the local chiefs a stirring note from Haile Selassie, in which he told them:

> . . . we have entered into a covenant with the British Government of military cooperation to restore freedom to Ethiopia. Azaj Kabado Tesemma [Selassie's representative on the mission] has been ordered by us to proceed to Ethiopia and tell you the good news and he brings with him English commanders under orders from the British Government to help the patriots. Therefore we tell you to receive him with every possible assistance, to see they encounter no difficulties, and to help them speedily on their way.

To reinforce the Emperor's message to the chiefs the RAF flew over the region, dropping copies of the message directly to the villages. Nine days later, and well rested, Sandford and his band were off again, heading deeper into Ethiopia with the objective of finding a suitable base to house Haile Selassie and spearhead their campaign.

Much to the chagrin of both Thesiger and Wienholt, they had been left behind at the camp not far from Gallabat. Thesiger had been told by General Platt that he 'wished me first to gain experience of more orthodox soldiering'. As for Wienholt, Thesiger said, 'being short of mules, Sandford had left Arnold Wienholt at our camp, to follow as soon as he could raise transport. We suggested he should join us in the stockade we had built, but he preferred to camp nearby.'

Wienholt's arrival at the camp had caused something of a stir with another officer, Ronnie Critchley, an imposing sight at

6 feet 6 inches who had ended up in intelligence after unsuccess-
fully trying to fold himself into a tank. Critchley said of his first
encounter with Wienholt:

> The strange excitable figure of Arnold Wienholt suddenly
> appeared and announced he had been working with Sylvia
> Pankhurst . . . stirring up trouble against the Italians. Tough and
> rangy, with a goatee beard and ramrod-stiff back, he was years
> older than everyone else. In his unconventional rumpled bush
> clothes, topped by his own creation of a shako-type sun helmet,
> he looked a little more odd than most.

Wienholt was, however, wearing his medals, making a clear point that
he knew a bit about the business of war. When he arrived, he brought
with him 11 donkeys, six armed Ethiopians and a Sudanese cook
who apparently had a bowler hat as his preferred form of headwear.

From the outset, Sandford was not terribly keen on having
Wienholt as part of the mission, so being left to his own devices
wasn't a great surprise. According to his biographer Wienholt
hadn't bothered to formally accept his commission in the army,
which, together with his long and well-known passion for making
his points clearly and publicly, served to add to Sandford's disquiet.
Sandford's other problem was one of age; though he ignored his
own not-insignificant number of years, he was none too keen on
the 62-year-old Wienholt with his partially disabled right arm.
Sandford wanted a cohesive force to get the job done, not a group
of quirky, strong-willed idealists who just might be past their
use-by date. Ronnie Critchley observed, 'the veteran Wienholt was
inclined to regard the others as a bunch of inexperienced amateur
"Lawrences" who would not get very far'. It was a view reinforced
by Wienholt in a letter to his wife when he said, 'I could go ahead
quietly at any time with no fuss, all so nice and easy to me, but
such an effort when you have not the long practical experience.'
Wienholt was not a team player.

Though usually a loner, Wienholt could be quite sociable on
occasion, and was delighted to receive visitors at his camp. A mutual
respect developed between Wienholt and the 30-year-old Wilfred
Thesiger who, despite his youth, was a highly experienced bushman and hunter and had spent years in some of the most dangerous
parts of Africa. Thesiger later wrote of Wienholt:

I often walked over to his bivouac, shared the 'dampers' cooked and the strong tea he brewed. Quiet of speech and unhurried in movement, he had a spare body, steady, watchful eyes, a lined face and grizzled hair cut short. He reminisced most frequently about the time he had spent with the Bushmen in the Kalahari. To me he personified the great African hunters of the past.

Another young officer, Captain Ran Laurie, also popped by with Thesiger, and he commented of Wienholt:

He entertained us for hours with recollections of battles long ago, especially German East Africa, and imparted to us much of his store of bushcraft. I shall always remember him as the most remarkable man I ever met. His humility was touching and his dedication to the cause, inspiring.

Wienholt relished the task ahead and he shared his excitement with his wife Enid in a letter, writing:

In the bush, Aug 23, 1940. Alive and kicking and indeed v. well. We are in the middle of the wet season and have rain practically every day. It rains most at dark or at night and my little tent keeps it out well . . . the grass is already enormous and if not already will soon be practically unpassable through – except for native roads. I find the young English officers are exceptionally nice to me at the various posts and stations. Many are police commissioners etc in private life.

He followed with another letter to her on 29 August; it was to be his last before heading off to join Sandford.

When he finally had sufficient animals for the trek, he ventured off on 31 August, intending to join Sandford but taking a slightly different route passing south of the village of Matabia and on to Kwara, close to the border. Wienholt departed with fewer men – he had found some of the Ethiopians and the cook 'useless' and sacked them. Of his reduced numbers he wrote, 'we have to cut things to the bone for transport and mobility but one never goes hungry'. Thesiger wrote of Wienholt's departure:

He had started down the path behind his two servants and the three donkeys. His rifle was slung over his shoulder and he had a long stick in his hand. At a bend in the path he stopped, turned round and waved. I was reminded hauntingly of 'Rocky', in *Jock of the Bushveld*, gun on a shoulder, stick in hand, starting with his donkey on his last journey into the interior.

Wienholt knew he was heading into dangerous territory. Laurie had warned him that many of the locals he may encounter were aligned, if only temporarily given their shifting allegiances, with the Italians. Intelligence reports in the days before his departure told of caravans of patriot supporters being attacked while travelling a similar path to the one Wienholt would take – in one case three men were killed and all the caravan's rifles were seized. To further add to Wienholt's problems, 50 colonial troops and 300 Gumz tribesmen, under Italian orders, had been stationed at the village of Matabia with the task of stopping arms traffic from the Sudan.

Thesiger and Laurie were the last of the Allies to see Wienholt. He didn't meet up with Sandford and nothing was heard from him. Two weeks later, on 15 September, two of Wienholt's party returned to Thesiger and Laurie's camp and told of Wienholt's fate. One servant, Isa Abu Jiar, told Laurie that their guides were very nervous about crossing the Gumz territory, and fled. They had camped near Matabia, and owing to rain they had broken their camp a little later than usual, somewhere between 8 a.m. and 9 a.m. Through a translator Isa said:

> . . . the Captain [Wienholt] was superintending the work, his rifle carried by his interpreter. Suddenly they were attacked from all sides and all was confusion. Isa snatched up his rifle and ran down the river bed firing as he went and was shortly joined by Osman who dropped his rifle when the attack started. Captain Wienholt who had no rifle ran off with the Ethiopians, but Isa only saw him for a few seconds and does not know what happened to him. He did not see if he fell down or anything.

Isa and Osman then made their way to the starting base.

Laurie reported to his headquarters: 'Two of Wienholt's servants just arrived. Reported his camp surprised five mornings ago while loading, by an Italian patrol assisted by local Gumz. The camp was just beyond Matabia near Rahad. They think Wienholt shot in the side, fell, but got up. Last seen making into the bush with one Abyssinian.'

At this point, another report, following Laurie's, came to light, stating that a telegram had been received from the officer in charge of troops at Gallabat, saying that:

> Lieutenant Wienholt had arrived at Sarako, destitute and starving, but that Fitauraru Warku Sinke had supplied necessities and he was proceeding to Gojjam. As this telegram was described as having been derived from a reliable source no further enquiries seemed necessary and it was assumed that Wienholt would join Col. Sandford. It was not until later that news came to Khartoum from Col. Sandford saying that Lieut. Drew at Sarako had wirelessed him on September 16th informing him that Wienholt had been ambushed and missing . . . it was then evident that the Gallabat information that he had gone to Sarako was wrong and on examining dates it showed, what had not been evident at first, that Wienholt could not have reached Sarako and the messenger have run with the news in the time from Sarako to Gallabat.

Local intelligence confirmed the Italians had attacked the caravan and that Wienholt was last seen heading into the bush. Despite the unreliable information, hopes were still held that Wienholt might make it into a British post. Rumours also did the rounds hinting that Wienholt, or another white British officer (of which there were very few) was being held prisoner in Gondar in Gojjam province. By the time the dust had settled and rumour was found to be just that, fighting in the area, and the passage of time, made a rescue party impossible. Another story had it that Wienholt, who was not travelling in uniform, had been captured and summarily executed as a spy. A romantic though still fatal variation on that theme had Wienholt, in uniform, captured by Italians and, presumably after a fair trial, draping himself in a Union Jack and then facing his death by firing squad.

Months later, a British patrol managed to get into the area where Wienholt and his party were attacked. They found Wienholt's topi (a lightweight helmet), bits of clothing and kit and a few bones. The report on the incident concluded, 'there was sufficient evidence when all was collected to assume death'. The report also criticised Wienholt's men, saying their 'tale was unsatisfactory' and they had 'left their rifles and bolted, never to return either to Wienholt's assistance or to find out what had happened'. The report concluded,

'Wienholt was last seen running into the bush holding his side as if wounded and it is evident he died of his wounds but was never found by the enemy troops.'

What the report didn't mention was that Wienholt had committed the same sin as he had during World War I: he had not understood the potential danger in the area and had placed misguided trust in local guides, whose loyalties obviously lay with the Italians rather than the British. Nor did he post a lookout.

Though Major Cheesman had reported this incident at the end of December 1940, Enid Wienholt was not informed until a telegram arrived on 31 January 1941, some four months after his disappearance, telling her that her husband was missing, believed killed. On 4 February a further telegram arrived, stating, 'Army Headquarters advise the following stop Arnold Wienholt at the time of his death was working individually and out of touch of Headquarters under circumstances difficult to provide details' – which wasn't correct, because they did in fact have details. Enid, after much badgering and pulling of strings and pleas directly to British HQ in Khartoum, finally received formal notification on 29 April 1941.

A letter was sent directly to her at her Darling Point home, from Lieutenant Colonel PS Airey in Khartoum, in which he wrote:

> The facts at present established are that your husband set out in late August with a party of natives following the route taken by Brigadier Sandford earlier in the month. Shortly after crossing the frontier he caught sight of an enemy patrol under Italian officers which he watched for some time under field glasses. Two days later, while loading up rather later in the morning than usual, the party was attacked from all sides and your husband was last seen disappearing into the bush as the whole party scattered. The native who gave these details says that your husband was wounded in the side. No further facts are known, but if your husband was not killed outright but wounded and taken prisoner by the enemy patrol you may rest assured that he received every attention, as the Italians are known to look after their prisoners. As we have no further news of him I am afraid we must assume he was killed.

11

MEANWHILE BACK IN KHARTOUM

In October 1940, while Enid Wienholt waited for official notice of her husband's fate in Ethiopia, Allan Brown, Ken Burke, Ted Body, Ron Wood and Billy Howell left the 2/1st AIF in Cairo for 'special duties'. Their mates were, unsurprisingly, extremely curious. While their interest in heading to Ethiopia was well known in the regiment thanks to Brown's overt lobbying, their orders from Allied command in Khartoum were marked 'secret'. As they packed their kit, their friends peppered them with questions. 'What's the strength of you chaps?' 'Where are you going?' 'How long will you be away?' 'Got a private date with Musso, I suppose?' The five simply smiled, and gave away nothing.

Before heading off to their secret destination, the five had a couple of days' leave, which they spent poking about the city in gharries and spending time at the Cairo Zoo. One contemporary report of their visit said:

> The Cairo zoo is a most popular spot with the men of the AIF. It wasn't the animals that attracted the troops. It was the unbelievable coolness and pleasant surroundings making for a complete relaxation and forgetfulness of camp routine. Beneath the eucalyptus trees and alongside the kangaroo enclosure men sprawled out on the grass.

What wasn't reported of the five was that they also managed to cause a bit of a stir, and this time the usually calm and well-behaved Allan Brown was part of the action.

Shortly before their departure, the five slipped into a local bar for a cold beer. A few beers into the discussion, Brown, usually the reserved sobering influence, joined his men in their skylarking and ratcheted it up a notch when he took out his Webley revolver, a standard issue for officers of the period and known as 'the wobbly' thanks to its indifferent accuracy, and tossed it to his men. In the crowded cafe the five played pass the pistol, throwing the loaded revolver to each other like it was a football practice drill. As other patrons dived for cover, and the management dived for the phone to call police, the five slipped away into the street, blending swiftly with the hordes of other soldiers.

The trip from Cairo took five days: the first leg was by train, then onto a paddle steamer along the Nile and then back onto the train to Khartoum. Throughout their journey their fellow passengers had no idea that the Australians' kit consisted primarily of the goodies they had collected during their commando training: all manner of explosives, fuses, timers, guns, knives and ammunition. Enough to start a small war, which was exactly what would happen in the near future.

Bill Howell described Khartoum as 'a very nice town really, many trees and good buildings'. Unfortunately for Bill and his colleagues, they weren't housed in any of the good buildings. Their lot was to camp just outside Khartoum with the other soldiers recruited to form the ten 'operational centres' that would eventually spearhead Mission 101. Of their companions Howell said, 'we were camped with a dozen or so South African officers and sergeants. They were great chaps, they were like Australians.' High praise and not the sort of comment ever directed at the British officers and troops they encountered on the mission. Ken Burke, never a man to offer respect merely based on rank, described most of the British officers he encountered in Khartoum as 'next to useless'.

Howell, who like his peers was an old private-school boy, went on to comment about his new South African colleagues, 'One was an Oxford blue (football), and a Rhodes scholar. They were all very big chaps and we may meet up with them later [on return from their mission].' Ted Body shared the enthusiasm for their new compatriots, writing later, 'They were a wonderful lot of men. One Dick Lieyt [Luyt], a Rhodes Scholar, was a sergeant – a very nice chap – now Sir Richard, former Governor of Guyana and Vice Chancellor of Cape Town University.'

Very soon they found out the true nature of the mission they were about to undertake. Colonel Sandford had been in Ethiopia for three months undertaking preliminary work ahead of a larger force, including Haile Selassie, which would sweep through when the Italians were at their most vulnerable, and the patriots well organised and effective.

The larger force would later be known as the 'Gideon Force' under the command of Major Orde Wingate, dubbed by Italian journalist Angelo Del Conte as 'the Napoleon of guerilla warfare'. Ted Body recalled that when the five Australians were finally told their role, they found, 'it was decided Britain would attack Abyssinia and a force called Mission 101 under Wingate was formed to be followed by the return of Haile Selassie. We were to be the advance party.' The advance party would follow Sandford's group into the Gojjam and get the patriots on track.

To get to that point, the operational centres – each comprising an officer attached to the British army, usually four sergeants and 'native' troops – were formed. Ted Body recalled:

> We were given 60 Abyssinians to train as we thought fit! They had fled their country and had been recruited in Palestine, the Sudan and Egypt. Some of them had been wealthy men with their own land, now they didn't have a bob!

The Australians raised a few British eyebrows when instead of instilling some British discipline by marching the men around the parade ground to learn the ancient military art of 'drilling', they started training their men in some of the arcane arts of war, such as hand-to-hand combat, attacking with stealth, field communications from hand signals to radio operations, and basic explosive use. The Australians doubted the ability to march in a straight line would be useful in the rough country that was ahead of them; mutual respect and shared abilities were much better investments in getting home in one piece.

As Arnold Wienholt had found before them in his various African adventures, language would always be a looming problem. To reduce the risk, the five were given a crash course in 'Sudan Arabic', a simplified version of Arabic with a vocabulary of around 800 words. It had the bonus of being a form of the language learned by the Ethiopian exiles. Ted Body recalled, 'We were given an interpreter each – mine was nearly a complete blob and eventually I was forced to communicate in very ordinary Arabic. It's a very easy language to learn enough to get by.' Over the following months, they would all add a smattering of Amharic, Ethiopia's dominant language.

Allan Brown and his men became the No 1 Operational Centre. The South Africans, a Canadian and other British officers took command of the other operational centres. The Australians, however, would be the first into Ethiopia, and the others would follow after a base of operations had been established by Brown and his men.

Sprinkled among the new comrades-in-arms were a few Sudanese soldiers. Trains, planes, trucks or steamers weren't going to get them and their supplies into Ethiopia. The local form of heavy haulage consisted of camels, donkeys and mules, so the expertise of the Sudanese with these animals meant training was a two-way street. The Australians passed on their commando and gunnery training, and the locals offered an insight into the ways of sometimes cantankerous animals.

Khartoum was alive with military and political activity when the Australians arrived in early November. At the close of October, it had hosted a gathering of the most powerful leaders of the Allied campaign in the Middle East: the Secretary of State for War Anthony Eden, General Wavell, General Cunningham who was leading the British Forces in East Africa, the Governor-General of the Sudan Sir Hubert Huddleston and the South African generals Pierre van Rynevelt and Jan Smuts.

One of the motivators for the conference was Haile Selassie's persistent nagging of Eden over the slow progress of his return. He was itching to get back into his country, and sitting about in splendour in Khartoum wasn't the progress he had had in mind. Though Selassie wasn't invited to the conference, Eden and Wavell visited him on 29 October and reassured him that action was imminent. It wasn't the easiest of meetings, as Peter Leslie recounted in *Chapman-Andrews and the Emperor*, Haile Selassie:

> ... left the Secretary of State in no doubt about the bitterness of his feelings in regard to the small number and the quality of the rifles issued to patriots, the manner of distribution and the tardiness of measures taken to train his bodyguard.

What Eden and Wavell hadn't considered was that, thanks to his friendship with Sandford, and his own intelligence network, Haile Selassie had a very clear and informed view of current events. The Emperor's displeasure apparently then flowed downhill, with Eden and Wavell convening another meeting with General Platt and Brigadier Scobie. Eden made it clear to the military commanders that Churchill, never the most patient of men, was keen to press on. Eden said:

> It is no less clear that there is some lack of coordination and I gather to some extent perhaps of interest on the part of the military here. Wavell was not satisfied either. As a result we had a meeting of all concerned after dinner which was at times a stormy affair. Wavell began the indictment and I followed it up. I fear that they must have all regarded me as intolerable, but there are times when it does little good to sit down to a pleasant evening party and I deliberately wanted to stir our folks up.

The mood in Khartoum wasn't brightened by the Italian invasion of Greece on the very day they sat down to discuss their plans for Ethiopia. It only got worse when a week later, on 6 November, the British, led by Brigadier William Slim (later the Governor-General of Australia) attacked the Italians in Gallabat with the intention of recapturing the fort they had lost months before. The attack was supported by around 12 tanks and 28 aircraft including 10 Gloster Gladiators, an obsolete biplane used as a fighter to protect the bombers. It was a brief victory that soon turned into a disaster.

In short order, the fort was recaptured and all went according to plan until their tanks started breaking down, thanks to land mines and the rough and rocky terrain. Nine were soon out of action. Then the Italian air support arrived. The Fiat CR42 biplane wasn't a cutting-edge fighter, but it was quicker and more manoeuvrable than the stodgy Gladiator. Four Gladiators were swiftly shot down, and the Italians regained air superiority over Gallabat. Wilfred Thesiger, who watched the battle, said of the Italians that they had 'suffered severely from the bombardment, but they fought back magnificently, their machine-gunners continuing to fire until the tanks ran over them'. Despite heavy casualties, the Italians recaptured the fort and maintained dominance in the skies. Brigadier Slim decided that a retreat was a prudent move. He later commented that another factor in his decision was that 'British troops behaved even worse than the Italians', which, though not reflecting the bravery of the Italian troops (many of whom were Eritreans), was intended to damn the British. The battle did little to enthuse

Haile Selassie, and for the Australians it confirmed some long-held beliefs about the abilities of their former colonial masters.

Something positive did transpire from the events of late October and early November. The meeting in Khartoum resolved, in accordance with the earlier plans formulated by Sandford, that they should 'generalise operations of the brigandage type, which are easy to execute, and which would give confidence to the rebels and so prepare them for operation on a more considerable scale'. What was needed, they agreed, was what author Peter Leslie described as an 'unusual and unconventional professional soldier who understood guerrilla warfare'. Sandford, though essential to the mission thanks to his expertise in all matters Ethiopian, wasn't the obvious choice. He had given up soldiering decades before and had no experience in the type of warfare needed to destabilise the Italians.

Fortunately Wavell already had the ace up his sleeve, and the conference presented the opportunity to play it. In September he had envisaged a role for an unconventional soldier, and had sent for a most unconventional man, Major Orde Wingate. At the time, Wingate was staving off boredom commanding an anti-aircraft unit in England, and after Wavell's summons he made his way to Cairo and then Khartoum, arriving there on the day of Brigadier Slim's disastrous attack on the fort near Gallabat.

Wingate was born in India into a British military family who were members of the Plymouth Brethren. His father's uncle was Sir Reginald Wingate, who had spent a significant slice of his career as Governor-General in the Sudan.

When his father retired from the military in India, the family returned to England, and after a strict religious upbringing, he followed his father into the army, training in artillery, and achieving his commission in 1923. For Wingate, the army was a fine chance to break away from the restrictions of his upbringing – he was a young man who gave the boundaries a significant push. He also became known as an officer who was argumentative, aggressive and not one to hold higher ranks in the awe in which they expected to be held. These traits were not ideal for a career in the British army, but they would later endear him to Lieutenant Brown and his men. One of Wingate's early commissions was a transfer to the Sudan Defence Force, where he spent a chunk of time in the Gallabat and Roseires areas on the border with Ethiopia, hunting for slave traders and ivory poachers. At the end of his commission, he led an expedition into the Libyan Desert on the hunt for the lost army of the Cambyses – something more of boys' own adventure than a military mission. The army remained lost, but Wingate learned quite a bit about operating in a harsh and remote landscape.

It was in 1936 that his unique approach to soldiering was rewarded. He was posted to Palestine as an intelligence officer. Palestine, at the time of his arrival, was in one of its inevitable states of uproar, with Arabs operating a guerilla campaign against the British and Jewish communities that were establishing themselves in the region. The commander of British forces in Palestine at the time was General Wavell, and the brash and outspoken Captain Wingate soon came to his notice.

Palestine, with its problems, history and intrigues was a perfect home for Wingate, and he readily cast aside the objectivity expected of a British officer and became a fervent Zionist. Wingate had a plan to sort out the problem with the local Arab community and their dabbling in guerilla tactics. Of his plan he wrote, 'there is only one way to deal with the situation, to persuade the gangs, that, in their predatory raids, there is every chance of running into a government gang which is determined to destroy them'. A key part of the plan was to involve Jewish police and intelligence officers, which was not well received by the British military, which preferred to keep its operations purely British. However, with the situation worsening, Wingate was finally given the green light and established 'special night squads'. These were combined British–Jewish counter-insurgency units who used guerilla-style tactics to break up Arab gangs who were frequently attacking the Iraqi Petroleum Company pipeline. One of his protégés in the squads was Moshe Dayan, later the famed bald, eye-patch-wearing face of the Israeli Defence Forces. Dayan was a Wingate fan, commenting, 'He was never wrong. I never knew him to lose an engagement. He was never worried about odds. If we were twenty, and the Arabs were two hundred, or if we were at the bottom of a hill and they were at the top, he would say: "All right, there is a way to beat them. There is some way in which with a decisive stroke, we can turn this situation in our favour."' Wingate also had the unusual approach, at least for many contemporary military leaders, of leading from the front – endearing to his men but not to some of his superiors.

His tactics against the Arabs were ruthless and effective, and in 1938 he was awarded the DSO for his services. However, his passion

for the Jewish cause proved to be his undoing. Training of the local
Jewish community in guerilla tactics didn't sit comfortably with
some senior military leaders, who felt that the tactics may be used
against them in the future.

While back in Britain on leave he took the opportunity to
speak publicly on the need for the formation of a Jewish state.
In May 1939, believing that Wingate was too compromised to be
an effective intelligence officer, his superiors ordered him back
to Britain, where he was given command of an anti-aircraft unit.
Fortunately for Wingate, his posting was only temporary. His move
to Khartoum was originally as an intelligence specialist, however
Wavell had always intended for Wingate to take over operational
command from Dan Sandford despite his lower rank.

Unsurprisingly, Wingate proved to be a divisive figure in
Khartoum. His occasionally abrasive attitude toward the British
officers didn't endear him to them, nor did his numerous eccentricities. Wilfred Thesiger, aware of Wingate's reputation in Palestine,
wrote, 'His personal service file described him as a good soldier but
a security risk, who as far as Palestine was concerned could not be
trusted since he put Jewish interests before British.' Thesiger pushed
the establishment view of him further, writing, 'Always an arrogant
and ill-disciplined officer, he now became increasingly aggressive
and resentful of authority. He was an ambitious soldier, but had
apparently wrecked his army career by the time war broke out.'

The aristocratic Thesiger was also a gentleman not fond of
eccentricities in other officers. When Thesiger arrived fresh from
the conflict at Gallabat, Wingate took him on a tour of Khartoum
headquarters. Thesiger later said of his superior officer:

> He shambled from one [office] to another in his creased, ill-
> fitting uniform and out of date Wolseley helmet, carrying an
> alarm clock instead of wearing a watch, and a fly-whisk instead
> of a cane, I could sense the irritation and resentment he left in
> his wake. His behaviour certainly exasperated Platt, who anyway
> had little sympathy with irregular operations. I once heard Platt
> remark, even before Wingate's appointment, 'the curse of this war
> is Lawrence in the last'.

Platt also reckoned that he disliked Wingate, 'more than the devil
himself'. It was destined to be a difficult relationship.

Thesiger also observed another quirk of his soon-to-be commander, saying:

> He would make appointments with officers at his hotel, and then receive them lying naked on his bed; one of them described to me how Wingate had been brushing his body hair with a toothbrush as he gave them his instructions. Behaviour such as this made him disliked wherever he went.

He did, however, admit that he found Wingate 'inspiring', a respect motivated by their common purpose and passion to see Haile Selassie returned to the throne and the Italians out of his country.

The Australians, not surprisingly, got on particularly well with the unconventional Wingate.

One of Wingate's first missions in Khartoum was to visit Haile Selassie, during which he surprised the Emperor by pledging his commitment to restoring him to the throne. Wingate told him, 'I pledge my life to restore Your Majesty to your rightful throne and ask only in return that you trust and support me absolutely.' Wingate also told Selassie that:

> ... the liberation of Ethiopia was an indispensable part of the British war aims; that it was also of the greatest importance that the Ethiopians themselves should play a leading role in the coming campaign, and, finally that he should take as his motto an ancient proverb, 'If I am not for myself, who will be for me?'

What Wingate knew – and was fairly certain Selassie also knew – was that not all the British political and military leaders were wedded to the notion of restoring the Emperor to his throne; another nice little colony was an idea that appealed to some. According to Australian journalist Wilfred Burchett, Wingate told the Emperor:

> These militarists and bureaucrats really don't count, you know. You appeal over their heads to the people – the people of England, America and China. They hate the Axis just as you do. They are all on your side. They know the shabby deal you had the last time. Appeal to the people of England, through their Parliament. Cable Churchill and state your case. He will back you up.

The theatrical Wingate had a cause again, and he left a very pleased Emperor.

Settling down to the business of getting things organised, Wingate found that Mission 101 – with Sandford in the field and the operational centres poised to depart – did not quite meet his expectations. He wrote:

> To sum it up it is fair to say that the conduct of the revolt at this stage showed poverty of invention combined with an intention to limit its scope below what was possible and from every point of view desirable.

Wingate decided it was prudent to cut to the chase and meet with Sandford, who was now in Sakala in the middle of the Gojjam. Sakala was located in a beautiful, tricky-to-access spot on a plateau described by Thesiger as 'an earthly paradise', surrounded by the Nile on three sides, and a 1200 metre escarpment plunging down on the fourth side. Flying was the only option.

12

GOOD MORNING, GOJJAM

Orde Wingate was many intriguing things, but a good flyer was not among them, so a trip behind enemy lines in yet another obsolete RAF aircraft, this time the Vickers Vincent biplane, was an unwelcome challenge. It was seat-of-the pants flying, using a rudimentary map, compass and landmarks, and with fingers crossed that they wouldn't get lost or run into Italian aircraft. The Vincent was an open aircraft, so leather flying helmet, goggles and a warm jacket were essential to surviving the flight. Barrelling along at a maximum speed of around 220 kilometres per hour through Italian-dominated skies also made it a sitting duck as the Italian aircraft were capable of almost double that speed. At the controls that 20 November morning was Flight Lieutenant Collis of the RAF, and accompanying a nervous Wingate were two Ethiopian liaison officers. Wingate used the trip to plan a route he could use when taking Haile Selassie back to his country. The land they flew over was mosquito-infested low forest in the heart of a malaria zone, leading to the escarpment, with Mount Belaya as the prominent point.

The Vincent made the journey without incident and landed at Sakala on a strip prepared by Sandford's irregular forces. Up in the high tablelands, the rainy conditions made landing both the high point and the low point of the flight.

Sandford and Wingate spent the next 48 hours plotting, and it was evident that Wingate had already envisaged himself as leader of the Allied forces, despite Sandford's superior rank. However, Wingate later noted of Sandford, 'his presence there made it possible for me to plan the campaign and convince others that it would succeed'.

The two men agreed that to be successful they needed to do much more than simply offer payment to the patriots in exchange for them fighting for their own – and for Britain's – interests. Though money wasn't a problem – around £400 000 had been allocated – they both believed that the local patriot commanders needed to be motivated, and the best way to do that was to enter the area with a small and well-equipped force and show the patriots they meant business. Just like he'd done in Palestine, Wingate believed the best lesson was to lead by example. Wingate later captured the thrust of the mission he and his operational centres were about to undertake, writing:

> Now the essence of this lesson is that to raise a real fighting revolt you must send in a *corps d'elite* to do exploits and not peddlers of war materials and cash. Appeal to the better nature; not the worse. After all what is the best we can hope for from any fifth column? We can hope that the rare occasional brave man will be stirred to come to us and risk his life to help our cause. This is of value to us. All the rest – the rush of tribesmen, the peasants with billhooks – is hugaboo. If you have a just cause you will get support only by appealing to the best in human nature; down-at-the-heel spies and pretentious levies are worse than useless.

Given the need to get men and munitions from Khartoum across desert, forest, rivers and up an escarpment, logistics were the key to success. Sandford reported that they agreed to purchase:

> ... some thousands of camels in the Sudan and that with these the British military authorities will undertake the transport of the arms and munitions and other supplies required for the Abyssinian campaign to at least as far as the foot of the escarpment. This is the course I have urged for the past five months and is in accordance with the policy approved by the War Office. It is lamentable that up to today (1st December) only a thousand rifles and a few thousand rounds should have reached Gojjam, and no money, no explosives, no machine-guns and no mortars.

Wingate's assurances that all of Sandford's wishes would come true led him to comment, 'I was encouraged by Major Wingate's optimistic forecast of the rate at which supplies of money, weapons, munitions etc would be forthcoming for the Abyssinian campaign.' But he would have been a lot happier if they had been on their way.

They also canvassed an item close to the heart, and the future, of Allan Brown and his sergeants, according to Sandford:

I was greatly interested to hear of the proposals for the formation of 'intelligence centres'. I understand these 'intelligence centres' are to consist of a British officer and four or five British NCOs and 200 Abyssinians, and are to be equipped with one or more machine-guns and a supply of explosives in addition to their rifles. I understand from Major Wingate that the Abyssinian personnel for the first three of these centres will have been already recruited and trained in the Sudan and that I can expect the first of these centres to cross the frontier in to Abyssinia in three weeks' time.

Their planning was aided by the web of contacts that Sandford had fostered throughout the Gojjam. He had found some sources less than reliable, thanks to the Italians' regular and generous bribes to prominent locals. He was, for example, no fan of Ras Hailu, an important chief in the region. Reporting to Khartoum, Sandford described him as 'a rather common looking man with limited intelligence, obese with grievances against his next door neighbour'. For some, cash came before patriotism, and it was also a chance to settle local rivalries dating back decades. To reduce the risk of information of dubious merit, Sandford relied heavily on what was perhaps the world's oldest network of spies, the Church. Much of the information that formed the basis of his discussions with Wingate came courtesy of the Coptic priests who were pivotal in the communities scattered around the province.

If the flight in had been dicey, the flight out was even more so. One of the Vincent's assets was a capacity to take off at low speed from rudimentary airstrips. Collis's skills as a pilot, and the Vincent's abilities, were sorely tested when the time came to leave Sakala. Two attempts to get the plane airborne from the very short and rough airfield failed, and on the third attempt Collis got the plane airborne precariously close to the end of the runway and the steep ravine that followed. It was the first mission in the partnership between the Royal Air Force and the SOE. For his skills, Collis was rewarded with the Distinguished Flying Cross.

Wingate's arrival and departure by aircraft, a rare sight in the Gojjam province, had a broader effect on the Ethiopian community than either man had envisaged. Sandford reported:

The visit of Major Wingate 20th November–22nd November, was extremely useful and the landing was a daring exploit finely executed by Flight Lt. Collis. The propaganda effect of the landing was excellent, and by the evening of 22nd November, I was receiving letters from distant leaders asking if the news of the landing was true.

Back in Khartoum, Wingate checked himself into the Grand Hotel and immediately set to planning tasks for his operational centres. Allan Brown was an occasional visitor, and warmed quickly to his eccentric and brilliant superior officer. In Brown and his sergeants, Wingate had found the lightning rod for his hypothesis, 'Given a population favourable to penetration, a thousand resolute and well-armed men can paralyse, for an indefinite period, the operations of a hundred thousand.' By 2 December, Wingate's plotting was complete and he presented his master plan to the senior military men in Khartoum, Generals Platt, Cunningham, 'Jumbo' Wilson, and Air Marshal Arthur Longmore. He told them that he intended to use the two operational centres that were ready to go, a battalion from the Sudan Defence Force and two Ethiopian battalions to move into the Gojjam and foster a revolt. The operational centres would go in ahead, with Allan Brown and his four sergeants taking the lead. The more conventional forces, called the Gideon Force by Wingate in a moment of Zionist-inspired bravado, would follow when the operational centres had caused as much havoc as humanly possible.

Wingate later wrote a broad synopsis of the mission, saying:

First we have to convince the Ethiopian that, contrary to his previous experience, these white men with whom he has to treat will give him a fair deal. He must see us first, not fighting by his side but in front of him. He must realise not only that we are brave soldiers but devoted to the cause of liberty. Cease trying to stimulate revolt from without, but let's do something ourselves. Enter the country with small fighting groups. Example instead of precept is what we want.

Who better to lead the charge than five young Australians?

With the tasks of Brown, Burke, Body, Howell, Wood and their colleagues in the other operation centres confirmed, the senior British officers moved to broader matters. They decided to do unto the Italians what the Italians had almost done to them: make them the meat in the sandwich, or more militarily, employ a pincer movement. The 4th and 5th Indian Divisions under command of General Platt would strike the Italians in Eritrea, to the north of Ethiopia. Cunningham's British East African forces would overrun Italian Somaliland to the east, and another force would land in the conquered British Somaliland to the north-east. Ethiopia would be the Italians' last stronghold, which is where the operational centres, and later Wingate's Gideon Force bringing in Haile Selassie, would come into play. Destabilising the Italians in Gojjam was a critical element in the battle to drive the Italians from East Africa.

Shortly after the meeting concluded, Wingate met with the officer who would be commanding the troops from the Sudan Defence Force and the Ethiopian battalions, Colonel Hugh Boustead. He had fought in World War I, and gone on to command forces in the Sudan until his retirement from the army in 1935. He had stayed in the Sudan as a District Commissioner in Darfur until the outbreak of war, when, like Sandford, he had joined up again. He was a seasoned soldier, a mountaineer, and he knew the region intimately. WED Allen described him as:

> . . . slight, wiry and nervous, he had the quality of a rapier in his character. His looks, his movements, and his mannerisms belonged somehow to the eighteenth century. Put a tricorn hat on that lean wrinkled face, add a sparse pigtail and a high tight collar and he might have been one of Clive's or Nelson's officers.

He was also a conventional soldier, which didn't bode well when dealing with a man like Wingate. The two had met on occasions in the Sudan and on tank manoeuvres on the Salisbury plain almost a decade earlier. Boustead's first meeting with Wingate in Khartoum did not begin well. When he arrived at the Grand Hotel, Boustead found Wingate naked in a bathtub full of cold water, idly thumbing through a copy of *Pride and Prejudice*, 'a suitable title, I felt afterwards, for the conversation that ensued'.

Boustead wrote that Wingate's 'strategic conception for the type of operation that lay ahead was arresting and brilliant. But his tactics were not at the time practical, taking into account the topography and means of supply.' The two would have a troubled relationship during forthcoming operations, with Boustead commenting:

His previous experience of commanding troops was limited to the command of a company of Eastern Arab Corps and small groups of Jews in the Jewish–Arab operation in Palestine in the thirties. In these latter operations he had distinguished himself. Our relationship during the coming campaign was rendered more difficult from my point of view by his acute lack of experience at this stage of soldiering and dealing with anything but small bodies of men. This inevitably led to his interfering in the chain and details of command, which I would not stand for, since my own position in command of my battalion would have been insupportable if I had accepted his attitude.

The conversation between the very proper officer and the naked man in the bathtub went on for 'several hours' according to Boustead, with the main topic being the route they would take with Haile Selassie, by that time codenamed 'Affidavit' (the operation to get him back into Ethiopia had moved from Scheme A to 'Anonymous').

Wingate preferred a direct approach, marching according to the map and his compass, something that worked well in the flat lands of Palestine. Boustead, infinitely more experienced, reckoned that heading directly to Belaya would in reality take them over 'stony ribs and escarpments of the Shankalla wilderness' and would be 'quite impassable to motor transport without months of preparation and an army of labourers', both of which were in short supply. Boustead suggested a more southerly route via Roseires. He also thought that Wingate's penchant for camels, leftover from his Palestine stint, was misplaced. Round one, camels and all, went to Wingate, but Boustead kept hammering away.

While the great military minds were planning, Brown and his sergeants continued training their men in the art of modern warfare. What had become apparent during their preparations was that they were missing a few vital bits of kit, in particular mortars. They had plenty of ammunition for the mortars, but just lacked the weapon. Ever practical, they visited the Khartoum railway yards and encouraged the engineers in the yard's workshop to improvise. The result was 3-inch mortars that only lacked a range-finder – a keen eye would have to suffice when they were put to use.

On 21 December 1940 the Australians and their collection of Ethiopians and Sudanese volunteers left Khartoum. Their departure was a well-kept secret, and even letters to family were discreet. Bill Howell, in his typical laid-back style, wrote to his mother and sister saying, 'I would love to tell you where we are going but I suppose it will keep. We are going on a pretty big adventure, which is terrifically interesting! Perhaps you can guess where we are going – hope you can.' What Bill didn't mention was that their task was the African version of Churchill's later command to the SOE, to 'set Europe ablaze'. The next letters from the Australians as they headed into Ethiopia would be passed to monks who would then send them on a haphazard journey on foot, mule and camel to Khartoum.

Fortunately for the Australians, sense had prevailed and the first leg of their journey would take them to Boustead's preferred starting point of Roseires, a small town on the Blue Nile, near the border of Ethiopia. It was also well south of the approach used by the ill-fated Arnold Wienholt three months before. As they had come to expect, winter in the Sudan merely meant daily temperatures hovering around Australian summer highs (100 degrees in the old Fahrenheit scale, high 30s in Celsius), so it was a hot and dusty train journey for the Australians, their men and their supplies – donkeys, mules and camels would come later. After a full day and night on the train, they disembarked and boarded a paddle steamer to chug the rest of their way up the river. Ted Body took the opportunity to sharpen his skills with the rifle, and his aim was true – the Blue Nile found itself short of a few crocodiles.

From the wharf near Roseires it was into the less-comfortable confines of a troop truck for the inevitable hot, dusty and bumpy ride to their new camp a discreet distance outside the town. At other camps nearby were the beginnings of Orde Wingate's Gideon Force that would accompany him and the Emperor across the border. The Force at that point was about half complete, with around 1250 soldiers, mainly Sudanese under the control of 14 British officers. Spies and divided loyalties of the locals meant that discretion was paramount, so the Australians tried to keep a low profile among the other soldiers. An Italian welcoming committee for the first operational centre across the border would not be a desirable addition to their travel plans.

Roseires was to be the launch pad into Ethiopia, and it was here that their camels were waiting. It wasn't to be a cinematic moment with the Australians charging into battle astride their faithful ship of the desert. Each camel had the unromantic task of carrying approximately 140 kilograms of supplies: 450 kilograms of gelignite, 225 kilograms of guncotton (an explosive), 1000 Mills bombs (hand grenades), 60 000 rounds of ammunition, detonators, rifles, food and water to last four weeks and 50 000 Maria Theresa thalers for the occasional purchase, incentive or bribe.

The Australians settled easily into their temporary home, and promptly went wandering. Bill Howell said, 'you see these big, black hunters roaming round in the bush with bows and arrows and spears and all the little villages are grass huts, round shape, and with a pointed roof on the tops'. Their camp, he wrote, was a little more sophisticated, 'cut out of the grass and scrub'. He told his mother and sister that, 'we drink the Nile water and swim in it too. There are numbers of crocodiles and [we] can't go in far and have to keep a good lookout.' In the camp they had a small taste of the good life of an officer, thanks to 'black servants who do our washing and clean our boots, make up our bunks etc'. A cold beer would have made for rural bliss, but refrigeration in this part of Africa was (and still can be) elusive.

On Christmas Eve, Orde Wingate arrived. The next morning he delivered a briefing to Brown, and to the officers – like Boustead and Major Donald Nott – who would follow in the Australians' wake. Wingate reinforced their lessons on guerilla tactics: never stick to a predictable route; never retrace a route; wear muted uniforms minus shiny buttons and medals that could catch the sun and give away their presence; develop hand signals for silent operations; keep an eye out for friendlies to avoid exchanging fire between allies; and, perhaps the most important trick, try to anticipate the enemy's actions. Brown's specific task was to get into the Gojjam province, link up with the patriots and start sabotaging anything and everything on the main road, and generally cause as much mayhem as possible – a task perfectly suited to the quirky talents of the Australians. Major Nott was dazzled, saying of Wingate, 'what a brain' and enthusing about what he called a 'scallywag show'.

Body, Burke, Howell and Wood spent Christmas Day 1940 in their camp. With Wingate's briefing over, Brown returned to the camp and the five did their best to have a traditional Christmas celebration, and he wrote they dined on 'fowls of some sort from the nearest native village'. An indolent afternoon followed, with the men all writing what would be their last letters to families and friends before heading off into an uncertain future. The talk was of petrol rationing in Australia, the AIF in Greece and the Western Desert. Bill Howell signed off saying, 'tell them I'll have a wonderful story to tell when I get back. It is a dashed shame I have not got photos of it all and kept a diary.' The secrecy of the mission meant that the men were permitted neither a diary nor a camera.

The only problem the Australians encountered while based at the camp was the small matter of a bit of big-game hunting. While out acquainting themselves with local flora and fauna, the exuberant five had wandered unknowingly onto a game reserve, and encountered giraffes and elephants. Unlike Arnold Wienholt, and unfortunately for the wildlife, they were good shots. Luckily the five were well on their way into Ethiopia by the time their encounter was reported. Douglas Dodds-Parker, later a prominent member of the SOE, received a complaint at headquarters in Khartoum about the five. He said, 'months later a letter arrived from the Game Warden's office, saying that they had shot, without a licence, a giraffe with a Bren gun, and an elephant with a Boys anti-tank rifle'. The fine imposed for shooting the animals without a licence was five pounds and 14 pence. The fine remains unpaid.

The five young Australians, all in peak physical condition, left Roseires on Boxing Day. Their first destination was Mount Belaya, at the foot of the escarpment that marked the beginning of Ethiopia's tableland. Waiting for them in Gojjam province was not only Dan Sandford and his four men, who made their base at Sakala, but three Italian colonial brigades (around 20000 men) and four Blackshirt Battalions (around 2500 men), tasked, among other things, with keeping some steel in the resolve of the brigades of the colonial troops they would be fighting beside. The Italians had secured themselves in a series of forts constructed since their colonisation five years before. The forts were sited on the high ground usually in range of the main road they had constructed. The road began at Addis Ababa, snaked its way down the Blue Nile Gorge, spanned the river on a modern bridge (that the Italians built) and then ascended the gorge and made for the regional centre of Debra Markos and then Bahir Dar on the shores of Lake Tana, then Gondar and through into the Italian stronghold of Eritrea. It was suitable for heavy military and supply transport and was one of the few easily trafficable roads in the country.

Gojjam had an additional problem aside from the Italians: a very powerful local chieftain, Ras Hailu and his son Dedjasmatch Mamu were in control. Ras Hailu was described by WED Allen as:

> ... the richest lord in Ethiopia. He was very old; some said that he was not less than eighty; but a curled black toupee still lent him some pretence of middle age. Slow-moving and corpulent, he yet held himself with grand nobility.

Neither Ras Hailu nor his son were fans of Haile Selassie, as an Australian press release of the time dramatically observed: 'years before [the Italian invasion] Ras Hailu had rotted in chains in the prison of Haile Selassie at Addis Ababa. With [Dedjasmatch] Mamu [now] were 6000 fanatical troops. His spies sought to trap the tiny force.' After fleeing prison, Ras Hailu exiled himself in Eritrea, until five years later he was seen boarding a train at Dire Dawa bound for Addis Ababa (and the bosom of the Italians) the same day that Haile Selassie passed through Dire Dawa bound for Djibouti and then into exile.

Ras Hailu and his family were the traditional rulers of the Gojjam, and the Italians gave him the honorary rank of general and reinstated him as the regional power based in Debra Markos. With intelligence tipping the Italians to Mission 101, they wanted Ras Hailu to make sure it wasn't a success. He was a willing party to their disinformation campaign, which targeted the Ethiopian people and painted Haile Selassie as nothing but a British lackey who was simply an accessory in the campaign to retake Ethiopia. What the Italians hadn't figured out was that the people of Gojjam disliked their new colonial masters far more than their deposed Emperor, and so the province festered nicely.

Departing from Roseires a few days before Brown and his men was Wilfred Thesiger, also making his way to Mount Belaya to join up with Dan Sandford. Unlike the Australians, Thesiger was travelling light, with just his orderly, Muhammad, a guide and three camels. He wrote:

> This isolated massif [Mount Belaya], about 80 miles away, had never fallen to the Italians. Our rough track ran through thick brush and the intervening country was almost waterless, so we averaged twelve hours riding a day, and spent Christmas night

without food or water at the foot of Belaya. Early next morning Muhammad and I set off on foot up the mountain, at first through thickets of bamboo and then through the forest where, in the dim light, cold streams tumbled down the mountainside and bands of black and white colobus monkeys peered at us from among the lichen-covered branches.

Two days before New Year's Eve 1940, Brown and the No 1 Operational Centre crossed the frontier from the relative safety of the Sudan, and into Ethiopia. They had been ordered to take the northern route to Belaya, through dense scrub that had rarely been traversed. The Italians, thanks to the web of informants both in Sudan and locally, had got wind of the first Allied force crossing the border. Fortunately, thanks to either poor intelligence or some deft rumour-mongering by Sandford and his colleagues from their camp near Sakala, the size of Brown's force was greatly exaggerated. Rather than the five and their 200 troops, local intelligence had the force at 2000 men, and instead of a couple of mortars cobbled up in the Khartoum railway yards, they were thought to have a battery of field guns. As they trudged through the wilderness, utterly remote from the rest of the world, they were unaware that some of their former colleagues, also under Wavell's command, had celebrated their New Year by capturing Bardia in Libya, and were now heading toward Tobruk, and into history as the 'Rats of Tobruk'.

Brown and his men avoided well-travelled routes and made do with rudimentary trails or carved out their own; it was heavy going from day one. Supplies were loaded on to 320 camels led two apiece by a soldier, usually one of the Sudanese, who were a little more acquainted with the camels than their Ethiopian colleagues, who preferred mules and donkeys. Ted Body recalled, 'we eventually got there and blazed a trail often only 4–5 miles a day through elephant grass 10–12 feet high which had to be cut with machetes'. Aside from the grass, there was bamboo, which the locals used for building and to weave temporary shelters.

The camels presented their own difficulties, and when the track was suitable the Australians had their first taste of camel jockeying. Though Body, Howell and Wood had experience with horses, the rolling gait of the camel was a challenge for the first few days. For city boys like Brown and Burke, it took a little longer. Burke's only interest in four-legged conveyances had been from the members' stand at Randwick race course. He reckoned the camels were 'just plain mongrels through and through'. Thanks to the mongrels, the five added lower back pain to their growing list of miseries. It was better than walking, but only just.

The trek across the Shankalla wilderness, an extension of the Sudan plain between the Blue Nile and the Ethiopian escarpment, to Belaya was brutal. Water was scarce; in some cases the only unreliable supply was found by digging into sandy riverbeds. While the water was a welcome find, it also contained mica, which led to a little irritation as it passed through, resulting in blood in the men's urine. The 'Wajir Clap' as it was quaintly known, thanks to symptoms similar to a number of venereal diseases, passed when the water supplies improved. This didn't stop the men stripping off and diving into the water when they reached a waterhole. Their native guides kept a close watch just in case elephants or lions, which are also fond of waterholes, came visiting while the soldiers frolicked.

The heat was relentless, with daily temperatures rarely dropping below 35°C. At dusk, the temperature dropped dramatically and the men huddled around fires, wrapped in blankets for extra warmth. The scrub stretched kilometre after kilometre, for the 240 kilometres to their destination. Hugh Boustead described the place as being filled with 'hot stony ridges and shrub land burnt black by honey hunters'. Nights were spent fending off insects, and throughout the day the men held competitions to see who could swat the most flies in a 10-minute period.

As the sun finally slipped away each day, Brown and his men would stop and set up camp for the night. Camels were unloaded, hobbled by bending one of their legs at the joint and then strapping it in place so the now three-legged camel wouldn't stray, and allowed to graze on the slim pickings available in the inhospitable wilderness. The men's diet of canned foods was supplemented by game when possible; when an occasional eland or waterbuck strayed into their path it quickly became an addition to the soldiers' diet.

The journey took nearly two weeks. The five Australians were on a sharp learning curve. (On the first night, Brown and his sergeants were horrified to see that their men had set their bonfires beside crates of detonators, explosives and ammunition; it was a mistake that wasn't repeated the next evening.) Along the way there were wrong turns, due to a lack of accurate maps and the fact that their scouts were not as familiar with the territory as they should have been.

The conditions took their toll on the camels. Ted Body, talking about the whole of Wingate's operation into Ethiopia, said, 'the terrain killed the camels by the thousands. Eighteen thousand commenced the trek and only six or seven hundred survived to arrive in Addis Ababa at the end of the campaign.' As the camels keeled over, the more edible parts were removed and used to supplement a meagre and monotonous diet. The Gideon Force and operational centres that followed in a steady stream out of Roseires would find the stench of dead camels handy as a navigational aid.

Mount Belaya is at the foot of the western escarpment of the Ethiopian highlands. As Brown's operational centre got closer to their destination and began the slow climb, conditions improved, though for the camels used to the heat and sand of the Sudan, it was not a welcome change. The steep, twisting path that took them up 7000 feet to the top was not much fun for them.

Commenting on the Australians' trek, Hugh Boustead said the trip had been a 'death trap' for the camels and they had lost 'forty-seven camels in a single journey, with broken necks and broken legs where they had fallen over the cliffs and ravines, or dead from exhaustion'.

On top of the mountain, where the forward base of Mission 101 had been established, Thesiger reckoned it was a glorious location with:

> ... green meadows, stands of juniper, wild olive and a leafless tree with a white blossom like a wild cherry. Everywhere were flowers: wild roses and jasmine, delphiniums, yellow daisies and a variety of others, some of which I had seen on the hills near Addis Ababa and in the Arussi mountains. The air was refreshingly cool after the hot lowlands, and the view was immense. I looked westward towards the Sudan over the endless scrub-covered plain partly veiled in the smoke of many bushfires, and eastward to the Abyssinian escarpment that stretched in a seemingly sheer wall across my front.

In charge of the base was Peter Acland, a former member of Sudan's civil service who had worked with Boustead to establish his force. He had set up the base in November 1940 in the Burgi valley on the north-east end of the mountain. Thanks to its geography it was easily defended by a a small force. The other advantage was two large caves that made for natural bomb shelters in the event enemy aircraft managed to get through and drop their loads. The cunning Acland also set up dummy camps in nearby valleys, hoping to split any Italian attacks and waste their energy and munitions.

Acland's first glimpse of Brown's No 1 Operational Centre was five heavily bearded men entering the camp at the head of a camel train and a bevy of native soldiers. Journalist Carel Birkby said they looked to be 'a tough lot, and a tough looking lot'. On each of their heads was the digger's slouch hat, and, Birkby said, 'two revolvers girt their hips'. Following them into the camp a few days later was Major Donald Nott, who commented that the Australians were 'all gunners – very good type of chaps'. On the other side of the coin, one British officer who followed the Australians into the camp a few weeks later described the sight that greeted him at Belaya in less positive terms:

> The vast encampment swarmed with a tatterdemalion throng armed with an assortment of weapons. Some [of Acland's troops] were equipped with rifles and uniforms captured or looted from the Italians; others, half-naked, wore broad-brimmed high-crowned hats and brandished spears. Others still, blank-faced and seemingly at a loss, wandered aimlessly about, swigging talla [a local type of beer fermented from grain and mixed with herbs and spices] from enormous gourds slung around their necks, while messengers with self-important and purposeful expressions scurried hither and thither through the inferno-like atmosphere; it was compounded of the smoke from wood fires, the stench of camel dung and a hubbub of high-pitched voices.

The Australians took conditions of the encampment in their stride. They knew where they were headed and this was merely part of the adventure. They spent a few days resting, enjoying some decent food (although the local brew was a little too warm to be pleasant) and scrubbing off the wilderness in the plentiful water, although shaving was not on; Brown believed they would blend in better with their faces covered with their now-opulent beards – or as Ted Body neatly put it, 'my reason was not to stand out so much being white'.

13

THE LAND OF MILK AND HONEY

Fifty miles out from Mount Belaya was the Ethiopian escarpment rising 1800 metres from the wilderness. South African Captain Laurens van der Post, who led his own operational centre along the route a few weeks later, described the approach as:

> . . . the great escarpment of Ethiopia itself, a darker blue within the blue and there began to appear with increasing frequency around us pillars of broken hills, columns of rocks and walls of stone like the ruins of great cities, a tableland eroded by wind and water with a deep labyrinthine system of canyons and river cuts, rivalled only by the Grand Canyon. A land flowing with milk and honey.

The crew that set off for the escarpment and into their operating area in Ethiopia's Gojjam province was still heavily laden. At Belaya, the remaining camels ended the journey and were replaced by 600 mules weighed down by 80000 rounds of ammunition, 11 machine-guns, two mortars, a generous supply of Mills bombs and explosives, and 250 more native troops. By comparison the mules made the camels appear easygoing, according to Ted Body: 'Mules I think are even worse than camels – they were forever wanting to buck their loads off.' It took two mules to carry the load carried by one camel, and it was hard going. The men were heading into their operational area, and the Australians had to make sure they arrived with their supplies intact; operating behind enemy lines meant that resupply was not an option. On the bright side, the five Australians were given horses. For a superb horseman like Bill Howell, it was a godsend, for Burke it was not so. 'I'm too big to be a bloody jockey,' he complained. But as with the camels, it beat walking.

The route up the escarpment was rocky and shrouded in smoke from bushfires, and the men were forced to dismount and trek through still-smouldering bush in some areas. The Australians' bush experiences kept them out of the path of the blazes that dotted the escarpment. Like the wilderness before, it was gruelling. Boots collapsed, both man and animal were dog-tired. To add to their miserable lot, Italian aircraft patrolled overhead, hoping for a glimpse amid the smoke so they could attack. The only respite was an occasional mountain stream the men dived into to wash off the soot and dirt.

It took them around four days to climb the escarpment to van der Post's land of milk and honey. They skirted the southern end of Lake Tana, the source of the Blue Nile and a region well defended by the Italian forts. Their main camp was struck in bush an easy distance from Dangila and Injibera, both towns featuring Italian forts and well stocked with troops.

Brown's group quickly set to work. Their priority was to link up with the patriots, and get down to the business of blowing things up. Their mates in the 2/1st Field Regiment were doing fine work hammering the Italians in the Western Desert, so it was time Brown and his small band followed suit in Ethiopia. Ted Body wrote:

> The Italians had built a series of forts from there [the escarpment] through to the capital. These were occupied with Italians and the locals they had persuaded or coerced into their army. We dodged these forts with the help of local patriots who had resisted the Italians, and set up a base in a forest behind the first three of the forts.

The fort close to their new base was at Dangila and it was the first of the Italian strongholds near the top of the escarpment. The town was home to around 10 battalions, over 10 000 men, commanded by Colonel Adriano Torelli.

The patriots were expecting them. Leading the patriots were two gentlemen, Mangasha and Negash. Ted Body described Mangasha as 'a fine old man, wearing a pair of army boots with no laces . . . and spotless white robes'. Negash was 'a more flighty type, younger than Mangasha'. Wilfred Thesiger shared Body's view of Mangasha, describing him as a 'large, dignified man with an agreeably open face and courteous manners', however his view of Negash was less diplomatic, saying he was 'small, unimpressive in appearance, looking ill-tempered, sensual and cruel'.

Of their first meeting, Body recalled, 'it was rather spectacular. The Patriots, in their always clean robes, formed a very long double line up which Allan Brown led us (minus Ron Wood who was guarding our base) to meet Mangasha who was seated on his throne (a box) at the end of the line. There was much bowing which is their form of greeting. This procedure was repeated a week or so later with Negash.' The Australians 'gave both these chieftains rifles, ammunition and some Maria Theresa thalers, big silver coins worth approximately 1 shilling and ten pence.'

Between them these men controlled a large slice of western Gojjam and had vowed to Sandford a few months earlier to cooperate with each other and the impending Mission 101.

Mangasha and Negash commanded around 18 000 men, ranging from early teens through to late middle age. They knew the area well, but were armed only with an assortment of ancient rifles, and not much ammunition; Brown and his men had exactly what they needed. However, as Body later recalled, the numbers might have been impressive, but the patriots 'wanted to die for their country, but few of the hundreds who had started out with us were still there when a fort was reached, usually at night'.

Brown observed:

It seems a funny war, as we are about 150 miles behind Italian lines and camped within two hours of one of their forts. However the local hillmen are favourable to us – thank Heaven, as they have rather nasty habits of dealing with whites, and they have the art of torture down to a fine art.

With the camp established, the mules were returned to their former owners, no doubt for sale or rental to another British force a little later on.

In the five years since the Italians' invasion, the colonisers had upgraded the road from Addis to Eritrea, and sealed it in many sections. Chasms, gorges and rivers had been crossed with superbly designed and constructed bridges. Ideal for the colonists to keep their forts and troops well supplied with ammunition, arms and men; also an ideal target for Australians with a penchant for explosives and bent on destruction. It was the ideal location for Brown,

Burke, Body and Howell to put into practice the skills learned during their commando training.

The Italians and their local allies were in for a very nasty surprise. Brown and his men were acting with complete independence, they had no radio and any messages came by runner, often over long distances. The selection of targets and the methods they used were entirely theirs. Brown later remarked, 'There were only five of us, but the poor blighters had no chance.' Roads were booby-trapped with mines that exploded under trucks, causing havoc to the convoy that moved along with them, and ammunition dumps that were secreted around the area were located, ransacked for supplies that could be carried, and the leftovers blown up. The Australians made it even harder by ambushing convoys of Italians who thought the night was on their side, only to have the Australians and their men open fire with mortars and machine guns from their hiding places on the roadside. After a quick, brutal and effective attack, the Australians would slip back into the scrub, leaving the hapless Italian convoy badly damaged and the men in it badly shaken.

While Brown, Burke, Howell, Body and their men were out on their sorties, Wood and a small force of his men kept the camp and their precious stores of food, ammunition and explosives secure from the Italians and their cohorts. He taught the native cooks to make damper with their limited supply of flour, and to prepare chickens bought from local friendly villagers to supplement the bully beef and other tinned staples of British army cuisine. It was almost comfortable. The camp was on high ground, affording Wood and his sentries both an excellent view of anyone coming and a murderous field of fire. Scattered in the bush outside the camp area were more sentries to provide an early warning. They didn't make the same mistake as Arnold Wienholt. The first days of their operation were more like a boys' own adventure than guerilla warfare. Though in the middle of enemy country, no-one was shooting at them – the Italians, no doubt apprehensive because of wildly inaccurate rumours of the force's size, had decided to keep to their forts – so it was open slather for the Australians. They had the opportunity to range around their local area unimpeded, with the exception of the regular enemy aircraft.

Bill Howell later wrote to his family, saying:

I have been blowing any odd Iti [Italian] bridge and mining roads etc in Iti territory and then ripping back again. I have fifty Abyssinian troops with me, dashed good coves most of them. It is not a bad life. I am on horseback most of the time. The Iti bridges are solid and take some blowing.

He was also impressed by the Italians' road-building skills:

. . . their roads are hellish hard to mine. I would have loved to have blown up an Iti steam roller the other night, but the bridge didn't go up until 2 am. We'd gone back a mile and stone landed all around us. We were very close to an Iti fort so could not go back . . .

And thus saved the Italian steam roller from a dreadful end. What it also meant was that Bill Howell was from the 'more is more' school of demolition.

The chaos on the road did eventually encourage a response from the Italians. Their planes, regularly patrolling the sky, moved into attack mode. The Australians were lucky, thanks to vigilance and the terrain. Bill Howell wrote:

The Itis seem to be looking for us as we have very frequent visits from planes that come and drop their bombs here and there hoping to hit us. One day we were out and a plane flew over low and saw Ken, Ted and I riding along. He came back and let us have a lot of little bombs, but we ripped off into the scrub and got away in time.

He finished his letter dramatically, saying, 'There is one handy here now – I must go and man the machine-gun!'

While the Australians were firing the first shots in the campaign to oust the Italians, the story of their arrival in Ethiopia had leaked to the British and then the Australian press. The secret mission was not much of a secret anymore and the Italians' fears were confirmed. On 23 January 1941 Australian newspapers published a cable from Britain reporting that five Australians were in Ethiopia leading Haile Selassie's new Ethiopian army and giving the Italians hell. The next day the *Daily Telegraph* proclaimed, 'Harassing Italian Army – Abyssinians Led By Australians', and *The Sun* entered the fray with 'Four NSW Pals in Abyssinia'. With the smoke from the Australian's initial attacks in the Gojjam barely cleared, the press office at headquarters in Khartoum decided to launch their own attack armed with their weapon of choice: the press release. Not surprisingly, this attack coincided with General Cunningham's advance into Somalia and southern Ethiopia, and General Platt's advances into Eritrea and northern Ethiopia.

Some phrases are considered hackneyed simply because their regular use is prompted by their uncanny accuracy, and though there is a debate about who muttered 'Truth is the first casualty of war', its accuracy was born out by the reporting of the foray into Ethiopia. The hacks pounding away on the typewriters must have mixed their Browns, because Allan Brown the bank officer and city dweller was reported in Australian newspapers as 'a young grazier from Hay (NSW) [who] has been appointed to command the first contingent of regular troops in the new Abyssinian army'. *The Sun* went even further, declaring, 'the party of Australians promised to provide this war's counterpart to the exploits of Lawrence of Arabia'. The five were later amused to learn they had joined TE Lawrence in history, and that their 200 ramshackle troops were in fact the new Ethiopian army.

Though the names of the five weren't disclosed, the papers provided plenty of biographical details to open up the human-interest side of the story. Suitably armed, the enterprising media scrum in Australia didn't take long to track them down. Ms Peggy Lamb, Ron Wood's fiancée, told the press:

> We have had letters that leave little doubt. Ron, Ted Body, and Bill Howell have been companions since boyhood and they went together to The King's School. They have often spoken about one another and the cabled descriptions tally exactly. Ron, for instance, was a rubber planter in Papua as the cable says and Ted Body was a grazier at Trangie. We all know Bill Howell was a station manager at Longreach. They often spoke of Ken Burke of Newcastle, [as] a very fine chap.

Ron Wood's mother added, 'I am certain. Apart from other things I had a letter just recently that said they were going "out into the blue". They have been friends for years and have always been together.'

More fuel was added courtesy of a 'military officer in Sydney' who had chapter and verse on Ken Burke. It may be just a coincidence that Ken's brother-in-law, Jack McCauley, was an air force officer in Sydney. (He retired from the RAAF as an air vice marshall and along the way was chief of air staff and collected a knighthood.) The 'military officer' commented about Burke:

> I don't know anybody that that description would fit better than Ken Burke. He is very well known in Rugby Union circles in Newcastle and in Sydney. He first played at St Joseph's College and later he played representative Rugby Union for New South Wales. He took part in the trials for the New South Wales team for abroad in 1927. Later he played in trials for the Australian team. He is in his mid 30s and is just the type for a mission such as this. The description in the cable fits him like a glove. I am prepared to bet anything that it is he.

The final authority came courtesy of Ken's mother, who told the press that she had just received a letter in which Ken had said he 'had some difficult work to do' and with his usual amused tone, told her his lifestyle had improved, as he had someone 'to clean my boots and prepare my food'.

The real purpose of the publicity was to denigrate the Italians and give the Allies a pat on the back – in war and politics, perception can be a powerful tool. The *Daily Telegraph* did its duty, and reported the Italians were disinclined to meet the forces of Generals Platt and Cunningham, and according to the London *Daily Telegraph*'s Khartoum correspondent, 'The Abyssinian deserters from the Italian armies have increased 200 to 300 per cent in the last week.' The paper also reported that down near Dangila the RAF were pounding the Italians with bombing raids that 'had an almost magical effect. A squadron of heavy RAF bombers circled nonchalantly over Dangila and blasted its objectives and returned without loss. Within 72 hours 1000 native levies deserted from the Italians.'

This was a little short on truth and high on colour. The heavy bombers were arthritic Wellesley single-wing light bombers, superannuated out of the European war, and scraping by in Africa. The numbers of deserters were more likely pulled out of a hat rather than based on sound intelligence, but at least it all read well. What was a little more disturbing was the press kerfuffle that also coincided with a significant event in the Gojjam, and one that was also supposed to be a secret.

Haile Selassie took the first giant step in his return from exile when he flew into Um Idla, not far from Roseires, on 20 January 1941. His Vickers Valentia biplane bomber, another obsolete aircraft consigned to the African campaign, was escorted by two South African Air Force Hurricane fighters, one of the few modern aircraft flown by the Allies in North Africa at the time. Aside from the usual regal retinue on board there were a few journalists sent to cover his return and Edward Genock of Paramount News was there to film the event.

The following day the Emperor headed for Belaya in an ill-advised motorcade of eight trucks and one car. As was Wingate's habit, he ignored the wise counsel of the more experienced officers, and the more recent experience of the Australians and their awful slog, and decided that the Shankalla wilderness could be readily traversed by vehicles.

Progress was slow, with the vehicles only managing a few kilometres per day – a similar pace to the Australians and their combination of shoe leather and camels.

In the appalling conditions the car and trucks overheated and broke down, some became stuck axle-deep in sand, tyres were shredded and one lorry rolled over on what was only a slight incline. Eighty kilometres from Belaya, common sense finally prevailed and they gave up, switching to camels and horses. One of the officers observed, 'First Wingate, then the Emperor (on horseback), then, if you please, the High Priest with his venerable beard gallantly padding on foot through the African bush with his black robes flapping and his prayer book in his hand.' Wingate went on ahead of the Emperor's party, and when he arrived at Belaya, Hugh Boustead, never a great fan, commented:

On the last day of January Wingate rode into the valley, bearded, dishevelled, filthy and worn, on a dropping horse. The party had been on the way for a fortnight and the route had been indescribable; he had left the Emperor ditched in a ravine, sitting dejectedly among some dead camels beside the overturned remains of the last lorry.

Wilfred Thesiger, commenting on Wingate's arrival, said, 'Wingate had already disconcerted his officers by his unseemly behaviour. He never washed now, and he grew an untended beard.' Kenneth Anderson, the Reuters' war correspondent travelling with Wingate, observed that:

> On the march to Belaya, Wingate's only ablutions were to lower his trousers and cool his bottom in the occasional waterholes, from which, incidentally, others would have to drink. He apparently carried no change of clothes except for a dressing gown, and in this and his battered Wolseley helmet he was not, at first sight, a figure calculated to impress the patriots, who expected their leaders to look the part.

The remainder of the group stumbled into Belaya on 6 February. Boustead and Thesiger may not have been entirely accurate in their observations but they did give a glimpse of the animosity that was fermenting between the traditional soldiers and the irregular Wingate, whose only comment on the journey was a curt, 'All went well.' Dan Sandford had arrived at Belaya a few days before, looking 'well but is sore in foot and spirit', to greet his old friend the Emperor. Shortly after their arrival, Wingate was advised he had been temporarily promoted to lieutenant colonel and given command of the Gideon Force. Sandford, though promoted to Brigadier at the same time, was Wingate's chief adviser to the Emperor on political and military matters. He accepted the situation with good grace; the operations of his men were now under Wingate's control.

While the Emperor was en route to Belaya, the Australians found that they had done such a fine job terrorising the enemy that traffic on the main road slowed to a trickle. The Italians, it seemed, were not keen to come out and play. With that in mind, Brown and his men decided to take the game to them. Rather than wait for specific orders from Wingate, Brown decided to launch an attack on the fort at Injibera, a small town scattered over a stony hillside adjacent to the road, and home to 1500 Italian troops. This would be the first time that Brown and his men had ever engaged the enemy face to face in battle.

Brown planned his maiden outing meticulously. He first established a forward base with his sergeants and their men on high ground a safe distance from their target. Behind the base, and deeper into the forest, were 1300 patriot troops provided by Mangasha; they would join the attack after the operational centre had softened up the target with bombs, mortars and machine-guns. He said, 'We took cover by day at our base, which was well hidden in the forest. At night we took our trench mortars within range of the fort.' Shortly after midnight on 2 February the Australians began what would become their ritual preparations for battle. Guns and mortars were checked and rechecked, ammunition was readied for fast and easy access, and burned cork was applied to blacken their hands and any parts of their faces that weren't yet covered by a beard. Ready for action, the operational centre began its stealthy move through the forest toward the fort. Brown observed that his men moved into position 'so slowly that even a twig would not be disturbed'. No-one spoke as they crept forward; all communications were by hand signals they had rehearsed over the previous week. A by-product of the signals was that their message was clear, and negated any misunderstandings inherent in a force made up of mixed languages. In battle, confusion over orders can be fatal.

Though short on firepower, Brown thought that if he could create sufficient commotion he could quickly rattle the troops inside the fort, who had little battle experience. The mortar crews closed to about 150 metres from the wall of the fort and waited. At 3.30 a.m., Brown gave the signal to open fire. It was the perfect time to seize an advantage, with the residents of the fort drifting into the deepest sleep of the night, huddled in blankets to keep out the cold. The sentries were drowsy, if not dozing, when Ted Body and his mortar crews opened fire. The peace was shattered by the first barrage of the mortars that had been cobbled together in Khartoum. Though the weapons lacked range-finders, the Australian gunners used the proximity of the fort, and dead reckoning, to make sure their aim was true, and after the first volley, aim was adjusted and soon their shells were blasting inside the walls of the fort. In rapid succession, the armoury, officers' quarters and ration store were hit and fires broke out; the buildings within the fort's walls were soon ablaze. Brown, Howell and their machine-gunners opened fire, sending a hail of bullets directly at the top of the fort's front wall. With chunks of masonry falling and the heavy-calibre machine-gun rounds flying, return fire from the fort was kept to a minimum.

Brown and his sergeants had another surprise in mind to play on the Italians' fear that they were under attack by a superior force. Ken

Burke, combining agility and speed – and supported by similarly agile men from their operational centre – made a run across the battlefield toward the native troop encampment just outside the fort's wall. In their backpacks were small homemade bombs with short fuses. Rapid fire from Brown, Howell and their men gave Burke and his team opportunity to get to their destination without being spotted or shot at. They slipped into the native troop encampment where they set and detonated their bombs. The explosions tore apart the huts, shrapnel whizzed through the air, gouts of flame erupted – often with more noise and flames than actual destructive power – and the native troops fled into the forest, their flight hastened by bullets fired relentlessly at them by the operational centre's gunners.

The combined effect had the Italians and their native troops believing they were in the middle of a major bombing raid, rather than an attack by little more than a handful of men. The air around the fort reeked with the smell of cordite, and the pall of smoke from the gun fire and explosions mingled with smoke from the numerous fires that had broken out in and around the fort.

The enemy force was completely rattled by the ferocity of the surprise attack. Instead of firing at their attackers, the Italians fired into the sky at non-existent aircraft. After half an hour of intense action, and with confusion reigning in the fort, the Australians called up the 1300 patriots provided by Mangasha to press home the attack and seize the fort before dawn arrived and revealed the true size and nature of Brown's force.

Unfortunately, Brown's enthusiastic and highly effective attack was undermined by the patriots who, as the fort was blazing and its occupants utterly confused, refused to act. Instead of rushing forward to where Brown and his men were holding the line, the patriot troops didn't move from their safe position in the forest, well away from the fighting, nor did they fire a single shot in earnest. Mangasha, who had provided the gun-shy patriots for the evening's attack, was apparently quite 'sheepish and said none of the 1300 [were] any good'. While the men would apparently die for their country, it seemed they were not keen to run the risk that particular night. It was not a good moment in the relationship between Brown and Mangasha. Ted Body summed the situation up, saying, 'They [the patriots] reasoned they had survived thus far and didn't want to take too much of a chance towards the end of the Italian occupation of their country.' With dawn close at hand, Brown and his men had no choice but to cease fire, slip back into the forest and return to their camp. It was a galling moment, and a very poor start to a relationship that was vital to the overall success of Mission 101 and the Gideon Force.

On the upside, while the Australians hadn't captured the fort, they had rattled the Italians. Brown said:

> We set fire to the fort with our mortars and withdrew until the following night. The Italian native troops had never seen or heard mortar before. During the daytime the Italians would fire their artillery at random into the forest, but they never succeeded in locating our positions and they were afraid to come out and look for us.

During the day back in their bush camp, Brown and his men caught up on sleep, ate cold rations – cooking fires would give away their location – and checked and rechecked their weapons and ammunition for the coming night's work. Sentries and scouts kept a vigil in the area surrounding the camp, making sure they would not be ambushed if their enemy became adventurous, and keeping an eye on activities in the target fort.

Though the patriots had been no help in rousting the Italians from their fort, Brown reckoned that his tactics had at least provided a psychological victory, so another night of terrorising the residents of the fort seemed a good thing. However, his best-laid plan came to nothing when in the early afternoon one of Brown's scouts reported the Italians were on the move. So badly rattled were they by the attack that they decided to evacuate to the larger fort at Burie, nearly sixty-five kilometres along the main road toward Addis Ababa.

When the coast was clear, Brown and his men slipped from their hiding places. They crossed the stream that ran through the town, noting it was heavily polluted and covered in a stinking green slime, with dead sheep and calves lying beside it. Inside the fort, however, they struck gold in the form of ammunition and food.

The Italians had left a mountain of tinned food, chunks of parmesan, piles of pasta, tea, coffee, flour, sugar, tomato sauce, butter, anchovies, olives and something that had been notably absent from the Allies' diet: fresh fruit. Their rations were running low by this time, so Brown and his men were delighted to top up the supplies at their camp.

Dick Luyt and a few British officers arrived around this time, and thought it was the perfect time to take some peace from the battle by having a dinner party.

Representing the Australians at the gathering was Ted Body, relishing the chance to catch up with Luyt, with whom he had struck up a friendship in Khartoum. One of the British officers said:

> We invited Body to sup with us, and gave him a fine six-course dinner, the most enjoyable meal since leaving base camp. Tadessa did the honours in our simple kitchen, and a good time was had by all. We even prefaced the 'bean feast' with an extra tot of brandy each. Unfortunately all the wine in the place had been in casks, which the enemy had stove in before departing.

The only downside to the evening was the chicken sauté with mushrooms, rice, heart of artichoke and French beans, of which a British officer noted, 'Dick Luyt thought the mushrooms didn't quite agree with him. I also felt a little "loose" the next morning, but was glad of a welcome change for the better.' The patriots, not interested in the vagaries of the European diet, added two field guns and 20 machine-guns to their growing arsenal from the loot at the fort.

The action at Injibera was the first time Brown and his men had faced the enemy and live fire, and not only had they survived, they had proven themselves capable fighters. Brown had selected his men well – Wood was the solid, dependable soldier watching their backs; Body on mortars proved his marksmanship in tricky conditions with rudimentary weapons; Howell worked his magic on the field and in the scrub; and Burke swapped his fullback position and moved his 'back line' to cause havoc on the field.

On 18 February, Wingate arrived in Injibera and offered a belated motivational 'Order of the Day', saying:

> The comforts which we now lack and the supplies which we need are in possession of the enemy. It is my intention to wrest from him by a bold stroke which will demand all your energies and all your devotion. I expect that every officer and man will put his courage and endurance to the severest tests during the coming decisive weeks.

He may not have noticed the Australians sipping a glass of brandy and wondering if their leader was merely stating the obvious.

To Mangasha, Negash and their men, who were also at the Injibera camp, he tried a rousing speech, saying:

> For five years you have refused to submit to the yoke of the oppressor; for five years rather than surrender your ancient Christian culture you have endured bombing and pillage ... Do you want to owe all the liberties, which the friends of humanity, who are fighting the totalitarian powers in land, sea and air have promised you, to their helping hands only? Rouse yourselves and put an end to this bickering and disputes which will disgrace your Ethiopian names amongst future generations.

To seal the deal, he added that he was speaking as 'Commander in Chief of the Forces of the Emperor Haile Selassie, in the field.'

14

BURIE OR BUST

In the wake of the successful attack on Injibera, Brown split his force for a short time so they could concentrate on fostering the support of the local villages and gather intelligence on Italian operations. Ron Wood kept their base secure from any enemy patrols or spies that may have been operating in the area, while Brown and Burke headed off into the villages to coerce the patriots, and any locals, into joining them in their dangerous work. Weapons – either seized Italian rifles or rifles that had made the trek from Belaya – and handfuls of silver Maria Theresa thalers were offered as incentives to sign on. It was also a handy exercise in gathering intelligence on the Italians and their sympathisers, and of course spreading untruths about the size and ferocity of the forces coming to roust the Italians.

Bill Howell, along with his 50 troops, resumed his program of blowing up bridges and mining roads. He focused his actions along the main road, destroying the small bridges that crossed the numerous creeks and gullies all over the Gojjam plateau, and laying mines at random locations along the road. What had been safe and easy travel for the enemy was now a hazardous and slow journey.

Ted Body took his mortars and, along with Wilfred Thesiger, headed to the fort at Dangila. With intelligence still reckoning on 10 battalions on hand at the fort, battle plans for the small guerilla force required imagination and élan rather than brute force. However, good fortune, and the rumour that the British had entered the Gojjam in force, had a very desirable effect on the Italians: the Italian High Command had ordered the fort commander, Colonel Torelli, to pack up and head as quickly as possible to a fort at nearby Piccolo Abbai, and then on to the Italian stronghold at Bahir Dar.

The original plan had been for Boustead and his company of Sudanese regular soldiers to spearhead the attack on the fort at Dangila, but with the shift in command from Sandford to Wingate,

Boustead decided to await orders from the new commander. Wingate, however, was more interested in heading with all speed in the direction of Addis Ababa rather than heading back up the road to Dangila, so Sandford's original plan passed into history, and the patriots and their British cohorts got the job instead.

When Thesiger and Body arrived at Dangila, they found the Italian retreat in full swing. Cars and trucks laden with men, ammunition and any supplies they could cram on board had taken to the main road, their column flanked by the native troops on foot. Torelli, in an attempt to deny any comfort to his enemy, had set the small town on fire, but many of the fires died out quickly, leaving much of the town intact. With the support of Mangasha's men, a more reliable and enthusiastic group than those he had sent to Injibera, Thesiger and Body engaged the fleeing Italians. Thesiger and his men focused on a direct confrontation, moving quickly through the scrub on the side of the road and firing with rifles and light machine-guns. Body and 800 patriots moved behind them and headed up the road ahead of the fleeing column to target a road bridge which if destroyed would effectively prevent the Italians' flight to the relative peace and safety of Bahir Dar.

While the plan was a fine one, the usual problem in battle is that plans, even brilliant ones, seldom survive the first volley, and this one was no exception. Torelli was an astute commander and a fine tactician, and he knew the road bridge would be a tasty target, so he had sent a force ahead of the column to make sure the bridge remained intact. Under merciless fire, Body got to within 20 metres of his target, but the patriots weren't as keen, and in a repeat performance of the fight at Injibera they stayed well back from the frontline. David Shirreff noted that the patriots who should have supported Body and the men from his operational centre 'would not follow him and the patriots fired off a lot of ammunition but refused to get to close quarters to attack'. Their unwillingness to step up left Ted Body and his men in a vulnerable, dangerous spot with few options.

Body, a betting man, decided the odds were against him, so he withdrew and hooked up again with Thesiger and his patriots who weren't shirking the fight, and were still pouring bullets at the retreating Italians. (Meanwhile Mangasha withdrew a large chunk of his force, primarily the men who had let Body down, and sent them off to loot and forage for food, which they did with more vigour.) As night fell, Torelli and his battalions made it to the fort at Piccolo Abbai, with Body, Thesiger and their force, though out-numbered, still in hot pursuit. They set up their mortars in the bush around the fort and began sending their lethal calling cards over the wall. Any soldier stupid enough to put his head above the fort's parapet was rewarded with a volley of bullets. It made for a long, sleepless night; though not particularly lethal, Thesiger and Body's work ground down their enemy's will to fight.

Shortly after dawn the next day, Torelli and his troops left the fort and headed toward the safety of Bahir Dar. The patriots, under Thesiger and Body, followed closely behind sniping at their heels. With Torelli suitably distracted by the efforts of the pursuing force, he marched straight into an ambush – at least this part of the plan had worked.

Overnight, Mangasha had been persuaded to send a large force of his more reliable men to Aba Aragat, a small settlement on the road between the fort and Bahir Dar. As Torelli and his men moved across the plain, with Thesiger, Body and their team gingering them along, Mangasha's men slipped out of their hiding place in the low scrub and attacked. Torelli was forced off the road and into the rolling bushland, country more suited to the locals than the Italians. Mortar teams safely located on high points in the surrounding bush fired continuously into the vehicles on the road as the patriots and men from the operational centres moved swiftly through the scrub, pour-ing machine-gun and rifle fire at the Italian troops as they moved uncertainly in the unfamiliar terrain. The battle lasted for three hours; Torelli and his men were only saved by two raids by Savoia-Marchetti three-engine bombers flying to their rescue from Bahir Dar. The patriot forces sensibly took cover as the bombers unloaded their cargo, which allowed Torelli to regain some control over the road. With the bombers still threatening from above, his convoy made for safety, reaching the town of Meschenti around dusk. In the wash-up of the battle Torelli, whose force totalled around 5000, lost around 600–700 men, killed, wounded or taken prisoner. The patriot losses were just a handful of men either killed or wounded. Body, Thesiger and their comrades made it through unscathed.

The patriots collected rifles, machine-guns and ammuni-tion from the dead, wounded or captured. Thesiger ensured the wounded received medical attention, and the captured were kept as prisoners, though some showed a flexible approach to soldiering and offered to swap sides in return for freedom. Thesiger observed that the patriots with him had 'fought magnificently'; he was less complimentary about Mangasha, who was quickly gaining a reputation for unreliability, noting 'he is no soldier' and that, 'during the battle Mangasha had exercised no control, leaving its direction to his subordinate chiefs and remaining throughout at a distance from the fighting, regardless of my attempts to induce him to take a more active part'. Thesiger, in hindsight, considered Torelli's decision to withdraw, 'the greatest mistake the Italians made during Wingate's campaign in Gojjam'. Thesiger believed that had the Italians fought on they could have won the battle and controlled the escarpment, thus preventing Wingate's Gideon Force gaining a foothold on the plateau.

With the moderate success of Injibera behind him, and Body and his mortars back in the fold, Brown decided the best course of action was to head the same way as the fleeing Italians, and attack the forts at Burie. One British officer didn't share the Australian's view and observed:

> The hundred miles of upland between Engiabara [Injibera] and the Blue Nile canyon at Safartak is not ideal for guerrilla war. It is an open landscape swept by strong and dusty winds and, even in the dry season, occasional violent storms. Every dozen or so miles the ravines of streams falling to the Blue Nile offer cover with their belts of thick undergrowth and woods. But over the plateau there is no cover, except for occasional coppices of trees round the scattered villages.

Brown, however, was optimistic, and said, 'the Italian position here is very dicky, and if we can rush this fort [Burie] one of these nights it will weaken them quite considerably. For a do like that we collect around 5000 tribesmen and then take off. At the moment we are packing up camp and going to move off to one of the forts – Burie. We are going to give them a shock tonight, I hope.' Brown was soon proven correct.

Burie was, and still is, a major market town on the main road. Like Injibera, the town is in rolling country with the occasional hill, and to the north-east the peaks of the Choke Mountains are visible. According to WED Allen, Burie was:

... of the common character of country market-towns over the whole range of the Ethiopian highlands: clumps of huts among groves of rather mournful eucalyptus trees straggling over bare hillsides. The lack of stone buildings lends an impoverished aspect to these centres which is scarcely relieved by the few shoddy sheds and villas of the Italian occupation.

At the time of Brown's arrival, Burie had a population of around 20 000, most housed in the typical Ethiopian huts of grass and mud. There were around 8000 Italian troops garrisoned there in three forts laid out roughly in the points of a triangle and located on high ground. Fire from the forts was potentially murderous if you happened to stray into the triangle, and their placement afforded reasonable coverage if conventional forces attacked. What they weren't prepared for was attack by mortars – and Burke's lethal gifts.

Their first attack took place on 20 February 1941. This time Brown varied the tactics, opening fire with the mortars at 8 p.m., just as the Italian officers were sitting down to dinner. When the troops in the fort finally managed to return fire, they did so effectively with rifles and heavy machine-guns. Body and his mortar crews found the bush around them erupting in a storm of tree bits, rocks and hot lead, but they kept on firing. Behind the fort's walls, the mortar shells were also doing fine work, starting fires in storage areas and ammunition lockers. At the same time, Brown, Burke and their men moved around the town with more homemade bombs, setting off a string of explosions, targeting fuel supplies and anything else that would burn nicely. The attack was intended to soften up the garrison, with Brown later reporting:

... we didn't get into the fort. However we managed to get in and burn the town, and it looked like Guy Fawkes Night, with thousands of bonfires. These garrisons are very nervous, and open fire with every machine-gun and field gun they can raise. Moreover, the last time they kept firing for 36 hours, and we were miles away at the time, sitting on a hill looking at them. One certainly gets a grandstand view of the war on occasions.

The fires in the town spread rapidly thanks to the flammable nature of the local buildings, and then moved into the dry bush and long grass around the township, starting bushfires that finally burned out nearly 16 kilometres away. The occasional enemy shell also contributed to the blaze. The encounter only lasted a few hours, and having ruined the Italians' chance of a good night's rest, Brown and his men withdrew to their camp a few kilometres away in the bush. They did sleep well, and were ready for round two.

The next evening the RAF managed to get some Wellesley bombers into the air; it was one of their rare appearances in the Italian-dominated skies. Just on dusk, guided by the smoke and fires from the previous night's battle, the bombers swept over Burie at low level, concentrating their bombs on the three forts, before roaring off into the deepening night. As they flew off, Brown and his men again closed in on the town and its forts under cover of the smoke that was now hanging over a few square kilometres of country around Burie.

This time Brown ordered his main force to set up positions with their machine guns and mortars around 200 metres from the town. And then they waited. Around midnight he signalled his men to begin the attack, firstly with machine-guns and Mills bombs. The machine-guns kept the enemy troops' heads well down while Burke and his men zigzagged their way across the open ground toward the forts, and close enough to lob their Mills bombs over the walls. An athletically inclined person like Burke could reliably throw grenades 25–30 metres; it was simply a matter of removing the pin that held the activating lever in place, and throwing, preferably as quickly as possible as it would explode seven seconds later. The problem the thrower had was that when the bomb exploded it would hurl shrapnel much further than 30 metres, thus making it potentially lethal to the thrower as well as the target.

Burke and his men knew they had to get close enough to the fort wall to make sure the bombs went over; they then needed to use the fort wall as protection against the razor-sharp bits of steel that would fly back in their direction. Despite the fact that they were horribly exposed to fire from all three forts, Burke and his men pressed home their attack, using the swirling smoke as cover as Brown, Howell and Body and their men kept up their machine-gun and rifle fire to suppress return fire from the enemy.

For over an hour they moved quickly and decisively while delivering their bombs, and with the combination of the machine-gunners regularly shifting positions, smoke and repeated explosions, the enemy had great difficulty finding targets. With Burke's work done and he and his men safely back with their colleagues, the mortars joined the battle. After inflicting as much damage as possible, Brown and his men disengaged and slipped back through the bush toward their camp for a well-deserved break from the clamour and threats of the battlefield; unlike their targets, they could rest in relative peace.

A press release from Canberra some months later said of the attack on Burie that Brown's tactics:

> ... succeeded beyond believing. The town roared into flame. Three protecting forts, sited in a triangle, panicked, poured artillery fire into the hapless town for hours. Fire swept the country for 10 miles around. And 1500 yards away the guerrillas sat and relished their handiwork. This was dramatic warfare.

Meanwhile, as Wingate's larger force drew closer to the beleaguered town, Brown and his men went about their business. Their local intelligence network had reported a large number of trucks at Burie, and Brown was keen to make sure that if the Italians decided to run they wouldn't get far, so he sent Howell and his crew to keep an eye on the road between Burie and Injibera. On that stretch of road was a concrete bridge, recently built by the Italians, and it was a tempting target for Bill Howell. After placing his men on the high ground around the bridge to provide cover and warning of any unwanted visitors, Bill got to work on his preparation to blow the bridge. Not one to stint on explosives, Howell used around 130 kilograms of gelignite and 112 kilograms of gun cotton (an explosive often used in blasting), and after retreating to a safe distance, he pushed the detonator. When the dust from the ferocious explosion finally settled, Bill found that he had reduced the bridge to little more than a pile of rubble. There wasn't time to sit back and enjoy his handiwork, however, because their intelligence proved to be accurate, and shortly after their ears stopped ringing, Howell heard the rumble of an approaching convoy.

This was too good an opportunity to miss, so he and his men slipped in behind the convoy and mined the road over which they had already passed, leaving their surprises for the next convoy they thought might be close behind. However, a bit of bad luck came their way as they were spotted slipping back into the bush after laying the mines. The numerically superior Italians set off after them.

The fight was close and brutal. In the heavy scrub on either side of the road the Italians found that Howell and his men were keen to scrap. The Italians opened fire with machine-guns and rifles from the cover of their vehicles on the road, and then split up to chase Howell and his men into the bush. What they didn't expect was that rather than make a strategic retreat, the Australian-led men decided to stay and fight.

As the enemy troops moved through the scrub, Howell's men sprang from hiding and opened fire at point-blank range. Despite the intense fire the Italians kept coming, and hand-to-hand fighting began, with Howell and his men using their rifles as bludgeons, their bayonets taking their grisly toll. Though Howell lost two of his men, the Italians' losses were much greater; they found that well-trained and experienced guerilla fighters were not going to be easily overwhelmed just by superior numbers. For the fierce Ethiopians and their Australian leader, there was no such thing as a backward step, and soon the Italians decided on a strategic retreat back to the main road and then back to Burie, and of course straight into the minefield. Howell and his men watched as the mines whittled down the enemy even more, and then slipped back into the bush.

Back around Burie, Brown and Burke kept the pressure on the forts with their nightly short-and-sharp sorties, and awaited the arrival of Wingate and his large force. Brown described this time:

> We are camped about 4000 yards south west of Burye [Burie] – only two of us being whites and the remainder of the 'army' being just wild Abyssinian tribesmen – and believe me they are wild too. They're very much like Fijians, with great mops of hair, only here they are not as clean. I am sure they have never combed their hair since birth. Things seem to be going along alright at the moment, as we have just made a battalion from this side retire into Burie just by annoying it. No doubt these dagoes can't stand much, as they had twice as many men as us, more machine-guns, and the top of a ridge to defend. Still by sniping at them day and night and keeping them awake, they tossed in their position in two days.

During the day, they kept an eye on the town, and watched as the convoy that had encountered Howell and his men limped back into Burie, joining the battalion they had just 'annoyed'. Brown said:

We are on a hill where we can see into the fort, and at night we just head over to their hill and wake them up with a hand grenade or two. After which they will stay awake all night firing machine-guns and their artillery pieces. In fact, we did that last night and the sergeant and I came back to bed, and from our beds watched the flashes of their guns. They look quite good at night time too.

His plan was to:

> ... within the next four or five days ... bring enough pressure on the garrison of the town to either make them evacuate to Addis Ababa or surrender. I think they will take the former course, but it will be a most unhealthy one for them, as all the local hillmen are just waiting for loot and spoils, and if they leave the fort it may develop into a massacre.

While Brown and Burke were awaiting the capitulation of the Italian garrison, their men caught someone snooping around their encampment and decided to interrogate him, Ethiopian style. Brown said, 'the fun started by giving him a hell of a hiding just to make him talk; I am afraid his life is forfeit now. They have rough justice, but are very fair in their own savage way.'

Wingate and the Gideon Force made it into Injibera on 23 February, and the following day they were around 10 kilometres north of the action. Two days later Wingate made a strategically clever move, and despatched part of his force, the 2nd Ethiopian battalion, to skirt around Burie and head for the road to Debra Markos, which would effectively put them in the middle of the Italian escape route to Addis Ababa, and dovetailed beautifully with the plan of his young Australian subordinate.

The following day some dodgy intelligence came Wingate's way, suggesting that Burie was in the process of being evacuated. Fortunately for him, Brown and Burke were still causing damage with their regular nightly attacks and had a very clear idea of what was happening at Burie, so the attempt at disinformation failed. On 27 February, the Gideon Force joined the fray, and though Boustead and the Australians counselled against it, Wingate was keen to push matters along and commenced his attack during daylight.

Body teamed up with Hugh Boustead and his men of the Frontier Battalion and clobbered Burie with mortar fire – and it was deadly accurate. Despite Brown's relentless attacks over the preceding days, the men inside the fort still had some fight in them, and for Body, it was reminiscent of his earlier fighting at Dangila. Boustead recalled:

> ... the Ethiopian mortars, under Sergeant Body, brought down a heavy response. Every machine-gun and mortar in the fort let go at once, and the woods where the mortars were concealed was a mass of flying twigs and branches as bullets whined and ricocheted through the trees.

Body's men were mainly Sudanese and didn't suffer from the reticence of some of the patriots, with Boustead saying of them:

> ... the Sudanese grinned, undisturbed. This was a comforting reflection; the rending tear of the Italian mortar shells, the whining crack of the bullets, skidding off the bark of the trees, left these young soldiers quite undisturbed in this, their first baptism of fire.

Body kept his mortars firing through the night while Wingate divided his force and attacked the three forts, constantly moving his men around the field to keep the enemy off balance. The Italians returned fire in the hope of finding a target, and joined in with their own mortars, though to little effect. In the darkness they had to rely on the flashes from the muzzles of weapons in the bush, but by the time they got their aim right, their targets had shifted. They were frustrated and failing in their defence of the fort.

In the heat of this battle the Australians, temporarily on the high ground, had ringside seats to one of the first cavalry charges of the war, and one of the last cavalry charges of any major war. As dusk approached and the mortars, machine-guns and rifles were still going about their deafening and deadly business, the men saw a cloud of dust rising from the long grass. It was a group of the Italians' native troops heading toward them at speed. Boustead said:

> I heard a sound of galloping hoofs, and the long drawn out 'Lu-Lu' of rushing horsemen in the heat of a cavalry charge. The next few minutes were critical. Bill Harris and Hassan Mussad, acting with great coolness and firing their Bren guns from the

hip in the grass, drove off the mounted men, only twenty yards from their front and flank. The enemy left both men and horses dead and wounded.

Wingate's secretary, Akavia, who was seldom separated from his leader or his portable typewriter, reported 30 horses were killed but omitted to mention the number of men. It was a single act of bravery and desperation, and one that earned the respect of the British force.

The battle raged until midnight, when Wingate and his force withdrew out of range for a break. Boustead reported seeing Wingate around 2 a.m., 'heavy with fatigue, men and animals camped in the black darkness somewhere on the forest edge'. It turned out to be a less than desirable location, because as dawn arrived the British found they had blundered perilously close to one of the forts to the east of Burie. Boustead noted, 'swiftly, stupefied with sleep, we loaded and turned back into the soot-stained sheltering forest as the mist lifted'.

Brown and Burke had spent the night a little more constructively, with their small band moving around the covering bush near the fort and maintaining machine-gun fire. With both aimed and ricocheting bullets whipping around, Burke wisely decided to keep his Mills-bomb raids to a minimum. The RAF made their second outing of the campaign, with the Wellesleys swooping overhead and bombing the forts. Their aim was good and the bombs, according to Akavia, 'caused great discontent' particularly among the native troops. As the bombers came into view, Brown, Burke and their men withdrew to a high point to watch. Brown said in a letter home, '[we] had a grandstand seat on the hill yesterday for the RAF bombing of the fort. It should have been most unhealthy inside. Unfortunately one of ours crashed, but one can't get off scot free every time.'

While his friends were watching the spectacle, Ted Body and his mortars were still in the thick of it. On 1 March Wingate ordered him to attack the nearby fort of Mankusa, one of the last obstacles on the road to Debra Markos. Ted took his team to a secluded position around 1000 metres from the wall of the fort, and then they opened fire. Shells were a little scarce, so Body made each one count. By the end of the day the fort was ablaze, and Akavia reported that 'there were a number of deserters during the day and

the night'. In an intriguing addition to the usual weapons of the
battlefield, the 'Field Propaganda Unit went into action during the
night. The Ethiopian officers of the unit crawled towards the front
and, using a microphone, called upon the native soldiers to join the
Emperor's force.' Akavia reckoned they were so persuasive that 'a
great number of the deserters were reported to have joined'. He
was right, but the Australians weren't happy about the addition to
their numbers. Brown said in his usual laconic way:

> I expected this place to be nice and quiet, but just to make things
> awkward the native troops of the Italians decided to desert to us.
> They outnumbered us 15 to 1, but we luckily got wind of events,
> and were able to provide sufficient escort. Deserters are no good,
> as they would do the same to us if things didn't go too well, but
> still it reduces the Italian strength.

The tide was turning rapidly against the Italians. The morale of
their native troops was heading toward rock bottom, and their air
superiority in the Gojjam seemed to have evaporated, with only a
lone bomber making an appearance. It bombed a church close to
Body's position, and even closer to where Boustead and his men
were located, but aside from some flying masonry, there was little
damage and it didn't put a dent in the rate of fire.

The Italians' next likely move was to evacuate Burie and make a
dash toward Dambacha fort and then on to Debra Markos where
they could make a stand on the high ground. If that failed, then
it was a final retreat into Addis Ababa. In the way, of course, was
Wingate's force, including Brown and his men. At dusk on 3 March,
Wingate, hugely outnumbered by the Italians, decided to move his
troops to the north of the road to Dambacha and Debra Markos, so
if the Burie garrison decided to move they could chase them along
the road, which was a much safer option than the small Gideon
Force confronting a much larger Italian force. At least chasing them
also meant everyone was heading in the desired direction, and the
Gideon Force was getting closer to Addis Ababa.

At seven o'clock the next morning, all hell broke loose, with the
Gideon Force's machine-gunners sending barrages ripping through
the air around the church and fort at Mankusa. Wingate's propaganda team joined the battle, broadcasting in Amharic and Arabic
through loudspeakers they had strung up in trees around the fort.

Their message to the Italians' colonial troops was clear, 'Surrender or die'. In the clamour and the smoke Brown and Burke, still observing from a nearby hill, couldn't work out whether the Italians had started their evacuation from Burie, or were trying to reinforce Mankusa, or both.

At around 8.15 a.m., they saw a large force of Italians, at least 5000 men, appear through the smoke drifting over the main road between Burie and Mankusa, and any confusion about what they were up to evaporated. In a repeat of the Italians' earlier evacuations, trucks and cars were packed with troops, and native troops and local banda swarmed on the roadside beside the column. The recently absent Italian air force appeared overhead, peppering the scrub on the roadside to keep attackers away from the swiftly evacuating force. Outnumbered and exhausted, Wingate and his men withdrew to a camp in the nearby bush. Boustead and his force were despatched to pursue the Italians on their way to Debra Markos.

While all this was going on, Brown, Burke, Howell, Wood and Body, who had handed over the mortaring task to Boustead's men and rejoined his mates in the No 1 Operational Centre, slipped into now-empty Burie. Their first task was to quell the Ethiopians' penchant for looting, which the Australians found unpalatable. Brown described it in detail:

> The Abyssinians have many queer ideas which it is impossible for Europeans to understand, but one gradually learns them. One of their customs does not impress me and that is the looting after a scrap. Every available article, even clothing, is stripped from the dead and then they are left for the vultures. They refuse to bury opposition dead and after a day or so the stench here was terrific. However, I now understand the value of the vultures, as they clean up the mess in three or four days – not to mention those animals, hyenas.

Luckily they arrived in time and, according to Brown, found the prizes left behind by the Italians: '21 trucks, hundreds of tons of food and four field guns with about three or four thousand rounds of ammunition'. The food and trucks would come in handy to maintain the pursuit of the enemy, and the patriots always got a kick out of using Italian guns to fling Italian ammunition back at the Italians.

The fort was not an appealing location, described by WED Allen as a:

> ... grim and dismal place sitting on the crown of the principal of five hills of Burye [Burie]. It was made up of stone huts giving onto a barrack yard – the whole surrounded by a wall; trenches, dugouts, wire, dead mules and dung, human and animal, covered the hillside. Flies were myriad. In the afternoon violent dust storms of the khamsin type enveloped the countryside and when the wind dropped, the dust hung in the air like a fog.

Over the next few days the Australians put the fort to good use, helping the medical officers establish a field hospital, and driving trucks to ferry supplies up to the Gideon Force in pursuit of the former fort residents. In the evenings they returned to their camp just outside the fort and upwind of the various fragrances.

The battle for Burie was finally over, and as part of the mopping-up campaign the press office in Khartoum entered the fray. Of their conquest of Burie, Brown observed drily:

> ... needless to say we are very proud of that, as we got a mention on the BBC News for the capture of Burie, and there were only the four white sergeants, and the local Abyssinians. That it was evacuated and not captured we have glossed over, and in a year or two I suppose it will develop into a story like the siege of Troy.

It didn't quite take on epic status, but much to the delight of their families back in Australia it was reported in the local media. News of their exploits in Ethiopia had been scarce, and letters required a two-week trek on foot from the frontline into Khartoum, and then a long sea voyage. The *Sunday Telegraph* of 9 March ran the headline, 'Abyssinians rout crack Italians' and reported:

> Led by Australians, Abyssinian troops are driving the remnants of a crack Italian force of 8000 toward Addis Ababa, the capital. Advancing eastward from the captured fortress of Burye [Burie], the Abyssinians are 25 miles along the main road to Debra Markos. Burye [Burie] is 150 miles north-west of Addis Ababa and Debra Markos, a vital military and air base, is 30 miles farther east. An Australian lieutenant, 6 ft 5 in tall, and a young London

officer lead the Abyssinians towards Debra Markos. Burly Australian sergeants organise the flank guards. The retreating Italians are harried from the flanks while mobile squads under Australian officers and sergeants sweep ahead to destroy roads and lay mines. The line of retreat is strewn with wrecked lorries. Ditches are choked with the bodies of men and horses, piles of food and equipment. Already 2000 of the Italian force have deserted to the pursuers. Deserters say every tree seems to hide a native sniper and ambushes are laid at every bend in the road.

The battle of Burie and its aftermath made the news for a few days, but in an event like World War II a single battle was soon consigned to history. The smaller fort of Mankusa went the same way, with the Italians withdrawing toward the fort at Dambacha. The Australians managed about 36 hours of peace at Burie – their first break in nearly a week of 15–20-hour days of close-quarter fighting – before heading off toward Dambacha. The morning of 6 March brought news that the Italian force was heading quickly toward Dambacha, and it was growing in size. The enemy column now included the evacuating troops from Injibera, Burie, Mankusa and Jigga, a small fort between Mankusa and Dambacha.

Hot on the Italians' heels was the Frontier Battalion, made up of mainly Sudanese troops; further down the road was the 2nd Ethiopian Battalion, which had been sent forward a few days before to lie in wait and cause as much disruption as possible. It was inevitable that something would go astray for the Allies, and it did. Akavia reported:

> . . . while the enemy's rear guard was trying to keep the Sudanese at a distance with the help of cavalry and machine-guns, the head of the enemy's column collided with the 2nd Ethiopian Battalion – about 300 Ethiopians and 8 British NCOs. The Italians came on in waves but the first attack met with a very hot opposition, so that it was quickly repulsed with losses. The enemy advance guard was driven off to the right. It made for the camel camp and started destroying the camels. The Italian attack then became general.

The single instances of fighting developed into a fierce engagement that saw great bravery on both sides. An Ethiopian lance corporal,

seeing the Italians despatch two Lancia armoured cars bristling
with three machine-guns apiece in the direction of a cluster of his
troops, grabbed a Boys anti-tank rifle and, under heavy fire, crossed
the road and engaged the armoured cars, stopping both and fortunately managing to escape being killed.

Akavia reported:

> The enemy advance continued in spite of losses and by their
> immense superiority in numbers and fire power at last, after
> some hours fighting, forced the Ethiopians to withdraw to the
> forest on the right, after making some small counter attacks by
> small groups.

Akavia estimated that at least 650 Italians were killed or wounded.
The bridge over the Charaka River, near the centre of the fighting,
was nicknamed Dead Man's Bridge, and Akavia bemoaned the usual
lack of air support, noting, 'RAF action while the enemy column
was wedged between the Sudanese and the Ethiopians (with some
patriots on the flanks) would have caused the disintegration of the
whole enemy force.'

Leading the Ethiopian forces were the South Africans
befriended by the Australians at Khartoum and Injibera. Brown
and his men would catch up with them again very soon, and of
that meeting he said:

> The South Africans at the moment are just licking their wounds
> as they had rather a nasty scrap the other day. The retreating gar-
> risons of Burye [Burie] and Mankusa came on to them, much
> to the surprise of both sides, and a decent scrap started – 8000
> Italians against a handful; but the handful held them for four
> hours, and actually counted 150 dead to our losses of 17 natives
> and one white officer captured. The Italian losses no doubt will
> be much heavier and their wounded quite considerable com-
> pared to our 16.

One reason advanced for the high Italian casualty count was that
many of the Eritrean colonial troops wore red stripes on the shoulders of their uniforms, and in this area of the highlands covered in
scrub and high grasses, the stripes were readily visible as the troops
moved, making them ideal targets for the sharp-eyed Allies.

After the fracas on the road, the Italians, now close to Dambacha, made camp for the night on a hill with a clear view of the road and the countryside around; a sound strategic move. On the outer perimeter of their camp were nests of machine-guns, which quickly deterred a brave attack early the next morning. The attack, ordered by Hugh Boustead, had been to assess the Italians' defences; they had found them to be formidable and so a larger attack was not an option.

By this time the Australians were back from Burie and rejoined the fight. Ted Body joined Wingate and his main force, while his mates went about their usual business, as the AIF news put it, of 'a secret service job – sabotaging the enemy's resources, destroying his lines of communication and inflicting damage upon him whenever and wherever they could'. Their target was Dambacha fort, where they expected the Italians to stop and make a stand. As Brown noted:

> We have a complete freedom of action in our doings of getting the Habishis [the patriots] to drive out the Italians, and so far have been quite successful, but if they are to stand at all, there must soon come a time when they decide to hold a fortified line, or we will have the whole of the country.

Hugh Boustead, who had been slipping through the scrub on a reconnaissance mission, had also reported 'the enemy was holding a very strong position'. Dambacha looked like it would be the scene of the pivotal battle of the campaign, and Brown and his operational centre were tasked to soften the enemy with their usual blend of machine-guns, Mills bombs, explosives and sleepless nights.

Wingate, however, had another plan in mind and decided it was Addis Ababa or bust, and rather than waste time and effort on Dambacha, he would simply go around it. The fort was on a rolling plain and partially obscured by a grove of eucalyptus trees. Navigating around it and out of the range of its guns would not have been especially problematic, except that the Italians came up with their own unexpected plan: they chose flight instead of fight, and left Dambacha bound for Debra Markos, the next major town and fort down the road to Addis Ababa, and the seat of Ras Hailu. This move forced Wingate to come up with a quick plan B.

Wingate's force was gravely outnumbered by the Italians, who already had around 14 000 men. If they managed to consolidate with Ras Hailu's forces in Debra Markos they would field around 20 000, which could lead to a protracted battle with the odds of victory stacked against the Allies. Debra Markos was on the highest ground in the area and was well suited to defence rather than attack. Wingate decided the prudent course would be to isolate the town and, as Akavia wrote, 'pass Debra Markos by the south and prey on the enemy's lines of communication with Addis Ababa'. Wingate also radioed Khartoum headquarters and encouraged them to cobble up a series of bombing raids to run day and night on the town. He hoped that the RAF's arrival would coincide with the arrival of the Italian column and increase the number of opportunities for havoc.

As was rapidly becoming a habit, Brown and his men were first to arrive at Dambacha fort after the Italians had departed. The fort was a mess, with dead and rotting sheep and calves scattered around, and according to one British officer, 'mountains of papers, shells, detonators, macaroni, rice and sugar scattered everywhere. There is no latrine accommodation, everything being incredibly filthy.' At this point, Wingate had no particular tasks in mind for the Australians, and with fresh troops arriving in force in the region, it meant that the men of the No 1 Operational Centre could take a brief break. They had been travelling and fighting since Roseires, almost three months before. Their clothes and bodies were in desperate need of a good scrub. Boots were in poor condition and their feet had been battered by the countryside and the ever-present irritation of tinea. Each man had had his first taste of malaria and that other Gojjam staple, dysentery. Fortunately neither ailment had been severe up to this point and they had pressed on, doing their best to ignore the symptoms and stopping only when necessary. They were all exhausted and had lost weight, increasing their vulnerability to opportunistic diseases. What was needed was some decent food, sleep and a break from battle. Dambacha, after a bit of housekeeping, would be their holiday resort in the Ethiopian highlands.

Brown said:

Sunday [9 March] once again and for the first time in six months or so it is going to be recognised as a holiday. And it is going to be a most welcome change too, for months past now we have been working seven days a week, and of late about 16 to 20 hours per day. Of course, the long hours are necessary, as the Italians have been withdrawing from this part of the country, and at a fast rate too, necessitating long hours to keep up with them.

He went on, 'At the moment we are safely settled in one of their old forts – Dambacha, with its room and other working facilities. Still, after so long in the open, I feel better under a tree.' His desire to slip back under a tree may have been prompted by the peace of the fort being shattered with the arrival of Orde Wingate, a bevy of British officers and a large chunk of the Gideon Force. The fort was an ideal spot for them to relax and plot. And the food wasn't bad either, because the Italians had yet again decided on a hasty departure and left behind plenty of supplies including staples such as tea, sugar, salt and jam to replenish their larder. Burke, who agreed with Napoleon that an army marched on its stomach, took a liberal approach to Wingate's orders to only use transport for ammunition resupply, slipping behind the wheel of a truck borrowed from the Italians and undertaking a few supply runs back to Burie to collect food items that were in short supply. He also shopped for local chickens and eggs, and the Ethiopian cooks turned out regular meals of pancakes with eggs, curried chicken, macaroni and tea. Brown reckoned 'we have [had] this menu about a couple of months now, and are a bit sick of it; one certainly misses vegetables a lot'.

While the Australians and their men enjoyed the respite of the fort, some of the British officers were not keen on their fellow guests. Brown's troops had earned a fearsome reputation, with one British officer describing them as 'a bunch of cut-throats . . . drunken, quarrelsome and intractable'. The same officer was apprehensive about the behaviour of his own orderlies and had disarmed them just in case, so his view may have been a little jaundiced.

One thing the Australians did find in the fort was a note from a British officer taken prisoner a few days earlier. He had anticipated a brief residency there, and had left a note for the lads to explain his recent absence, saying, 'I am a prisoner here and quite well. Good luck to you all.'

While taking a break at Dambacha fort, the men took the opportunity to move around the district to gather intelligence and see how the local population was reacting to the fighting. The news they came back with heartened Wingate. Many of the local population had been sitting on the fence, unsure of what would happen if they supported the British and the patriots and they lost; after five years of colonial rule, they knew the Italians could be unforgiving. However, what the intelligence gathering revealed was that the locals had slipped off the fence and were now firmly on the side of the Allies. The fleeing Italians had few, if any, supporters left.

15

THE BEGINNING OF THE END

During a lull in fighting, Wingate and his Gideon Force officers took to plotting the next stage of the campaign, while Brown and his sergeants, never men to be idle long, added ambulance driving to their retinue of skills. For their inaugural trip, made at night to reduce the risk of air attack, they loaded the wounded into two of the captured trucks and a staff car and drove back to Burie, where they were greeted by the genial Dan Sandford, who had recently taken up residence in the fort. One British officer recalled Ken Burke arriving behind the wheel of a truck, 'looking like Father Christmas, with a big woolly beard and his language is as racy as ever'. Burke was becoming well known around the Gojjam as the resident 'character'. The captured fort was not only being used as a hospital, but was being tidied up in readiness for the arrival of Haile Selassie. The Allies had also established an airstrip so that the seriously ill and wounded could be airlifted to Khartoum, and supplies could be flown in. One of their passengers to Khartoum was Ted Body.

Body became the first casualty of the No 1 Operational Centre. He'd got through the attacks on the forts completely unscathed, but while working directly with Wingate en route to Debra Markos, he badly twisted a knee and was reduced to a 'hobble', and though it didn't impede his skills with the mortars, the problem that followed shortly after did. The country in which the Australians had been operating up to that point is known as 'fever country', with the risk of illness diminishing the closer you get to Debra Markos. At the heart of 'fever country' is Lake Tana and the towns on the edge of the escarpment and through to Dangila – the hub of the Australians' operational area. Though all five Australians had had minor bouts of malaria that had slowed them down or put them out of action for short periods, Ted Body had the dubious honour of becoming the first to be incapacitated by the parasitic disease. While drugs helped to lessen the severity of the symptoms, time and rest still topped the list of treatments. Ted would be out of the fight for around a month, and his recollection of the first weeks in Khartoum was blurred by the severity of the malaria. He eventually fully recovered from his knee injury and malaria, joined a motorised convoy and was soon heading back to Ethiopia, this time along a more civilised route than they taken just after Christmas 1940.

Wingate and his force left Dambacha on 12 March, still intending to circuit around Debra Markos and establish themselves in the country between the town and the Blue Nile Gorge, which had only one road and one bridge, thus making it a perfect natural choke point. Control of this area would mean the Italians' force at Debra Markos was isolated from their compatriots in Addis Ababa and Bahir Dar. The move was timely as General Platt, then in Eritrea, launched his final and decisive attack on the strategically important town of Keren on 15 March. It was significant to both the British and Italian forces because both road and rail heading to the capital of Asmara, and the port city of Massawa, had to pass through the town. Seizing Keren meant disruption of the Italians' supply line. Platt and his forces had been at it since early February, but success had eluded them. Though Keren wasn't fortified, it was located in dreadful country for anyone bent on ousting the incumbents. Steep mountains, escarpments and ridges gave the Italians the high ground and natural protection from which to repel their attackers. It would take two weeks of bitter fighting for Platt to finally drive the Italians from their position and send them in retreat toward Asmara.

To the east, General Cunningham and his force recaptured the port city of Berbera in Somalia on 16 March and were tapping on Ethiopia's door. With the port under their control, the lifeline of supplies for their rapidly advancing army could be guaranteed. In Bahir Dar, Colonel Torelli found himself cut off from support by a recently arrived British force. The Gojjam province was looking like the soft centre of Ethiopia, and Prince Amedeo, the Duke of Aosta and the gentleman unfortunate enough to be the commander of Italian forces in East Africa, wanted to establish two lines of resistance, one at Debra Markos, and one at Gondar to the north of Lake Tana and on the route to Asmara.

The Duke was none too pleased at events in the Gojjam, and replaced General Natale with his deputy, Colonel Saverio

Maraventano. The new leader was told to aggressively defend Debra Markos, and as Wingate would soon find out, Maraventano was not a man who liked to slip into reverse gear when confronted by an enemy.

WED Allen observed of the period:

> The Italians had, in fact, within a fortnight, evacuated the whole of western Gojjam; and they were retiring behind the forts of their last and most formidable stronghold to the west of the great loop of the Blue Nile. But the weary conquerors who now went boldly forward with a strength of not more than 300 men, to reconnoitre the defences, were themselves in a perilous enough position.

Haile Selassie and the royal entourage had reached the Gojjam on Sunday 2 March and were cooling their heels awaiting news on the fighting around Burie. Allen described their camp in the bush thus:

> The heir of the House of Solomon was sitting under a tree at a camp table, covered with a red plush cloth and lit by a single candle-lamp. A common brown Kurdish rug was on the ground. We were regaled with sufficient whiskey, Turkish Delight and pistachio nuts. The Emperor looked frail and rather tired.

On 5 March, after promising news from the front, they broke camp and moved forward. Selassie's adviser Edwin Chapman-Andrews had a knack for travelling in style, no matter what the circumstances, and noted that he departed around 2 p.m. after he had 'pink gins with the doctor and then dined'.

Ken Burke, under Brown's orders, headed back yet again to Burie in a captured Fiat staff car, where he collected Dan Sandford and his colleague, the former Vice Consul to Ethiopia, Maurice Lush. The three then set off along the main road to meet the Emperor, who was now en route to Burie. They met up at the Fatham River, around halfway along the road to Injibera. Ken Burke met his first Emperor, and the Emperor met his first famous Australian football player. Despite the dramatic differences between the men, the two had an immediate mutual rapport and respect. Burke was surprised to be taken directly into the Emperor's inner circle as an afternoon of political and military discussions followed. In typical style, Burke remembered the Emperor as 'a terrific little bloke – he certainly had some guts'.

After dinner that night, the Emperor, Burke and Lush chatted and listened to the latest developments in the war to their north and east courtesy of the BBC. Chapman-Andrews, who along with Sandford had been out meeting with some patriots, returned to the camp around 9 p.m., 'cold and hungry'. When those problems were remedied, Sandford and Lush headed off on the long haul back to Burie, this time on the back of a mule rather than in the back seat of a Fiat.

When the Emperor retired for the night, Chapman-Andrew and Burke paid a visit to one of the patriots, Mesfin, in his nearby camp. Mesfin was an affable host and travelled with a decent supply of the favourite local tipple, tej, a honey-based wine similar to mead. The strength of tej varies according to its length of fermentation, and Mesfin liked a bit of kick to his tej. Burke, a man of immoderate tastes, managed a reasonable hangover; Chapman-Andrews wasn't quite as healthy, noting in his diary the next morning, 'Vow not to drink tej.'

The Emperor's mule train bearing his servants and luggage headed off at 7 a.m., with Haile Selassie, Burke and the less-than-healthy Chapman-Andrews leaving for Burie at the more civilised hour of 11 a.m. They arrived in Burie just as all hell was breaking loose courtesy of a violent thunderstorm that brought with it driving rain and high winds. Burke stayed at Burie for the next week, helping prepare defences for the airstrip, transporting the wounded from the front to the hospital at the fort, and chauffeuring the Emperor to meet local patriots and visit the wounded. The Emperor was also keen to hear details of both the Australians' and the patriots' exploits over the previous few weeks. It was a brief but welcome break from the frontline. Burke's peace ended on 23 March when Brown and the rest of the team were ready to go back to work and begin making life as miserable as possible for the residents of the fort at Debra Markos. Wingate had rethought his plans and Debra Markos was now a target.

In the intervening period, the RAF had met with reasonable success in sorties over the town; troops under Wingate had directly attacked the outlying forts, mainly at night; and Debra Markos had been subjected to regular attacks by mortars and artillery. Wingate surprised his soldiers by taking a hands-on approach, working with the mortar crews to load and fire their weapons as they moved around the target. The Australians had proven the value of the hit-and-run actions and Wingate adapted their tactics for use by his larger force. He was also painfully aware that in attacking Debra Markos he would be taking on a vastly superior Italian force, so this type of attack was his safest and most effective option. A bonus was that the unpredictable nature of the action had a marked effect on the morale of the colonial battalions and Ras Hailu's men, which was evidenced by a sharp increase in desertions.

However, not all was going Wingate's way. In an aggressive move Maraventano ordered a battalion back along the road to a small fort at Emmanuel, which they had deserted on the flight to Debra Markos. The fort was occupied by around 200 Sudanese troops and 100 natives. After a short and decisive exchange, the occupants realised they didn't stand a chance and headed out of the fort and into the cover of the bush. The Italians promptly re-established themselves in the fort, an action the British thought may have been a prelude to a counter-attack back along the road to Burie, but their fears were not realised. For his part, Colonel Maraventano was very pleased, saying that the event marked 'an improvement in morale and the aggressive spirit of the troops and the restoration of our prestige'. Akavia also noted a change, writing in his diary that the action had made some of their patriot chiefs a little rocky: 'information received from reliable sources that some Abyssinian chiefs who joined us contemplate treacherous acts.'

The intelligence was found to be reasonably accurate, though the 'acts' were more of lethargy than outright treachery. Thesiger and his men had been despatched on 17 March to close the road between Debra Markos and the crossing of the Blue Nile Gorge. To give them a hand with this mission, they had teamed up with the patriot leader Belai Zaleka, a small, mean-faced and humourless gentleman everyone believed to be the finest and fiercest patriot in the Gojjam. However, 'everyone' was wrong. Unknown to Thesiger, Belai Zaleka had been contacted by the other side, in the form of Ras Hailu, who, to garner Zaleka's support, had offered his daughter as a bride. It seems Belai Zaleka was something of a social climber and not much of a realist, so he jumped at the chance to advance his standing by marrying into the province's leading family. Thesiger found that prodding Belai Zaleka into action was far more difficult than he had expected. Rather than enthusiastically attacking the enemy, Zaleka simply trotted out a litany of excuses to remain in his camp. When he wore out 'lack of supplies', 'waiting for more troops' and 'waiting for better intelligence', he moved to petulance and told Thesiger that it was *his* army and he would act when he wanted to. Thesiger, well behind enemy lines and relying on the patriot leader for support and basics such as food and ammunition, had no choice other than to wait and hope.

When commenting on the incident that left a blot on his formerly pristine copy book, Thesiger observed that, 'to Belai Zaleka's peasant mind, the chance to marry into the Takla Haimanot family proved irresistible'. What Zaleka failed to factor in was that the Italians and their compatriots were still likely to be losers. Payback came four years later when Haile Selassie, then restored to power, had Zaleka and Ras Hailu's son Lij Mammu thrown into prison for the trouble they had caused in the Gojjam. After a fair trial, both were hanged.

This problem with the local help didn't affect the four Australians. With Burke back in the fold after his chauffeuring duties, they left Dambacha and headed toward the action around Debra Markos, where they joined up with troops from the Sudan Defence Force and returned to their favourite routine: swiftly and brutally attacking enemy positions around the township with mortars and Mills bombs; ambushing any patrol foolish enough to leave the fort; attacking convoys; mining roads; and, in their spare time, joining Wingate on his nocturnal attacks on the town. Their particular area of interest was the stretch of territory reclaimed by the Italians between the Emmanuel fort and Debra Markos; in their advance back to Emmanuel, they had reoccupied the small forts of Gulit on the north side of the road and Addis to the south. Both forts were perfectly located to provide a withering defence for traffic on the road, and to catch the unwary in a murderous crossfire. Brown and his band were again back in the lead, with these two forts as their targets.

In company with Hugh Boustead and his force, the Australians attacked Gulit each night while other British forces moved closer to Emmanuel. From 27 to 29 March the 2nd Ethiopian Battalion pounded away at Emmanuel with artillery, mortars and machine-guns. Brown, Burke, Howell, Wood and their group joined them at the front, using their well-honed tactics of machine-gunning and lobbing Mills bombs then changing positions and attacking again, keeping the Italians constantly on edge. It was dicier than ever for the Australians as they were constantly on the alert to avoid being hit not only by enemy fire, but by friendly fire from the large force they were now working with. Radio communication on the battlefield was patchy, so Brown and his men relied on sharp eyes, quick reactions, well-rehearsed hand signals and hearing attuned for the differing sounds of battle to keep from harm as they darted about the battleground.

Unfortunately all was not going as well for their associates in the battle. On the morning of 29 March, Lieutenant Michael Tutton was heading back to the Ethiopian Battalion's position after reconnaissance closer to their target. He was moving quickly because he had noted, from harsh experience, that a bout of dysentery was about to hit him. What he found when he rejoined the battalion was that 60 men of A Company, then commanded by New Zealander Captain Allen Smith, had mutinied. Rather than fight, some had decided to head to Burie and try for an audience with their Emperor.

The following day at around 5.30 p.m. Tutton, who had spent the day enduring the pain and indignities of dysentery, dragged himself up to see what the battalion had achieved as the day drew to a close. What he found was that more men had followed the mutineers, and that 'several others were dead drunk and incapable of moving'. Unfortunately his commanding officer, Major Ted Boyle, wasn't handling the problem well. He had lost his temper and was using his fists to try to restore some order. Wingate later sacked Boyle for the debacle. The only redeeming moment of the ill-fated engagement was that the Italians had decided to withdraw from the fort and head to Gulit, a short distance along the road toward Debra Markos.

Fortunately the Australians were still operating quietly and effectively; by that stage of the war, their No 1 Operational Centre was one of only two of the ten operational centres that had seen battle, and one of the few still capable of fighting. One operational centre near Bahir Dar had come to a halt when its commander, a Canadian Captain MacKay, was shot in the stomach. One other operational centre was still back in Dambacha, laid low by dysentery.

For the Italians retreating from Emmanuel, Brown had a little surprise. Late on the night of 30 March, the Australians set off from their camp, using the cover of darkness to get close to the road, where they waited in the low scrub, scanning for any light from campfires, or the rumble of approaching traffic. With no man-made noise interrupting the peace of the Gojjam night, they crept forward and onto the road to lay their charges. It was tricky work in the dark, particularly when handling explosives that were known to be sensitive. The Italians fleeing toward Gulit would run right into the Australians' trap.

Unfortunately for Brown and his men, they had only just finished their task and were about to retreat toward a high point in the bush just off the road to watch their handiwork, when they heard a convoy approaching. They quickly packed their explosives away and prepared for a hasty exit into the bush, but it was not quite hasty enough. As two laden trucks exploded, the convoy came to an abrupt halt and the troops guarding it noticed the cause of their woes heading into the nearby bush. The Australians didn't have time to set up their machine-guns and mortars for the ambush, and were caught on the hop. After a few days of pounding by the Allies followed by exploding trucks, the Italians were keen on payback, and having a much larger force was handy. What the Italians didn't expect was that the Australians and their patriot colleagues had no intention of running.

The brief, brutal action took place on a wet, cold and windy night in the high scrub at the side of the road. Though utterly outnumbered, the Australian force made it to higher ground with better cover and better visibility. They let rip with concentrated machine-gun fire and Mills bombs to slow the enemy advance. The Italian troops that made it through the fusillade were in for an even bigger surprise when the commando training of the four Australians kicked in and old-fashioned hand-to-hand combat started. The Italians were not trained for this type of warfare, and as they rushed uphill toward the Australians they found themselves fending off skilled, swift and savage attacks by the four and their compatriots. The zeal of the larger attacking force was whittled down by an unrelenting barrage of punches, well-aimed kicks, slashing and stabbing with knives and bayonets, and, for those unlucky enough to get close to Burke and Body, a rugby-style head butt. The sheer ferocity and fearlessness of the Australians' attack turned the tide, and so with 23 of their troops killed, the Italians decided to retreat back to the road, and take their chances with the landmines. In the engagement, only two of Brown's patriot troops were killed.

While they escaped intact from the battle, it was a turning point for the Australians. After the close combat, any vestige of a boys' own adventure in which they righted wrongs and liberated the oppressed was gone. It was a sobering moment. In the few months they had been in-country, they had been able to put aside the violence and aftermath of engagements that had been conducted at a distance, and the toll of the rough life they had been living. This engagement brought the deadly reality of their situation home to them.

The remnants of the Italian force made it to Gulit fort and prepared for their final withdrawal to Debra Markos. Boustead, commanding the action in the absence of Wingate, who was back at Dambacha miserably enduring a bout of malaria, received intelligence from patriot sources that the Italians would soon depart Gulit, so he decided it would be a fine idea to attack them after they had left the relative safety of the fort. Boustead was unlucky in his choice of men to attack the retreating Italians. At this point, he was not aware of Boyle's problem with his reluctant troops, so his order to attack the fleeing Italians was not obeyed. As a consequence, the Italians managed to escape from Gulit without a shot being fired at them.

Their colleagues across the nearby Addis fort were having a much warmer time. Just before midnight on 31 March, Brown and his operational centre crept up to the fort, and with the mortars (now under the control of Bill Howell) dug in, they opened fire. Their machine-gunners poured suppressing fire into the fort while Burke and his team made regular sorties close to the wall, and threw their Mills bombs over. The attack was relentless, and by the early hours of the following day the Italians, feeling decidedly isolated with the departure of their neighbour, made a strategic retreat toward the road and Debra Markos. The Australians then took up residence in the fort and with the arrival of dawn were brewing tea in the remains of the officers' quarters.

What Wingate and his commanders didn't know was that while the Italians were being driven back to their stronghold at Debra Markos, their commander, Colonel Maraventano, had been summoned to urgent talks in Addis Ababa. He flew to the capital, and at 8.30 a.m. on 30 March General Trezzani updated him on the 'grave military situation' of Italian forces in East Africa. On 27 March, Major Platt had finally succeeded in taking Keren and was in pursuit of the Italian force that was hot-footing it toward Asmara.

To the east near the Somalian border, Dire Dawa, Ethiopia's second-largest city, was under merciless attack and was not expected to last much longer. Addis Ababa was next on the Allies' list.

Maraventano was then ushered in to meet with the Duke of Aosta, who gave him orders to return to Debra Markos immediately and concentrate all his forces there as the prelude to the complete evacuation of Gojjam province. The Duke also told him to disband his irregular native forces or hand them over to Ras Hailu. The evacuation was to be swift and orderly, and anything that couldn't readily be carried was to be given to Ras Hailu or destroyed. Rather than evacuate to Addis Ababa, which itself would soon be under threat, Maraventano was ordered to lead his force toward the town of Dessie, an 800-kilometre slog along the main road toward Addis, across the Blue Nile Gorge and then through rough country and mountains. All of this was carried out in a country where the Italian positions and fortunes were constantly changing, and always for the worse.

To add to his problems, 1 April 1941 dawned with Boustead and his force, and Brown and his three sergeants and their men, attacking Debra Markos. General Platt later noted in his report on actions in the Gojjam that in this battle, 'the disparity of the forces opposed had reached something fantastic; 12 000 Italians and colonial troops were contained by two companies of the Frontier [Battalion] supported by the mortar platoon (4 mortars) of the 2nd Ethiopians, totalling 300 men'.

The town of Debra Markos is on a high point of a rolling plain and, in the typical style of the Italian occupation of the Gojjam, was ringed with small forts. The citadel was on a rise in the centre of the town and surrounded by a grove of trees. The Australians joined Boustead and his men in sniping at the Italians with machine-guns and rifles throughout the day, and when night fell, they got very serious. Though Brown's preferred time of attack was between midnight and dawn, when the enemy was at their lowest ebb, orders came through requiring an attack as soon as possible. It was another wet, cold and windy night when Brown and his men linked up with Colonel Colin MacDonald and his Sudanese soldiers from the Frontier Battalion.

They slipped around the entrenched Italian defences that surrounded the town, and gave the enemy a nasty shock by attacking them from their rear with machine-gun and rifle fire. The mortars were silent this night, and Burke's Mills bombs were too dangerous to use in such an unprotected location. While a fine strategy for the element of surprise, there was one problem with sneaking up behind the Italian defences. They closed to about 15 metres from the Italian positions, and then opened fire at point-blank range with their machine-guns and rifles. It was a devastating attack on the enemy until one of the Italian machine-gunners managed to turn his weapon around and opened fire on the exposed attackers.

The gunner's aim was good and his first victim was Colonel MacDonald, shot through the temple. Despite the maelstrom, the Sudanese soldiers kept advancing. The death of their officer and a man they deeply respected was unforgivable. Retreat was not an option.

The Australians and their men poured fire into the Italian positions, trying to provide some relief to their Sudanese comrades as they advanced the short distance toward their prey. They were astounded when the Sudanese, nearly close enough to touch their enemy, dropped their rifles and withdrew their pangas, a lethally sharp knife around 14 inches long and 5 inches wide, and the preferred weapon of African bushmen. What followed became etched in the Australians' memory. The Sudanese overpowered the Italian gunners, many of whom hadn't been able to reverse their weapons and bring them to bear. They moved quickly and systematically along the 100 metres of gun emplacements, wiping out the machine-gunners with slashing strokes of their pangas. The screams of their victims joined the roar of battle. The enemy gunners who tried to run were chased and, as Brown noted, 'cut down like corn before the hail'. With the Italian defenders either killed or scattered, and silence on the battlefield, the Sudanese soldiers picked up the body of Colonel MacDonald and carried him back behind their lines – a 13 kilometre walk at 2 a.m, Brown told a journalist later that morning. Wingate sent a letter to Boustead, suggesting he contact Maraventano and recommend the Italians surrender. Wingate required the 'unconditional surrender of Debra Markos on pain of heavy bombing', and in the event of their surrender, 'all Italian nationals, colonial troops and banda to be guaranteed their safety'. The message was relayed to the Italians by wireless telephone, with Boustead stirring matters along by telling them that the bloodthirsty patriots were amassing around the fort and that 'while regretting the useless shedding of the blood of brave men, there can be no alternative for those who resist stupidly and use-lessly when all hope has gone'.

After a lull in the fighting, and a lack of response from the Italians, it was back to business as usual. Mortars coughed their projectiles and machine-guns resumed their hail of lead directed at the forts and Italian positions. Sergeant Clarke of the less-than-enthusiastic Ethiopian Battalion managed to save some face by leading a few of the more reliable men into skirmishes on the outlying forts: they targeted Italian rather than native troops and were spectacularly successful, killing 18 of them.

Sensing that victory was soon to be had, Boustead sent a small force from the Frontier Battalion under Lieutenant Henry Johnson to move around Debra Markos and head to the Blue Nile Gorge. If the Italians decided to evacuate rather than surrender, there was only one road they could use. Boustead wisely attached part of No 1 Operational Centre, under Bill Howell, to accompany Johnson. Howell's team, now very experienced and reliable, brought their mortars with them.

As the fight to take Debra Markos drew to a close, the Australians had their second casualty but, just like Ted Body, it was because of the country in which they were fighting rather than wounds from battle. Ron Wood, suffering from malaria and various other ill-effects from four months of continuous fighting and travelling in the Ethiopian scrub had kept his end up during the battle, but when it was over he was in a bad way and beyond the limited capacities of the field hospital. He was transported to Khartoum for treat-ment and rest. Unfortunately one of the other ill-effects that beset Ron was a growing addiction to *araki*, a common tipple throughout the highlands made from a mix of ground, fermented *gesho* leaves (a common local plant) and distilled into a lethal beverage with an alcohol content of around 45 per cent. His mates thought a little rest away from the stress of constant battle would see him back in form.

Brown, Burke and their men remained back in the centre of the action in the Gojjam at Debra Markos. Bill Howell, now heading toward the Blue Nile Gorge, didn't have long to wait for trouble to come his way. On the morning of 3 April one of Maraventano's transport columns, heading back from the Blue Nile Gorge to Debra Markos after delivering supplies, came into range. The column – around 30 empty trucks, a Red Cross vehicle with an escort of two armoured cars, 50 of Ras Hailu's men and a platoon (about 50 soldiers) of Blackshirt troops – were making their way up a ridge when they were spotted. The British force opened fire with Bren guns and the Boys anti-tank rifle from their positions of cover on the crest. Their timing was perfect because the armoured cars couldn't raise their guns sufficiently to engage. The Boys rifle quickly disabled both armoured cars before joining the Brens and attacking the trucks. Twenty-five trucks were destroyed, and the Italian-led force suffered – 12 men were killed and 12 more were wounded. The Italians left standing loaded into the remainder of their trucks and drove as quickly as possible back to where they had come from. There were no casualties on the British side, and, after scooping up food and ammunition from the remnants of the Italian column, they slipped back into the scrub to hunt for another position in which to lie in wait.

Debra Markos lost its occupants on the morning of 4 April 1941, when Colonel Maraventano and seven colonial battalions, plus around a thousand native troops, and a column of around '4000 women and children, the families of Askari [the colonial soldiers], 500 native civilians who had compromised themselves by acts done in our favour, and about 100 nationals' according to an unnamed correspondent, departed for Dessie, around 220 kilometres away if you were travelling in a straight line. It was potentially a march of two weeks or more depending on the weather and other obstacles they might encounter. Ras Hailu remained, and sent his men to the outlying forts and key parts of the town to keep looting to a minimum. He then waited for the British to come knocking on the door of the citadel. At midday they did just that.

First into the town was one of Boustead's officers, Major Peter Hayes, who carried a letter demanding Ras Hailu surrender and hand over the town. Hayes approached the citadel under the protection of a white flag and a small squad of heavily armed troops. After the pounding they had dished out, Hayes was surprised by a hospitable welcome: 'I was met by a large crowd and Ras Hailu. They started kissing my feet and Ras Hailu took me into a small inn and plied me with Tej.' Hayes later returned to Boustead with Ras Hailu's 'somewhat vague answer', which may have been caused by exuberant consumption of the tej. That evening, and in the absence of any further word from Ras Hailu, Boustead tried again, this time without kid gloves: he sent a message telling Ras Hailu that if he did not surrender, aerial and land attacks would resume.

The following morning Boustead appeared at the citadel and was greeted by Ras Hailu, looking the picture of military chic in an Italian general's uniform bedecked with ribbons – and ready to negotiate. Observing the meeting was WED Allen, who said of the old Ethiopian: 'cunning and arrogance disguised the anxiety in his face'. Boustead didn't negotiate. Hailu asked to be placed in charge of public security and to live in the citadel 'in a style consonant with my dignity and my position'. Boustead said no, a gutsy call considering Ras Hailu had around 5000 of his men still in the town, greatly outnumbering Boustead's force. Ras Hailu knew, however, that the end of the Italian era in Ethiopia was at hand, so with long-term survival in mind he relented and handed over the keys to the citadel. In the wash-up of the battles to take Debra Markos, Wingate's secretary Akavia prepared a butcher's bill. He noted that the enemy had suffered 245 killed and 800 wounded. On the other side of the coin, Wingate's force had two killed, 18 wounded and two missing. British stores and armaments were bolstered, with two field guns, 18 heavy machine-guns, six light machine-guns, two armoured cars, two trucks and a large supply of ammunition, clothing and equipment. Any plans Ras Hailu may have harboured to use the supplies abandoned by his former comrades had long since evaporated.

If Boustead wasn't impressed by Ras Hailu's requirements, he was even less so the next morning when the patriot leader Negash, who had been scarce during the recent battles, turned up. According to Negash, he had been appointed, though he didn't state by whom, Governor of the Gojjam, and he demanded the citadel and all its contents. Boustead took the view that the patriot leader was 'pompous and bombastic', and banished him to the outlying forts until Haile Selassie arrived. 'This is most shameful,' Negash said. 'It is an order,' replied the armed and resolute Boustead, while quietly hoping that the Emperor would arrive sooner rather than later and take on the political squabbles that were brewing. Boustead's men made the point of who was boss later that day when Negash's men were found looting the hospital. Major Jock Maxwell, a fair-complexioned, boyish and no-nonsense Scot who was second-in-command of the Frontier Battalion, was unimpressed, and when the men declined to discontinue, Boustead reckoned Maxwell 'shot one dead at 300 yards and scared off the others, making them drop their loot as they ran'.

Fortunately for Boustead, the Emperor was close. Wingate arrived the next day, 6 April, and in the early hours Chapman-Andrews dodged Brown's mines on the road between Emmanuel and Debra Markos and arrived at the citadel. Haile Selassie, accompanied by Dan Sandford, followed in a suitably regal convoy of six cars, arriving in the early afternoon and raising the royal standard over the citadel. That day General Cunningham's army also reached the outskirts of Addis Ababa.

Greeting the returning Emperor was an honour guard made up of the 2nd Ethiopian and Frontier Battalions. The patriot leaders Negash and Mangasha, and their forces, along with locals, were on hand to pay their respects. Colonel Boustead and Colonel Benson, the newly arrived commander of the 2nd Ethiopian Battalion, were formally presented to the Emperor. Ras Hailu made an entrance, half an hour after the appointed time, when, as Major Donald Nott recalled, 'he drove up in a motor car and got out. He bowed stiffly, a formal obeisance to the Emperor, and muttered something, and then stood upright.' He went on:

> Haile Selassie then read an address in which he praised the Frontier Battalion and the 2nd Ethiopian Battalion. He sat on the Palace steps, which we had hastily cleaned as his dwelling, and held a reception of notables.

Nott didn't think much of the locals and their new-found enthusiasm for the British and their returning Emperor, saying, 'HM received patriots who danced before him, reciting their prowess, mostly lies.'

Later that evening the Emperor put the Italians' reserve supply of champagne to good use, hosting a cocktail party to celebrate Cunningham's arrival in the capital. Ken Burke wasn't presented to the Emperor, or invited to the party, but later that night when the formalities were over, he 'popped by' to see the Emperor, much to the chagrin of the British officers. Allan Brown tagged along, and together they listened to the BBC broadcast the news of General Cunningham's success: 'Addis Ababa has fallen,' the announcer intoned. The Emperor was delighted but at the same time frustrated that he was still trapped in Debra Markos. He shared with Brown and Burke his disappointment at General Cunningham's insistence that he remain at Debra Markos. There were still around

40 000 Italians in Addis Ababa and the General was worried that the Emperor's return may have provoked a wave of retribution against the Italian colonists that would end as a bloodbath.

Wingate, in between social engagements and sorting political issues with the Emperor and local worthies, hatched a plan to add stimulus to Maraventano's flight toward Dessie, and quell any desire to return. On finding that a phone line was still working to Dejin, a small village on the road between Debra Markos and the Blue Nile Gorge where the Italians had paused briefly, he persuaded Edmund Stevens, correspondent for the *Christian Science Monitor* who was one of the journalists travelling with Wingate and his Gideon Force, to ring through to the village and speak to the Italians. Thanks to his fluent Italian, Stevens made for a very convincing Dr Digrofino, allegedly a prisoner of war who was risking his life to give the fleeing Italians a warning; he told the Italians' switchboard operator that a British division had just arrived in Burie and that a terrible fate was in store the Italians on the Blue Nile, and that they should get out as quickly as they could.

Suitably stimulated, Maraventano and his column managed 28 kilometres on the first day of their march toward Dessie, stopping for the night at the scene of Johnson and Howell's ambush of the transport column. Johnson, still nearby, decided that an attack on a column that size would have most likely been fatal for his men, so they moved out of the way of the camping Italians.

Two more days of marching, including a brisk downhill trot from the top of the plateau to the base of the Blue Nile Gorge, had them crossing the river and into relative safety.

The day after Haile Selassie arrived in Debra Markos, Boustead headed toward the Blue Nile Gorge, hoping that his advance forces – led by Thesiger – had managed to corner the fleeing Italians and deliver the *coup de grâce*. He was disappointed. Thanks to Ras Hailu's successful conning of the patriot leader Belai Zaleka by offering his daughter's hand in return for Zaleka giving virtually no support to his so-called allies, in particular to Thesiger, there was no chance of cutting off the fleeing Italians before they reached the Blue Nile Gorge. Thesiger, according to Boustead, 'was mortified' when the truth of Ras Hailu's successful move was found out, and he was sent back to report the debacle to Wingate. Thesiger said that 'Boustead was furious but Wingate was unexpectedly understanding', so much so that he sent Thesiger back to rejoin the pursuit.

Under Boustead, Johnson's men, along with Howell's crew, began the long descent into the gorge. Boustead described the gorge as 'an astonishing spectacle, a huge deep gorge cut like a miniature Grand Canyon into the Abyssinian plateau, with extremely precipitous sides covered in bush and scrub down which a road had been cut'. What they found at the bottom was that the only bridge had been badly damaged and was impassable. On the other side, the Italian rear guard were busily blowing up the only road that snaked its way to the top of the gorge. Boustead was disappointed and angry, commenting, 'having seen the escarpment I feel confident that Belai Zaleka could have completely destroyed the Italian Force'.

From their position on the other side of the river, up the steep and winding road out of the gorge, the Italians opened fire with artillery and mortars. It was an effective move because Boustead and his men had only one exit route: back up the gorge on their side of the river, which the Italian guns were doing a fine job of making a very unsafe place. The British elected to stay under cover near the river and see what eventuated. Luckily for them the Italians had no desire to wade back across the Blue Nile.

When the Italians finally decided to move on, Boustead ordered Johnson and his force to continue the pursuit. At around 3.15 a.m. on 9 April, they crossed the river. The force totalled 137 men, including Howell and 15 of the men that had fought with the No 1 Operational Centre since training in Khartoum, and they were chasing around 8000 troops under Italian command. Thesiger, very keen for the chance to prove himself after his recent debacle, rejoined the fray with his Sudanese orderly and nine patriots, adding to the men from the Frontier Battalion. The original force had been larger but, as was becoming a habit, some of the men decided they weren't interested in proceeding. The Sudanese Nuba soldiers told Johnson that it wasn't in their deal to cross the Blue Nile, and that home and their wives beckoned. The fight had gone out of them. Johnson marched them off to Debra Markos under the command of their sergeant.

The pursuit of the Italians across the Blue Nile wasn't without incident. Though the main force was making its way up the gorge, Maraventano had left behind the 13th Colonial Battalion, which did its best to make the crossing as perilous as possible before heading up the hill to rejoin the main force. In the firefight around the rocky and slippery sides of the river, Johnson's tiny force suffered one man killed, with the colonial battalion losing seven men and suffering 13 wounded.

Though it was a ridiculously small number to send in pursuit of a force nearly 50 times larger, it had some bite – and Johnson had clear orders from Boustead to chase the Italians and cause them as much trouble as possible.

The crossing of the river marked the departure of another of the original Australian five to an uncertain immediate future. Bill Howell was a long way from his mates, at the beginning of what would become a long venture across Ethiopia. Ron Wood was still in Khartoum recovering from malaria and the toll of the last few months. Ted Body had recovered from his leg injury and the first of many bouts of malaria, and returned to Ethiopia on 7 April. He was travelling on four wheels rather than four legs this time, and planning on catching up with all his mates on a shady balcony somewhere in Addis Ababa. It was a fine plan that wouldn't quite work out. Brown and Burke were still in Debra Markos, poised to begin one of the more intriguing and successful moments of the entire Ethiopian campaign.

16

TROUBLE IN THE RANKS

Back in Debra Markos, Brown and Burke were about to have their first industrial-relations dispute. Colonel Torelli was still in Bahir Dar and wasn't showing any desire to capitulate. To Torelli's east, on a secondary road that ran from Bahir Dar and joined the main road to Addis Ababa just south of Debra Markos, was the Italian-held town of Mota, its fort occupied by the 69th Colonial Battalion, nicknamed with tongue firmly in cheek as 'The Glorious 69th'. Ousting the Italians from Mota would put even greater pressure on Torelli and on the remaining Italian forces in Dessie in the north-east. As WED Allen put it, 'vigorous mopping-up operations were essential if all Italian resistance was to be eliminated before the rains'. The rains, less than two months off, could readily turn the entire Gojjam province into a quagmire.

Lying close to the Abay River, Mota was a major market town in the area and at every Thursday market it became the commercial hub of the region. The market attracted local farmers, villagers and merchants who trekked down the road from the regional cities of Bahir Dar and Gondar to the north. For many Ethiopians, the war was little more than a sideshow to their daily lives that hadn't changed in generations.

Hugh Boustead was very keen to dislodge the Italians, saying, 'It is essential to try and get Torelli out of this and to operate on him as we have been doing at Debra Markos every night, and to attack with bombs, rifle and bayonet.' As usual, the No 1 Operational Centre would spearhead the task. Brown, Burke and their men were tasked to head north into the Choke Mountains to rally the local patriots and secure the road, thus cutting off another line of supply or evacuation for Torelli. Mota fort would be their first big target, and it would not be an easy trip. Getting there was a 130-kilometre trek north into the rough, steep country of the Choke Mountains and included crossing the 4000-metre Chaigul Pass. Spring had barely touched the mountains and the temperatures along the trek would hover around freezing.

Some of Brown and Burke's men, a mix of their own force from Khartoum and additions from the Sudan and the Ethiopian Frontier Battalions, didn't warm to the task. It was obvious to them that it was only a matter of time before the Italians surrendered, so heading off into the misery of the Choke Mountains wasn't what they had in mind; staying warm and comfortable in Debra Markos was their preferred option. On 10 April, Wingate ordered them to move out. Fifty-eight of the men refused, so Wingate ordered them to be disarmed, arrested and locked away pending a court martial.

Burke, who had fought side-by-side with many of them, was not impressed by Wingate's abrupt treatment of the men. He believed they deserved better treatment in consideration of their brave service, and was confident that a more lenient approach would get them back on track. This was where the Australian view sharply contradicted the British view. Burke went straight to Wingate to plead the case for the men. Donald Nott reported that Burke failed dismally, and that Wingate, in response to Burke's plea, 'went through him like a dose of salts'.

The 58 recalcitrant troops were brought before a court martial the next morning, with the bulk of the Debra Markos force mustered to watch. Fortunately for the troops, Burke's pleas on their behalf the previous day did have some effect on the outcome, and all were discharged from the service rather than suffering any harsher penalty. Nott said, 'The men were marched up and their sentence read out with a warning they would be shot if they enlisted again. They were stripped of all uniform except shorts, and chased down the ranks out of the fort while the big drums in the corner of the fort were beaten.' Haile Selassie watched the event through his window. What this meant for Brown and Burke was that they headed off into battle with 19 troops at their command.

Being shot at by Italian troops wasn't necessarily the most dangerous problem to confront the Australians in the Ethiopian highlands. The local mosquito population carried malaria and yellow fever and had already infected a large number of the troops, both native and European. Old favourites like polio and tetanus were not uncommon either, and dysentery was commonplace.

What the Australians soon found on their trek into the Choke Mountains was that altitude sickness could be added to the menu of maladies.

On a more positive note, their progress was aided by the local patriots they met. Word of the arrival of Haile Selassie in Debra Markos had a positive effect on their reception, with Brown noting, 'as the first representatives of the Emperor here, we command a considerable amount of homage'. One of the acts of homage by a local chief was to present Brown with an iron-grey stallion, a much more comfortable animal than the mules that were often their transport in rough country. Journalist Carel Birkby, one of the small contingent of journalists who were travelling with Wingate and the Emperor, had earlier found the sight of the lanky Australian on a mule quite amusing, describing Brown 'with his black beard and long legs, which dangled almost to the ground as he rode in a painted wooden saddle on a little Abyssinian mule'. An iron-grey stallion was certainly more becoming.

Their progress to Mota was slow through what WED Allen called 'heart-breaking country' into what was nicknamed the 'roof of Africa'. In the distance were the four peaks of the Choke Mountains, each passing 14 000 feet. Though the rainy season had yet to start, the men got an early taste, with heavy rain and strong winds lashing the highlands, and adding to the persistent chill that got worse as the climb began. The landscape was bleak. They stopped at remote villages of no more than a few huts where they supplemented their rations with eggs and injera (a slightly sour tasting flatbread that is common throughout Ethiopia), and bought firewood and charcoal, a popular cash-flow product in the region and handy to blacken their faces for night attacks.

As they moved onto higher ground, the landscape changed to something bordering on the surreal: it was desolate, inhospitable and punctuated for kilometres by large local plants standing almost 10 feet high and topped by a prong that looked to them like a red hot poker – the cause of a few bawdy jokes. Their spirits rallied as they crossed the pass near the peak of Mount Kiero, Ethiopia's second-highest mountain and some 14 000 feet above sea level; from here the Mota fort came into view below them. Having spent days clambering uphill through rough country, they now had to descend to the fort, which was set at around 8500 feet about sea level. When close, they set up camp, reconnoitred the area, rested, ate their cold rations – a campfire so close to the target was out of the question – and began plotting their attack.

The next morning, rested, refreshed and more accustomed to the altitude, the force of a mere 21 men slipped into their well-rehearsed and battle-honed attack formation. Directed by hand signals and hidden by the high scrub, they encircled the fort and set up their mortars and machine-guns around 200 metres from the walls, and huddled down to wait for night. The Italians' plans for settling down for a languid evening in front of the fireplace, a good dinner and maybe a glass or two of Chianti were ruined when Brown decided to attack just after dusk. He wasn't keen on spending more nights outside in the cold and wet mountains than he had to. Following their well-practised habits, Brown signalled his men to open fire, beginning with machine-guns, which peppered the parapets and kept the Italians and their local troops cowering below the wall and out of sight as the bullets swooshed around them.

As the night deepened, the mortars joined the machine-guns, landing their bombs over the walls. Burke stepped up the action, leading his men in a zigzag through the scrub between their lines and the fort and hurling Mills bombs over the walls, yet again proving that his throwing skills were on par with his fullback kicking skills. Inside, it was chaos thanks to the ferocious and unpredictable attacks. Bombs and ricocheting bullets made moving around the fort hazardous. All around, it was deafening, dangerous and relentless. Rather than a good dinner and decent night's sleep, the Italians were served rations and an uncomfortable night in the bomb shelters and damp trenches behind the walls. The men of the Glorious 69th, under the leadership of Comandante Enrico Nazzarella, were cut off from their peers in Bahir Dar, and believed they were under attack from a large and well-trained force – they were half-right.

The machine-gunning, mortaring and occasional visits by Burke continued throughout the next day and into the night. There was no respite for either side. Brown kept his men on the move, and the brief lulls in the battle ended when the guns and mortars returned from the new positions. Smoke rose from the numerous fires in the fort and its inhabitants were battered and demoralised. The stone walls still stood, but behind them the destruction was vast. What had started as a disciplined return of fire at their constantly shifting targets was now ragged and without enthusiasm.

After nearly two days of pounding away, Brown and his men had the psychological edge on the fort's occupants and it was time to turn it to their advantage. Brown was also aware that his supply of ammunition wasn't inexhaustible, so he needed to bring this conflict to a suitable end quickly. What he couldn't do was overpower the vastly superior Italian force, but he could roll the dice and try something tricky. Under the cover of a flag of truce, Brown sent one of his Ethiopian men to the fort with a message telling the Italians they were surrounded by a large force with heavy guns and lashings of ammunition. Brown's ultimatum was concise: surrender or be wiped out.

Thanks to the stories swirling about the Gojjam province about the size and abilities of British and patriot forces so far, Nazzarella didn't doubt the integrity of the note, but to surrender so soon would have brought dishonour to the flag, and so Brown's offer was declined. Nazzarella did, however, suggest that Brown and he might have a chat. When the messenger returned with the response, Brown, with Ken Burke watching on apprehensively, and poised to open the bombardment at the slightest provocation, emerged from his hiding place in the scrub close to the fort and took a slow walk under the flag of truce.

Nazzarella, in a pristine, well-tailored uniform, greeted the scruffy and bearded Australian at the gate. Brown towered over the natty little Italian commander. As they entered the fort, Brown observed that its exterior was strongly constructed of stone, as were some of the buildings inside along with those made of mud and grass used for local staff and native troops. He also noticed the firing position of weapons, and trenches. What struck him was the appalling damage his men had meted out to the incumbents. Huts had been flattened, stone buildings damaged by shell and fire, but oddly enough the officers' quarters were virtually untouched. This intelligence would be vital should they need to battle on, and it confirmed in Brown's mind that if the Italians decided to call his bluff and counter-attack, the chance of his force winning a protracted engagement was remote, bordering on suicidal.

Brown also knew from recent experience that the Italian military travelled with a degree of élan that was in contrast to the Australians and the English, so he wasn't surprised when the Comandante addressed him in English and suggested they have a glass of champagne to lubricate their discussion. Three bottles remained in his cellar and sharing one with the Australian would be his pleasure.

The chat was amicable and Nazzarella was a fine host. Unfortunately military business did have to be discussed at some point, and eventually Brown got around to the subject of surrender – by the Italians, of course. The consequences, as Brown pointed out in his gentle yet matter-of-fact way, would be most unpleasant for the Italians. 'I told him he was surrounded by superior numbers, and that unless he surrendered the whole garrison would be wiped out,' Brown later said. The Italians' circumstances had changed, he pointed out, and Ethiopia was on the cusp of being returned to the Ethiopians, and their friends the Allies. Addis Ababa had fallen, Haile Selassie was in Debra Markos and poised to make his triumphal return to his capital after five years in exile – and it would be better and safer to surrender to Brown rather than risk being captured by the patriots who had unpleasant habits when dealing with prisoners. The aftermath of the Battle of Adwa was something the Comandante had not forgotten, but the need to save face was still strong, and Brown said, 'Much to my surprise, he told me to come back the next morning after he had discussed the matter with the other officers overnight.'

What neither the Australians nor the Italians knew was that Boustead and reinforcements were heading toward Mota and were very near. Wingate, well aware of Brown's tenacity and capacity for blowing things up, thought his men might be running short of mortar bombs over the course of the engagement, and ordered Boustead to help mop up.

Just before dusk on 18 April, Boustead and around 400 men had headed for the hills, thus missing a cocktail reception for the British officers hosted by Wingate the following night. Haile Selassie and his two sons were in attendance, and Wingate, according to a British officer at the reception, 'made toasts with champagne cocktails'. Boustead enjoyed a simpler evening on the trail. With mules scarce, his men had been forced to load their supplies onto camels, an animal known to dislike mountain conditions, particularly when it was cold and wet. It was going to be a particularly uncomfortable trip. Boustead reported of the appalling conditions:

> As we went up and up the cold became intense and it was clear the men from the Sudan plains were suffering from mountain sickness. A high wind rose and was followed by snow which then worked up into a blizzard. The men only had one blanket for covering

and we spent a miserable night below the pass [the Chaigul Pass] shivering with cold and suffering with mountain sickness.

Toward the end of their journey, the orders were changed. Over the radio, Boustead was ordered to send the bulk of his force back to Debra Markos so they could join the march into Addis Ababa. He was left with only around twenty Sudanese troops and a few mortars. Unlike some of their compatriots, Boustead reckoned his force was frustrated at having endured the journey only to be 'desperately disappointed at not being in on the attack on Mota'. What the men didn't know was that Brown and his team were doing quite nicely, and the capitulation of the Glorious 69th was at hand.

When Brown returned for a chat around 9 a.m. the next day, he found Nazzarella looking composed and tidy just as he had the day before. Tea was offered instead of champagne, which was just as well because it would not be a celebration for the Comandante and his beleaguered garrison. Brown soon found that his ploy had been successful and the Italians lacked the heart for another night of bombardment. In one of the more civilised moments of World War II, Comandante Nazzarella agreed to Brown's request for unconditional surrender. Brown said, 'In the morning I returned and the whole garrison then marched out under the escort of a few of my men.'

The surrender of the Glorious 69th was painless and came as something of a surprise to Boustead, who had expected a decent fight. When the Italian force marched out of their fort and were greeted by only 21 men, Brown and Burke had a brief moment of concern. However, after the misery of the previous days, the Italian troops had no intention of fighting, nor were they deeply disappointed at being so neatly duped. Brown and Burke were pleased to report that none of their men had been killed or badly injured in the battle. The last two bottles of champagne were shared by the officers of both sides, with the enlisted men making do with tea.

A press release announcing the capitulation of the Italians at Mota rather unkindly said, 'The Glorious 69th was true to the fighting traditions of the Italian army today. It surrendered at once before the real bloodshed became inevitable. Honour, and the flag, were satisfied. Why not? The garrison had fought for 30 hours! Comandante Enrico Nazzarella gave tea and champagne to the victors. The Glorious 69th marched into captivity. Vale Glorious 69th!'

The Italians' first night in captivity was as civilised as their surrender. The native troops who had formerly occupied the fort, on hearing that the Italians were on the run and the Emperor poised to return to his capital, pragmatically decided to switch allegiances rather than merely surrender. They were readily recruited into the service of Haile Selassie and his rapidly expanding army. Boustead joined the Australians in the fort for a good night's rest and some decent food. In a large room nearby, the Italian officers and NCOs, relocated from their bunks to more simple accommodation, had also settled in for the night. George Steer, correspondent and friend and adviser to Haile Selassie, wrote of a colourful moment that evening when Boustead, snoozing happily in his room, was stirred from his slumber by a very annoyed Burke bursting into his room. Burke said to the drowsy officer, 'Who has won this bloody war, sir, us or them?' 'It looks like us,' replied Boustead. 'That's just what it doesn't look like!' replied the agitated Burke, who ushered Boustead along to the room where the Italians were spending the night. Burke wasn't impressed that each of the officers and NCOs was not spending their first night in captivity alone, but in the company of their Ethiopian mistresses. One wit later observed, 'in miniature we had the end of a hit-or-mistress Empire'.

With Mota in safe hands, Wingate ordered Boustead and his small force to head toward Bahir Dar to increase the pressure on Torelli and his garrison there, and on the garrison at Gondar on Lake Tana's northern tip. On Anzac Day 1941, Brown and eight of his men headed back on a 70-kilometre trek through the mountains, escorting the captured Italian officers and NCOs, minus their Ethiopian consorts, to the nearest British camp. Burke and his 11 men took charge of the fort and would wait there for Brown's return. A little stocktaking was in order and as usual, it proved to be a treasure trove, with Burke discovering two mortars, 30 machine-guns, around 2 million rounds of small-arms ammunition and enough provisions to keep a battalion in the field for two years. More than enough for their needs and to equip Boustead for the next stage of his journey.

17

THE TRIUMPHAL MARCH

While Brown was taking his prisoners to their temporary home, Burke was holding the fort and Bill Howell was in pursuit of Maraventano, Haile Selassie was heading toward Addis Ababa. His five years of exile were about to come to an end.

The Emperor left Debra Markos on 27 April, much to the annoyance of General Cunningham. The general was concerned that the route into Addis, along the main road, wasn't completely cleared of Italians and their sympathisers. He was also apprehensive about security in Addis Ababa; the city still contained 12 000 or so Italian troops who had surrendered, as well as 5000 Italian civilians living and working in the city, and law and order had not yet been established to his satisfaction.

Cunningham, however, was fighting a losing battle to keep the Emperor at bay, and he had few allies. Brigadier Lush commented:

Pressure to bring him [Haile Selassie] back was intense – from London from my CPO [Chief Political Officer] Mitchell, from the representatives of the press who had somehow appeared in Addis Ababa and of course from the Emperor's HQ vociferated by Dan [Sandford] quite calmly and by Wingate loudly and without thought; by British officers who were bored by the inactivity at Debra Markos and wanted to 'get shot of the little man and get on with the war'.

The 320-kilometre journey was by open car for the Emperor, commandeered from Ras Hailu, and an assortment of cars and trucks for most of the others. Accompanying him was a large force of the Ethiopian army cobbled together by Wingate from the Gideon Force, including Boustead's team recalled from Mota, to give a suitably impressive public-relations effect. Wingate and Sandford were keen to see the Emperor with 'his' army to dispel any suggestion that the British were having a few colonial thoughts of their own. Mingling among the Ethiopian army and the Emperor's personal guard were around sixty of the Sudan Defence Force and their Bren guns – public relations was one thing, but the security of Haile Selassie was paramount.

The motorcade traversed a temporary bridge that had replaced the one across the Blue Nile destroyed a few weeks earlier by the fleeing Italians, then tackled the winding road up the gorge, a tricky trip thanks to rock falls, the escarpment plunging down one side of the road and the over-friendly families of local gelada baboons. The Italians had done a fine job in blasting sections of the road to smithereens, and the British engineers did an equally fine job making the road trafficable for the Emperor and his column. Part of the trip up the gorge was literally a cliffhanger, with the trucks moving slowly, only inches from the precipice. Some trucks were unloaded for the journey and their contents hauled up by hand. Akavia recalled that he carried bags and put his shoulder to the task to push the trucks up some of the trickier spots. Next stop was the ancient monastery of Debra Libanos where Haile Selassie paused to pray, and then the motorcade moved on.

On 3 May they arrived at Ficce where Cunningham's representatives were waiting for them to confirm the final arrangements for what Akavia termed 'the triumphal entry into Addis Ababa'. At Entoto, on top of the hills surrounding the capital, they paused to take in the view of the city, and again so the Emperor could pray. Carel Birkby wrote:

> . . . he stepped out of the open car in which he was travelling, Bimbashi Le Blanc at the wheel and old Ras Kassa by his side and walked past the crowds who sought to kiss his boots as they never sought to kiss the Italian viceroy's. Coptic deacons clad in gorgeous robes of sky blue, scarlet, purple and gold held up gold crucifixes which he saluted. Bareheaded, he entered the octagonal Coptic Church of the Virgin Mary. For a few minutes he retired into the inner sanctuary, where he unburdened the overwhelming gratitude of his heart to God. I stood close to him in the dim half-light of the ambulatory and saw tears start in his eyes. He went down on his face, like the humblest subjects did before him, and kissed the carpet on the floor of the church.

Birkby's fellow South African, Dick Luyt, was similarly moved, and commented, 'We had arrived as we had set out to do with Gojjam conquered and the Emperor with us. The stage was set for a new era in Ethiopian history.'

Along the road that wound down into the capital, men and women wearing white shammas, long white cotton dresses, crowded to watch the return of their Emperor, five years to the day that he had left the city and headed into exile. The red, white and green flag of Ethiopia fluttered from poles and any other object it could be attached to.

At the head of the procession was Orde Wingate, quite the picture mounted on a white horse and wearing his inevitable Wolseley helmet and shorts. He was accompanied by the loyal Akavia, and Dick Luyt, who was marching ahead of the 'woolly headed patriots', many of whom had vowed not to cut their hair until the Italians had been kicked out of the country. Despite Cunningham's orders that a maximum of 700 patriots be allowed in the parade, around 10000 turned up and marched. The weather was perfect, flowers were in bloom on the hillside and the scent of eucalypts sweetened the air.

The procession headed to the palace on top of a hill in the centre of Addis and close to Haile Selassie's residence, where he gave a speech imploring his people to 'not repay evil with evil ... do not stain your souls by availing yourselves on your enemies'. Bands played, children's choirs sang songs of welcome, and the Italians fretted in the three safety zones in which they had been sequestered under Cunningham's orders. Selassie then headed to his residence where, according to Carel Birkby:

> The vast throne-room had been cleaned up, painted and refurnished since the day we entered Addis. The Fascist insignia on the walls had gone. The Emperor's old throne had long since disappeared, but a new one had been built, the immense traditional divan-throne of King Solomon's descendants with glowing cushions, gilt pillars and a velvet canopy. The Emperor went into the throne room, senior Imperial officers behind him, and after presentations, he stood with dignity before the throne, wearing a simple khaki uniform bearing the badges of rank of a general.

As the various chiefs entered the room, they came forward to:

... fling themselves at the foot of the throne where Haile Selassie now sat, to kiss the dais, to fall on each other's necks, kissing cheeks and clinging to each other in the deepest emotion while tears coursed down their smiling faces.

The British did not join in.

A formal dinner for the British officers and significant Ethiopians followed that night. Wine and congratulations flowed, with Haile Selassie thanking Britain for restoring him to his throne, and pledging a government with 'liberty of conscience, and democratic institutions'.

The Australians were, as usual, back at work, with Allan Brown heading back to the Mota fort and Ken Burke. After resupply and rest, the partially reunited No 1 Operational Centre followed in Boustead's steps toward Bahir Dar and their old sparring partner Colonel Adriano Torelli.

Like the trip to Mota, the next stage of their journey was miserable. The rainy season was upon them, and it was still chilly in the highlands. Dry clothes were a fond memory, and ground sheets did little to keep out the damp during the nights. The jigga flea, a particularly nasty parasite that burrows into humans and can cause unpleasant problems like swelling, ulcers and skin lesions that turn septic, added to the misery of the journey. The female of the species, when pregnant, likes nothing more than a warm human in which to lay her eggs, which eventually hatch inside their host. The jigga flea tends to lurk in the soil, so feet and toenails are popular targets, and by the end of the journey quite a few of the men were lame thanks to these bugs.

While Boustead and later the Australians were heading through the Choke Mountains toward Bahir Dar, a small force under Major Tony Simonds finally had Torelli on the run. In a sour note to the campaign, the force had nearly been even smaller, due to one of the operational centres, under the command of a young lieutenant who, according to one unnamed British officer, was a 'rather sheltered and religious young man', or in Simonds's view, 'a coward and a disgrace'.

The lieutenant had the misfortune to be placed in command of four lacklustre sergeants whose idea of organising the locals saw all four with venereal disease and not much in the way of local resistance to the Italian colonists. Simonds found that rather than fighting the Italians, the British soldiers from the operational centre were walking toward an Italian fort with their hands up. Fighting wasn't on the British soldiers agenda it seemed. Simonds took a dim view of their actions, and picked up a machine-gun and fired a burst over their heads. They got the message, and as Simonds dryly commented, 'Fortunately, despite being a bad shot, I didn't hit them.'

Simonds and his men, including the very effective No 2 Operational Centre under the Canadian Lieutenant MacKay, had been harassing Torelli for nearly two months since 12 March. Simonds had used both day and night attacks to annoy the superior Italian force, and had managed to kill or wound around 300 troops and six officers, including wounding Torelli. In these actions, MacKay had been wounded and was replaced by Lieutenant 'Billy' McLean, later to be a very active member of the SOE in Europe, and even later a Member of Parliament.

On 28 April, General Nasi, then in Gondar, ordered Torelli's withdrawal from Bahir Dar, and a rather stylish one it was, with the force heading toward Gondar by steamer across Lake Tana. By the time Boustead arrived on 1 May, and the Australians a few days later, the fight had gone out of Bahir Dar. Brown and his men broke away from the main force, and toured the region looking for the remnants of the Italian forces, but didn't meet with much luck. It seemed targets were getting scarce, at which point Orde Wingate stepped in and ordered them to join the long-winded chase to catch Maraventano. Brown and Burke were about to be reunited with Bill Howell.

Howell and his men, now under the command of Major Donald Nott, had been busy. Around mid morning on 29 April his force had made it to the foot of the escarpment near Dera, roughly in the centre of the country. On the plateau at the top of the escarpment, Maraventano was secure in a fort complete with his colonial troops and around one hundred Blackshirt troops. He commanded the high points, and greatly outnumbered his enemy. Nott was a professional soldier with a creative bent, and he came up with a plan to put the Italians on the back foot, and get his men safely up the escarpment.

He despatched Lieutenant Ken Rowe, a wily Rhodesian ex-oil man, and a small group of troops to advance, light fires and, to give the impression of camps, keep them burning throughout the night.

The Italians, thinking that the British were on their way in force, were neatly conned, and directed their artillery fire at the 'camps'. During this one-sided battle, Bill Howell and two other sergeants led their men up the escarpment, in the dark – a hazardous journey. Once up the escarpment, the Italian gunners, busily firing at what they thought were the British troops, were easy to spot. Howell and his cohorts crept close to the Italian positions and opened fire with light machine-guns, scaring the hell out of the Italians, who had considered themselves unassailable. When the Italians counter-attacked, Howell and company slipped away into the night.

Nott used this diversion to get his remaining force safely up the escarpment, and set up a camp in a deserted church with a good view of – and not far from – the Italian fort. Fortunately it was also a spot that could be well defended by his small force. On 3 May, after hearing rumours that a large British force was camped nearby, Maraventano sent some of his troops to give his enemy a prod and see just how strong and well entrenched they were. At 8.30 a.m., the Italian force of around 800 men, armed with rifles and machine-guns, attacked.

The British force of barely 80 men returned fire with every gun they could muster. Nott, who was meeting with a Muslim sheikh from a nearby village, heard the attack and ran toward the sound. Thesiger, Howell, Rowe, and their men were busily engaging the probing force, with the Sudanese troops holding back, hiding behind cover and waiting for the Italian force to come within point blank range. When the Italians were very close, and lulled into thinking they had the upper hand against a small force, the Sudanese emerged from their cover and opened fire. Mills bombs followed. The Italian troops dived for any cover they could find and returned fire.

Shortly after midday, the Italians withdrew. They speculated the British force was around 1000 men, which meant it was also a public relations victory for the small pursuing force. Both sides had fought bravely that morning, and for the Italians, casualties were high with one officer wounded, 19 troops killed and 53 wounded. Nott lost one man and had two wounded. He reckoned the event made for 'the most thrilling day of my life', while Maraventano praised his own men, particularly one group who 'pressed forward to the closest quarters with superb courage and dash'.

Not only did the battle give the Italians pause, it did wonders for the local population, many of whom were the new best friends of

Nott and his men. Nott said that the locals 'swarmed in with gifts of cattle, sheep, eggs, tej, honey, bread and bananas. Several have offered to fight for us.' It represented a change in the area, which was predominantly Muslim and not Coptic in faith like the supporters of Haile Selassie. The local Muslim population had not been opponents of the Italians. With the success of the British forces against the Italians, though, the locals decided to place themselves on the side of the victors. Nott's force was also growing in size, with around 500 armed patriots joining him, all keen to take the fight to the Italians.

Following the success of the Australian-led actions earlier in the campaign, Nott set his men the task of grinding down the enemy's morale with harassing attacks day and night. Bill Howell was at the forefront of the raiding parties, leading his patriots into mortar range, bombarding the Italian positions and then slipping back into the gloom. For his part, Maraventano didn't take Nott's tactics lying down, and began sending out his own small bands of troops to harass the British raiding parties who were slipping and sliding around in the muddy, misty conditions. Neither side was having a good time, thanks to the onset of heavy rain, the unyielding cold and the lice that had replaced jigga fleas as a constant irritation. Despite fine efforts on both sides neither scored a decisive blow.

The tide turned on 14 May when Wingate arrived. As biographer Christopher Sykes said of Wingate's arrival at the battle, he was, 'throwing his own fire into the dispirited force'. He had left Addis Ababa on 10 May, moving fast and hell-bent on forcing the surrender of Maraventano. In Addis Ababa, Ted Body had joined Wingate, who was travelling with three assistants, a handful of Sudanese troops, and was closely followed by Ras Kassa and 120 patriots. En route, Wingate added Brown, Burke and Ron Wood – now in better health and just back from Khartoum – and their men to his small force of Sudanese troops.

They travelled fast over the challenging country of gorges, escarpments and stony wastelands. Their shoes were shredded by the journey and the men were hungry, dirty and dog-tired, but Wingate didn't waste time with pleasantries and rest after arriving at their camp in the Coptic Church. Thesiger said, 'bearded and unkempt, he had got off his mule, stared about him with searching eyes, set face and jutting jaw and then called us together. He wasted no time. He had told us he intended to make the Italians surrender within the next few days.'

While Wingate conferred with his officers, the Australian sergeants caught up: Burke told of the neat con job at Mota fort, Body of his time with the eccentric Orde Wingate, and Howell of his experience with the local lion population. He had been much luckier than Arnold Wienholt. A few days earlier, Bill and one of his men, sneaking up close to Italian lines, came upon a pride of lions who eyed the two as a menu item. Firing warning shots would have been fatal so close to the Italians, so they remained immobile, not even daring to twitch. Bill reckoned they 'had an unpleasant few moments' before the lions just walked away.

As soon as Wingate's men had the wireless set up, he sent off an update of the situation to Cunningham. The Italian force from Debra Markos was 12 000-strong and it was now moving into country that favoured the Italians. Its destination was Amba Alagi, where it could join up with the 7000 troops under the command of the Duke of Aosta. Wingate intended to 'destroy them within ten days', well before they joined up with the Duke.

Amba Alagi was a mountain redoubt in the north of Ethiopia where the Duke believed his forces could hold off the British. It was close to being a perfect fortress, full of caves and galleries to store ammunition and afford safe firing points. The British hadn't shared the Duke's belief in the impenetrability of the site, and after capturing Dessie on 20 April, had moved on to Amba Alagi for the final showdown. By the time of Wingate's arrival at Dera, the Duke was surrounded by the British forces, and his mountain lair wasn't living up to his expectations.

The day after his arrival, Wingate received a wireless message from General Cunningham telling him to join Boustead in Gojjam, and for Nott to return to Addis Ababa after handing over the pursuit to his second-in-command. Wingate decided a blind-eye approach was appropriate, and sent a response to Cunningham, curtly saying, 'Read the appreciation I have sent you,' and ordered the wireless closed down. Not a great career move, but given their recent history, Wingate didn't really care. He later noted that, 'I intended, as far as possible, to comply with orders, but thought it legitimate to get to Debre Tabor by moving in the enemy's direction instead of away from him.' Thesiger approved of Wingate's disregard of the order, saying it was 'on the Nelsonic principle that it cannot be wrong to engage the enemy'. The Italian column was close at hand, and Wingate wanted to finish his task, so a very liberal approach to interpreting the orders seemed a fine idea. Thesiger reckoned Wingate, having sent his response, then stood up, gazed into the distance, and said, 'What stupendous country. It must compare with the Himalayas.' Also in his field of view was the Italian column, heading out of Dera and making for Amba Alagi, a move that Wingate intended to thwart.

That evening Wingate sent for Thesiger and the Australians and told them to leave immediately along with Lieutenant Rowe, his men and a handful of patriots. Their task was to move swiftly through the night to get in front of the Italians and then open fire. He said:

> Make sure you inflict at least two hundred casualties. I shall follow them up and attack from this side. Their morale is bad and we're damned well going to make them surrender. Don't take any animals with you, they could delay you. Go off and get ready.

They headed down the escarpment with only the moonlight to guide them, lugging mortars and a heavy machine-gun. There was no easy route, and the patriots, familiar with the local terrain, made easy work of it, but it was a demanding trek for the Australians. Brief moments of respite came from mountain streams and the warm air of the small valleys. The following afternoon they received information from the patriots scouting ahead in the local villages that the Italians had camped for the night on a nearby mountain. They were all exhausted and decided to rest until the early hours and then climb the mountain and attack the guard post at dawn. The attack was an anti-climax – the guard post turned out to be a hut containing an old man and his five sons, all asleep. It seemed the local intelligence-gathering wasn't reliable, so the small band moved on.

That night they slept in an empty fort at Wagidi on a plateau and, from their reconnaissance shortly after dawn, found they were in front of the Italians, who were having an equally hard time making their way up the escarpment toward them. For a small unit, being caught in a fort by a vastly superior force was not a good idea. They needed to be able to move fast and have a position to which they could safely fall back if the battle turned against them, so in the early hours of the morning they crept out of the fort and dug into a ridge on the plateau. From this position they had a fine view of the Italians coming across the flat plateau toward them.

The Italians had artillery in their arsenal, and so when they saw the Allied force they opened fired with these big guns, using the greater range of their weapons to begin the battle. However, their aim wasn't great and the artillery had little effect other than noise and smoke. As they drew closer, the Australians joined the fray, opening up with their World War I vintage Hotchkiss machine-gun, and the rest of the force joined in with their rifles. According to Thesiger, 'The Italians then made a rather half-hearted charge with their native cavalry, some of whom got close enough for us to throw Mills grenades among them.'

Despite the none-too-vigorous attack by the Italians, the British force was still in danger of being surrounded, so it withdrew to a ridge on higher ground known as a panhandle; it had slopes on both sides and was easier to defend than the ridge they had been on. In the retreat, 30 patriots were killed or wounded. Lieutenant Rowe was also badly wounded and captured. He was well treated by Italian doctors, but later died at an Allied hospital in Addis Ababa, after the Italian surrender.

The great chase and this final battle ended, for Thesiger and the Australians at least, with a whimper. After their retreat, it became quiet, with Thesiger saying, 'having crossed the panhandle, I knew we could beat off any attack, but beyond shelling us the Italians left us alone.' It seems the Italians were busy on their other flank, with Wingate moving into position.

Just after dawn on 18 May, Wingate's force attacked the Italians, who retaliated in equal measure. No ground was lost or won and both sides returned to their camps around 5 p.m. as the night drew close. The following morning the attack resumed, with Lieutenant Johnson observing the battle. He recalled seeing Ras Kassa, the Emperor's military adviser, and the gentleman in part responsible for the presence of Brown and his sergeants in Ethiopia, also watching the battle. Johnson said Ras Kassa was 'a very respectable old gentleman, charming manners. He sat on his shooting stick like an English country gentleman watching a pheasant drive.' The charming old gentleman had done some fine work by discreetly putting out the word among the local population that the British force totalled around 15 000 men on this front, with another 3500 under Thesiger on the panhandle. Belai Zaleka, the well-known and unreliable patriot leader, was allegedly on his way with another 4000 men.

Colonel Maraventano chose not to wait around to see if this intelligence was right or wrong, and on 20 May he broke off the engagement, with Akavia reporting that 'a running fight ensued, conducted exclusively by patriot forces who displayed great courage and frequently ran among the enemy's troops'. It was to be the last skirmish – the rapidly declining fortunes of the Italian colonists in East Africa had reached rock bottom the day before, when the Duke of Aosta surrendered to the British at Amba Alagi.

In the middle of the afternoon Wingate sent a runner, under the flag of truce, to Colonel Maraventano to advise him of Aosta's surrender the previous day. He gave the colonel 24 hours to decide whether or not to surrender and said that if he didn't capitulate he would withdraw British forces and leave the now isolated Italians to the hands – and knives – of the patriots. The colonel replied that he would keep on fighting, declaring with a flourish, 'danger, deprivation and fatigue we Italian soldiers will bear for the honour and grandeur of our motherland'. He then sent a message to General Nasi at Gondar, seeking guidance or permission to surrender. The general replied that the colonel should 'decide according to conscience and tradition how you think best'. Maraventano called his officers together.

In the interim, Wingate sent another strongly worded message, making it clear that the Italians must either surrender immediately or the British would depart and leave them to the patriots. The Italians came to the view that to fight on would simply be a waste of life; the prospect of mass castration by the patriots was a key point in the decision-making process. It was all a bit of a bluff, as neither side had much ammunition left to keep the fight going, and the chances of resupply by air were minimal.

Thesiger and the Australians were simultaneously doing their own form of negotiation. After climbing down the escarpment at night, they approached the fort held by part of Maraventano's force at Agibar early on the morning of 22 May. Out came the truce flag and Thesiger, flanked by the tough-looking Australians, suggested the Italians might be best to surrender the fort. After a brief discussion of terms, the Italians agreed to unconditional surrender. Wingate ordered that the garrison of the fort, around 2500 men, be marched into custody at Ficce, around a four-day march, with the Australian and British troops keeping a close eye on the patriots to make sure they didn't practise any of their traditions in dealing with the captured enemy.

Maraventano capitulated the following day. The surrender was taken by Wingate and Ras Kassa, both on horseback. The presence of the old Ethiopian leader was to reinforce the joint nature of their enterprise and to remind the enemy what the patriots might get up to if the surrender did not proceed smoothly. Though one Italian officer, Gastone Rossini, wasn't a fan of Wingate, describing him as 'an insignificant little fellow of miserable appearance', Luigi Silvi was more enthusiastic, saying of the surrender:

> The English Colonel, whose face was completely obscured by a beard and a large helmet, raised his hand in salute. Then he moved towards the group of officers with outstretched hand and said, 'I have never before fought against such gallant colonial troops.'

With their new captives in hand, Wingate and his men headed to Ficce. The combined captives marched into the town totalled 282 Italian officers, 800 other ranks and 14 500 native troops. The Allies had cleared the battlefield of Italian weapons, bringing with them 12 pieces of artillery, four mortars, 60 heavy machine-guns, 161 light machine-guns and 12 000 rifles, and their almost-exhausted supply of ammunition.

Mission 101 was drawing to a close. Pockets of Italian resistance were mopped up over the next six months by the regular forces, with General Nasi's stronghold at Gondar finally taken on 27 November.

One of the Australians' final duties before heading to Addis Ababa was to attend a formal parade reviewed by Haile Selassie. The Emperor had travelled to Ficce to take the salute of the troops escorting the Italian prisoners of war. The Italians would also be part of the parade. Maraventano was not keen on the idea of his men being forced to pay tribute to their former enemy, and protested that, 'It's not civilized. It's barbarous to humiliate the prisoners so.' His pleas fell on deaf ears, and he was reminded of some the actions of his peers when they invaded. At 10 a.m. on 29 May, the prisoners, the escorting troops and their officers paraded before Haile Selassie, who reportedly 'watched in silence, his expression sombre and rather sad'. The parade passed without incident, a happy state of affairs that may in part be attributed to the Sudanese troops having their Bren guns trained on the Italian prisoners just in case.

Shortly after the parade, Brown, Burke, Body, Howell and Wood headed down the main road toward Addis Ababa, where they met with Wingate to begin the administrative bits and pieces to wrap up Mission 101 and their operational centre. The fit, lusty young men who had left Khartoum in December 1940 arrived in Addis Ababa bedraggled and painfully thin. Their clean-shaven faces, bright eyes, sharp creases, shiny buttons and spit-polished boots were just a memory; in their place were uniforms blackened by charcoal and mud, faces heavily bearded, boots falling to pieces and bodies covered in cuts and scratches, some of which were infected. Ken Burke, the most solid of the group, reckoned he had lost around 20 kilograms in his six months in Ethiopia. All four men were simply exhausted. But as usual there was a bit of work to complete before a long shower, a good meal eaten in a real dining room with real utensils, a few cold beers and a long sleep.

When they set out from Khartoum before Christmas the previous year, they carried 50 000 silver Maria Theresa thalers. In the peace of Addis Ababa that late May 1941, Brown did his final accounting: their expenses for nearly six months of constant travelling, fighting and inciting had cost precisely 200 pounds.

18

THE WASH-UP

Despite the remarkable success of operations in the Gojjam, and the return of Haile Selassie to the throne, the welcome for Wingate and the Australians back in Cairo in early June 1941 wasn't quite as warm as they deserved.

With Ron Wood still 'somewhere in the Sudan' according to media reports, thanks to a bit of misdirection by his mates – he was actually in a Cairo hospital suffering from a minor infection caused by social rather than military action – Brown, Burke, Body and Howell enjoyed their first real break in over six months. They were thin and worn. Bill Howell's mother would later say of her son that the twinkle had gone from his eyes, and this was something that could be said for them all. One of the first tasks in Cairo was beard removal and a haircut, and their freshly shaven faces showed the toll of their time in Ethiopia. Reflected in the mirror were gaunt-faced men who looked every hour of their age, with a few more added. It would take a few months to restore some of the zest and vigour they had displayed when they first arrived in the Middle East a little over a year before.

Ethiopia had started out as a grand adventure, but had become a harsh lesson in the reality of war. Nearly six months of living rough and fighting hard had left an indelible mark on their health. Although they didn't know it at that point, all were destined for lengthy bouts of illness and hospitalisation thanks to their service in Ethiopia. Malaria and the lingering effects of dysentery and poor nourishment during their months in the countryside would stalk them all for the rest of their lives.

However, ignorance of what the future held, and the success of the mission, had them in good spirits; being billeted in one of Cairo's better hotels with a healthy supply of beer and good food did wonders for body and mind. Their tale, thanks to earlier leaks and the hush-hush flavour of the adventure, was a beacon for the journalists lurking about the hotel in search of a story.

Australian correspondent Reginald Glennie tracked them down, and now that secrecy wasn't an issue they were happy to tell their story. Information to their families had been sparse, with their infrequent letters, written during the brief and rare moments of peace, headed out of Ethiopia by runner to Khartoum and then into airmail, which despite the name, usually took around 10 weeks to get to Australia, if it arrived at all. Brown and his sergeants knew that their families would be chuffed to hear a little more via the press.

The men told of their arduous journey through the Sudan and up the escarpment into Ethiopia. They recounted their tactics and their victories. They told Glennie that 'when we had set fire to forts close together we would retire, leaving the garrisons blazing away at each other with their guns, apparently believing the other had been captured' – all of which Glennie duly recorded and published throughout Australia and New Zealand. The BBC followed up its earlier story on the battle for Burie, and took great delight in reporting that the Australians' swathe through the Gojjam was achieved at the cost of a mere 200 pounds.

Exciting as their brush with fame was, however, their futures were not at all clear. Ken Burke was not a man to hold a grudge, and his brief stoush with Wingate hadn't left any enmity between the two. All the Australians were deeply fond of their irregular commander, and were very keen to serve with him again. He led from the front, which the Australians found both encouraging and endearing; he had guts and he got the job done. Ted Body later reflected their views, saying:

> I had the greatest respect and highest regard for Wingate as all us Australians had . . . He was definitely eccentric but so are a lot of great men, also completely fearless and brilliant. Churchill wrote a foreword in one book on Wingate, saying he was 'a man of genius who could well have become a man of destiny' – Wingate asked us to go with him on his next exploit. He said if he was given 1000 men and a wing of planes he would undertake to disarm 100 000 men anywhere in the world. We, of course, thought the world of him and wanted to stay with him.

He also thought that Wingate's occasionally spiky behaviour may have been contrived to stimulate a reaction: 'He had no fear – he liked to shock – was extremely restless and had a very kind side to him . . . I think a lot of his moods and poses we read about could have been to emphasise a point.'

Unfortunately for the Australians, Wingate's eccentricities and forthright views conspired against them all. In the last weeks of the campaign in Ethiopia he knew the days of the Gideon Force and Mission 101 were numbered, and he had been busy in his rare quiet moments writing to London and Khartoum seeking a new appointment. Unfortunately for Wingate, his superiors didn't share the enthusiasm of the five Australians. His irregular approach to soldiering and life in general did not sit well with the military establishment. General Cunningham was still so miffed by Wingate's 'radio failure' and role in what he perceived as the premature return of Haile Selassie to Addis Ababa that he ordered him out of the country by air from Harar where he had met with Wingate for a report on the work of the Gideon Force. Wingate was bundled into an aircraft and flown via Khartoum to Cairo, where the boot was put in neatly by the loss of his temporary rank of lieutenant colonel, and reversion to the rank of major. His departure from Ethiopia was so swift that he did not have the chance to attend the Emperor's celebration dinner back in Addis Ababa or bid farewell to his loyal Australians. The Emperor, as a mark of appreciation, later sent Wingate a letter of thanks, a signed photograph, a gold watch and four gold rings.

General Wavell, his sometime patron, took Wingate's eccentricities in his stride – after all, the man worked miracles with small forces – but Wavell's resources were stretched to breaking point and he was unable to offer a lifeline this time. In June 1941 he was facing his own towering problems. Greece had fallen to Germany two months before, and Rommel had earned his nickname of 'The Desert Fox' earlier that year with his brilliant campaigns against Wavell's forces in North Africa. Churchill, in an off-the-cuff moment, said, 'Rommel has torn the new-won laurels from Wavell's brow and thrown them in the sand.' In a more reasoned and compassionate moment much later he wrote:

> At home, we had the feeling that Wavell was a tired man. It might well be said that we had ridden the horse to a standstill. The extraordinary convergence of five or six theatres, with the ups and downs, especially downs, upon a single Commander in Chief constituted a strain to which few soldiers have been subjected.

On 21 June 1941, while the Australians sipped beer in Cairo, and Wingate prosecuted his case for a new command, Churchill removed Wavell as Commander in Chief.

Wavell, with considerable dignity, remarked, 'The Prime Minister is quite right. There ought to be a new eye and a new hand in this theatre.' The new eye and hand was Claude Auchinleck. Wavell was appointed Commander in Chief of India, a virtual job swap with Auchinleck, and was in command there when Japan declared war. He would also be in command when Wingate returned to favour, thanks to his later exploits in Wavell's new backyard.

To add to his predicament, Wingate wrote an 'appreciation' of the campaign in Ethiopia, and as usual he was not diplomatic. The appreciation arrived the day after Wavell had been handed his fate, and thus not particularly good timing. While it offered his theories about guerilla warfare, and how some had performed in practice, he was critical of the initial planning. He described some of his – fortunately unnamed – superiors as 'military apes' and some of his officers as 'the scum of the cavalry brigade'. Wavell, busy cleaning out his desk, reportedly said to one of his colleagues that the appreciation had considerable merit, but could easily see Wingate arrested for insubordination. However, rather than suppress the report, he circulated it, with some of the more vitriolic passages removed, to a small circle. He also referred some parts for further investigation. Wilfred Thesiger said, 'the report caused great resentment, and the enquiries which resulted from it even more'. Wingate's problems – his return to the rank of major, the lack of another appointment, the absence of any reward for his work and the considerable annoyance and dislike caused by his 'appreciation' – had weighed heavily on him, and culminated in his suicide attempt in the first week of July. Thesiger also speculated that 'he became obsessed by the conviction that the British intended to deprive Abyssinia of her independence'. However, the real problem adding to his depressed state was medical in origin.

He was staying at the Continental Hotel, which was home to many British officers in Cairo. On the evening of 4 July, Wingate went into his bathroom, took up his hunting knife and attempted to cut his carotid artery. At the last second he flinched, cutting into his throat but not the artery. Wingate was resolute, however, and though covered in blood he tried for the jugular vein. Again he flinched at the climactic moment, and missed by a whisker. His blood loss was considerable, but not fatal, and he slumped to the floor of the bath-room. One British officer, Household Cavalry officer, Lieutenant David Smiley, speculated that on his way down to the bathroom floor, Wingate pulled the bell to alert the hotel servants.

The noise alerted some fellow officers, including Colonel Cudbert Thornhill, and Smiley, who had just returned from dinner. Smiley and his friends forced the door open and found Wingate lying in a growing pool of blood. He later offered the view that the suicide was staged by Wingate and that pulling the servants' bell ensured he would be found in time. Smiley was not a Wingate fan, saying he was 'half mad, partially a genius, partially a lunatic'.

Wingate was rushed to the 15th General Hospital, and blood was pumped into him as surgeons worked to close the wounds. Biographer Trevor Royle said he had been told the blood loss was so significant that 14 pints were pumped into Wingate, with the replace-ment fluid held in Gordon's Gin bottles, and 'if the spirit didn't get to Wingate, the tonic certainly did'. The sad truth is that doctors found that Wingate was suffering from a severe case of that old Ethiopian problem, malaria. He had had bouts of it since Debra Markos, and the last months of the campaign hadn't had much in the way of rest, recreation, peace or good food. Wingate had been concerned that if the severity of his malaria was on record, it would be another barrier to command, and he already had more than his fair share. Unwisely, he had found a willing local doctor, and began dosing himself with Atabrine, which was the state-of-the-art drug of the time to treat malaria. One of the side-effects of the drug is depression.

One of the first to visit Wingate was Sir Edwin Chapman-Andrews, recently returned to Cairo and working at the Middle East Intelligence Centre. Like the five Australians, he was recov-ering from the campaign, 'as I certainly needed rest and a change and a steady supply of good food as I had lost weight and had had dysentery very badly on the march through Gojjam'.

Chapman-Andrews found Wingate evasive on the reasons for his suicide attempt, with Wingate offering, 'I had a bit of fever and I was a bit beyond myself. I don't know why I did it but at any rate on the spur of the moment I did it.' Wingate then launched into a grisly lecture on the most effective way to cut one's own throat. Hugh Boustead, never a fan of Wingate, visited, and offered practical advice, telling him, 'You bloody fool, why didn't you use a revolver!'

The five Australians also visited, and it was a far more civilised conversation. They talked about future missions together, though all knew it was optimism at best. Despite the ravages of six months of hard living and constant fighting they were still keen to get back into action, preferably on another irregular mission. However, it was soon obvious to them that Wingate would not be fit for operations again for a very long time, if ever. He did lift their spirits, telling Brown that he had recommended him for the Military Cross, and the other men for a raft of decorations. What none of them knew was that the British command wasn't interested in celebrating their fine work in Ethiopia, and in particular the ten operational centres. Brown's Military Cross never eventuated, and though originally disappointed that he had been misled, he later found out that Wingate had recommended him but it had been quashed at a higher level. Ted Body fared a little better, being mentioned in despatches (a military award for gallantry) for 'Distinguished service in the Middle East during the period February 1941 to July 1941'. For the others, official recognition was precisely zero.

Wingate's doctors found that perhaps the most significant cause of his attempted suicide was not an overdosing of Atabrine, but rather cerebral malaria, with one of the doctors noting, 'It [the blood slide] was swarming with malarial parasites.' When sufficiently recovered from his injuries and the bout of malaria, he was sent back to England where he told Lord Horder, the physician looking after him, 'You know, I am not the only great soldier who has tried to commit suicide. There was Napoleon, for instance.' Surprisingly, Horder didn't find that Wingate was suffering from delusions of grandeur or a Napoleonic complex. He later told the War Office that Wingate was fit to return to the war.

In March 1942, Wingate was promoted to colonel and, again under Wavell's orders, was sent to Burma to wage guerilla war against the Japanese, commanding a force that became known as the Chindits. He died on 24 March 1944, when the B25 bomber he was travelling in crashed in Manipur in north-east India. He was on his way back from inspecting his operations.

The five Australians didn't have any luck staying together to fight again with Wingate – nor did they have any luck just staying together. Around six weeks after they returned from Ethiopia, the army doctors decided that all were fit enough to return to war. They were ordered to report to General Blamey, then deputy commander in chief. The good news was that the sergeants would be commissioned as lieutenants. The bad news was that a return to irregular operations with Wingate or anyone else in that theatre of war was not going to happen. Blamey was not keen on the five staying together, so instead the tight unit was split up and returned to the AIF. Brown headed back to the old regiment, the 2/1st Field Regiment; Ken Burke to the 2/2nd Battalion; Ron Wood to the 2/3rd Battalion; Bill Howell to the 29th Infantry Battalion; and Ted Body to the 2/1st Regiment.

Brown was soon back in the fight, this time commanding artillery against the Germans in the height of the North African campaign. Ted Body was the first to be whisked away to join the Officer Cadet Training Unit in Egypt. Burke, Wood and Howell volunteered for 'special duties', and were off the books for a couple of months. Though their activities never made it to formal records, Burke, never a man to brag about what he had been up to, did admit that he had been 'behind the lines' in the Western Desert. The three then joined Ted Body to be hewn into officers and gentlemen.

In the closing months of 1941, the five also had their first taste of their medical future. Though the doctors had pronounced them fit enough for active service, the quality of their health was erratic thanks to malaria, dysentery and a diet as irregular as the forces they commanded. Bouts of malaria and pneumonia would see them all hospitalised on a few occasions each, and Ron Wood had an additional indignity: a serious case of haemorrhoids – horses, mules and camels obviously hadn't agreed with him.

The five lieutenants began the new year in action: Brown, Wood, Howell and Burke were serving in the North Africa campaign around Benghazi and Tobruk, and Ted Body was leading a platoon in Syria. The five were now close to the end of their exploits in the Middle East. Japan had entered the war and Australia was in peril. Churchill wrote, 'We had lost the command of every ocean except the Atlantic. Australia and New Zealand and all the vital islands in their sphere were open to attack.' In the first two weeks of February 1942, one of those vital islands, Singapore, fell to the Japanese. Ken Burke's brother-in-law, Jack McCauley, was in Singapore as the Station Commander, mounting air attacks against the Japanese, and made it out just before the surrender. It was time to start bringing some men home to defend Australia. The five soon returned to Australia via Ceylon, and after little more than a moment of leave, they were back on the frontline, this time in the jungles of New Guinea.

The only formal mention of the Australians' work in ousting the Italians from Gojjam province came in General Platt's report to his superiors in London in September 1941. Broadly, he observed, 'The enemy had three colonial brigades (16 battalions) concentrated on three main forts, Dangila, Burye [Burie] and Debra Markos, with 4 Blackshirt battalions in support.' As for the Australians, it was a passing reference:

> The remainder of the Frontier Battalion (less No 5 coy), the second Ethiopian Bn, No 1 Operational Centre, a platoon of 4 mortars and a Field Propaganda Unit were formed into 'Gideon Force' under the command of Colonel Wingate and assembled in the former Italian Fort of Enjibata [Injibera] on the axial road of Gojjam on 23 February.

The only other operational centre mentioned in his report in action in the Gojjam was No 2 Operational Centre under the Canadian Captain MacKay. History has not treated MacKay well either, as not even his initials appear in any surviving records or contemporary writings. Archibald Wavell could have been referring to the work of the Australians and Mission 101 when he wrote:

> The part played in a great victory by organization and preparation behind the lines seldom receives proper recognition in military history, which is apt to concern itself with the more spectacular movements and chases of the campaign itself.

Platt did not recognise Wingate or the Australians for the tactics that had been pioneered and used so effectively by No 1 Operational Centre. He reported:

> In view of our great poverty of numbers, a new technique had to be thought out for these attacks, which were strikingly successful in inflicting casualties upon the enemy and in lowering his morale. The country was well covered and our forces were thus able to lie up in the daytime, only a few miles from the enemy's positions without detection by his air or native cavalry. Action was taken only at night, when approach marches

reconnoitred during the day were carried out by parties which rarely exceeded 100 men for a single operation and usually numbered 40/50. The alternative methods used were to lay LMGs [light machine-guns] from close range on the enemy's campfires when they were still burning or (more commonly, for the enemy soon adjusted himself to this ruse) to approach, armed simply with bomb, rifle and bayonet, bomb his position from 10 yards range, carry them with the bayonet, beat off the counter-attack, and withdraw before dawn. The hour chosen for these attacks was usually when the enemy was sleepiest, and his customary reaction was to continue with HMGs [heavy machine-guns] and artillery until dawn, thus waging a war of nerves upon himself.

Douglas Dodds-Parker, who spent a chunk of the war in the SOE (Special Operations Executive), ran logistics in Khartoum for the campaign in Ethiopia. In his book on their work, *Setting Europe Ablaze*, he said of Allan Brown and his men, 'They were to add a distinction to the ANZAC reputation for bravery and endurance, and to return safely home.' More significantly, the tactics of the operational centres had formed the basis for the SOE's tactics for the rest of the war. He said:

> The operational centres had proved to be of great significance. Small, well-led units, radio-linked, had served for local resisters to join. They were formed later by SOE as missions in the field, in the Balkans and Italy; and to support immediate operations as operational groups and 'Jedburghs' (teams of three who were part of Operation Jedburgh and were usually parachuted in behind German lines) in France.

While Brown and his men were enjoying a brief moment in the media spotlight, and being blithely ignored by almost all of the British command, the saga of the missing Arnold Wienholt was being resolved. Shortly after Enid Wienholt received the letter from Lieutenant Colonel Airey in which he indicated that Wienholt was missing and believed dead, his passing was publicly marked by the Sydney periodical the *National Journal* on 1 May 1941. The journal described Wienholt as:

... a modern Crusader. Zealous for a just cause, fierce against the aggressor and tender to the oppressed, he took his life in his hands to help the Ethiopians, who he counted his friends. His courage was absolute, matched, as in most great men, by his modesty.

Enid Wienholt was a pragmatic woman, and with her husband's numerous business interests now hanging in a legal limbo, she had to act. It was highly likely that Arnold was dead, so she wrote to British headquarters in Khartoum hoping for some guidance or finality. It wasn't until 11 September 1941, almost a year to the day that Arnold Wienholt died, that a definitive response arrived from Khartoum. It came in the form of a sworn statement by Lieutenant John Hood of the Sudan Defence Force. Neither Enid Wienholt nor the men of No 1 Operational Centre were aware that on 8 July 1941, Hood was ordered to take a patrol from Gallabat to resolve the mystery of the missing Wienholt. Accompanying Hood was Isa Abu Jiar, one of Wienholt's servants who had fled during the Italian attack. Their first stop was at the village of Mutabia where he met the head man, Damotie, who 'was very surly and appeared most unwilling to part with any information concerning the attack on Wienholt's camp on September 10th 1940'. With a bit of encouragement from Hood, Damotie finally 'told me a few things which proved to be lies'. Their relationship took a turn for the worse when Hood searched Damotie's house and found Wienholt's ground sheet.

The next evening, while camped outside the village, Hood had a visitor, Yasin Sageir, a local Gumz tribesman who was also the local representative of the 'Occupied Enemy Territory Administration'. According to Sageir, the nearby Italian camp consisted of one native corporal and 17 native 'other ranks'. The group had picked up Wienholt's tracks and persuaded 20 local Gumz tribesmen to track him down; as a sweetener for the deal they were given rifles and ammunition. One of the tribesmen was Damotie, which accounted for his reticence to tell the truth. Thanks to excellent tracking skills, they found Wienholt and his party, and the Italian troops attacked. According to Sageir, the Gumz held back and only fired the rifles into the air for effect. Wienholt and his party had dispersed by the time the Gumz had entered their camp.

Armed with an apparently reasonable account of the action, Hood and his men co-opted five Gumz as guides and set off to the scene of Wienholt's last stand, a four-and-a-half-hour march from Mutabia, and close to the Shinfa River. They found the camp easily, and Hood set about making an inventory. Among donkey bones, spent ammunition, remains of saddles and so on, he found a tube of Macleans toothpaste on the site of Wienholt's tent, and the remains of a leather boot believed to have belonged to him. Isa Abu Jiar then took Hood in the direction that Wienholt had taken as he made a break for the cover of the bush. Hood recalled:

> ... about three hundred yards away in a low boggy hollow there was a pile of bones in an advanced state of decomposition. These may be Wienholt's, as they were found in a place in which a wounded man may lie down for a breather.

Hood collected a selection for later inspection, and concluded:

> From the evidence still remaining there is no doubt that Wienholt's camp was taken completely by surprise – no empty British ammunition was found and it seems unlikely that Wienholt's party fired a single shot. The Gumz say that all camp equipment (tents, bed, basin etc) and the remaining donkeys were taken back to Gallabat on Metemma by the Italians.

Shortly after Hood's statement arrived in Sydney, Enid Wienholt received a letter from Major Robert Cheesman in Khartoum. He reiterated Hood's findings and added a little more, telling her that he had also taken a statement from Liji Wandin Agagaw, a local chief in the area around Gallabat. Wandin Agagaw had escorted Dan Sandford and his men in the advance party and had been told to expect another Englishman, Arnold Wienholt. However, the Englishman hadn't appeared, and he was later told that the Englishman had been deserted by his guides and had been killed.

Wandin Agagaw, under orders from Sandford, had sent out a search party that had finally found the remains of a small shelter, and 'two human bones were found at separate places near a camp site that might have been occupied by Arnold Wienholt's convoy'. Though hardly a definitive account, it married well with the results of Hood's inquiries and the statement by Isa Abu Jiar, and was sufficient to help Enid Wienholt sort out the family's affairs.

On 10 October 1941, the Supreme Court of Queensland declared that Arnold Wienholt was dead. Probate of his will was granted on 14 November 1941, and his estate totalled 180 079 pounds, 17 shillings and seven pence – a healthy estate considering you could buy a slice of Sydney real estate for a few hundred pounds. Enid Wienholt married Ivan Lewis, her late husband's former employee and sometime colleague in Africa, in March 1942. Like his five unknown colleagues in Mission 101, Arnold Wienholt, the once famous politician, grazier, activist, big-game hunter, soldier and spy, slipped into obscurity. Allan Brown, Ken Burke, Ted Body, Ron Wood and Bill Howell never knew of Arnold Wienholt's involvement in Mission 101.

19

LATTER DAYS

Bill Howell was killed in action at Buna on the northern coast of New Guinea on 18 December 1942. He was 33 years old. Buna was the main supply base for the Japanese positions on the Kokoda Trail. The battle began in November 1942, and the Australian and American troops didn't see victory until the beginning of January 1943. In the battle 2870 Allied troops were killed.

A soldier who had joined the 2/1st with Howell, Body, Burke and Wood – and like them had fought through the Middle East and then headed to New Guinea – recounted:

> We were all very sorry to lose Bill from our unit, and our little gang way back in 1940 when he went with some of our other cobbers on the special mission to Abyssinia. When I came up here I tried without success to locate him, our regiment never having been in camp anywhere near his battalion. A part of the regiment did, however, have guns in position where Bill was killed, and some of the boys who knew him have told me they saw him and he waved back to them as he went forward at the head of his men into action. They say he went along heedless of danger, in his natural old happy keen and fearless manner and must have been an inspiration to the men he was leading.

Bill's commanding officer, Major William Parry-Okeden, wrote to the Howell family shortly after Bill's death, saying:

> I want to express my very deepest sympathy to you. Bill was one of the grandest chaps I have known. Unfortunately in this cruel war all the best are either killed or wounded eventually. Bill's continuous devotion to duty and personal courage in leading his men were only equalled by a very few. These brave chaps lost

their lives saving many others and I cannot express in words the high esteem they hold with us all. You may like to know that Bill did not suffer, as he died instantly.

The remaining four Australians spent the balance of World War II ferrying between the battlefronts in New Guinea and the Solomon Islands, and back home to Australia for brief periods of rest, advanced training and longer periods of illness. They all suffered regular and ferocious bouts of malaria, as well as a return of dysentery and the addition of dengue fever – all this before they were ducking bullets, shells and strafing by Japanese aircraft.

Ken Burke's maverick disposition earned him a mention and a touch of respectful notoriety in October 1942 during the battle of Eora Creek. Author Paul Ham in his book *Kokoda* observed:

> More Australians died at Eora Creek than in any other battle in the mountains, with the exception of Isurava. For the first time, the Japanese had an overwhelming geographic advantage: the high ridge line above the Eora Creek gorge.

All too familiar type of country for Burke. The Japanese had set up their guns in reinforced bunkers, and when the Australians arrived it became a bloodbath. Paul Ham wrote:

> They halted on a partially exposed spur some 900 feet about the south bank. The Japanese on the north side had a clear view of this feature, waited for the soldiers to crowd up, then shelled and machine-gunned them.

The Australians withdrew, slithering back up the muddy slope with bullets whizzing around them, and clinging to trees and anything they could use to stop themselves from sliding back down and into the maelstrom.

Brigadier JE Lloyd decided to split his force, sending one group to outflank the Japanese to the west, and the others to try their luck crossing the log bridges, being horribly exposed to the Japanese guns. One of the officers charged with taking his men across the log bridges was Lieutenant Ken Burke, who knew more about tactics in a situation like this than most of his superiors put together. Paul Ham wrote, 'on the night of the 22nd an Australian reconnaissance patrol led by Lieutenant Ken Burke went down to the bank of the creek. A Japanese machine-gun raked them across the water, leaving thirteen dead or wounded on the bank.' Burke decided that to go further was pointless and suicidal and refused. He reportedly said to the commander of the 1st Battalion, Paul Cullen, 'Fuck Brigadier Lloyd'. Shortly after, he managed to offend his superiors again and in doing so inadvertently found an ally in General Douglas MacArthur.

Burke's brother-in-law, Jack McCauley, who spent some time during the war attached to General Douglas MacArthur's staff, was told a story about Ken by MacArthur himself. The battle around the Kokoda Trail was in full swing, and Australian intelligence from the front was telling MacArthur that the Japanese had the Australians outnumbered. What heightened the problem was that the bulk of the Australian troops were not regular army; they were horribly inexperienced and poorly equipped to fight any battle let alone one in the mud, rain and jungle of the Owen Stanley Range. MacArthur told one of his American generals to take his men and reinforce the Australians, and to 'lead your men, inspire your men, and if you get killed doing it, well, so be it'.

He took MacArthur's orders literally, and while leading his men up a track, was stopped by a burly, mud-stained and determined Australian who calmly stepped out of the jungle and pointed a Thomson machine-gun directly at the chest of the general. The general had little clue about whom he was dealing with and tried the 'Don't you know who I am?' routine, which failed, and then name-dropped, saying he was acting under direct orders from Douglas MacArthur. The gentleman with the machine-gun, Lieutenant Ken Burke, was not swayed and responded:

> I don't care if you're the Lord God himself. My orders are: nobody up the track, nobody down the track. So if you would like to take another step, I will be obliged to shoot the head off your fucking shoulders, sir.

According to Jack McCauley, MacArthur was highly amused by Ken Burke. For his numerous sins, Ken Burke was never even formally chastised, but instead he was seconded to the newly formed Z Special Forces, and ended up around Rabaul and Bougainville, doing what he did well: fostering insurrection with the locals and blowing things up.

Ted Body's knee injuries in Ethiopia caught up with him, but not before he had again been mentioned in despatches, this time for 'distinguished and gallant services in the south west Pacific area'. In July 1944 he was discharged from the army. Brown, Burke and Wood were still serving officers, and still fighting, when the war drew to a close a year later, following Germany's unconditional surrender on 8 May 1945. Victory against Japan soon followed, and on 2 September 1945 their surrender was signed on board the USS *Missouri* in Tokyo Bay.

The three men were soon discharged from the army and returned to civilian life, after fighting from the very first battles to the very last of a war that ran for nearly six years. Despite the close bonds formed in their early days of training and in the epic times in Ethiopia, they did not keep in close contact. Only Ken Burke and Allan Brown kept in touch, with Allan Brown often telling his family stories of his colourful mate. These were men who did not say much about their war. No bragging, no wistful reminiscences, no regular reunions and chat of the 'good old days'. The war was behind them, but the battering they had taken lived on.

Ron Wood was discharged from the army on 29 July 1945, and returned home to his parents in Manly. War had kicked the hell out of him both physically and mentally. Shortly before his discharge he had been diagnosed with 'mental strain', the beginnings of which may have harked back to the bout of illness that caused him to be sent to Khartoum for treatment and rest after the battle to take Debra Markos. The marriage he had planned before enlistment had also fallen through after nearly six years away fighting. He couldn't work, and he eventually moved away from his parents and spent his final days unemployed and alone in the less-than-salubrious boarding house known as the Carlton Private Hotel in Victoria Street, Manly. On 11 September 1950, Ron Wood was found dead in his room. The cause of death was 'disease of the heart – myocardial degeneration'. The small funeral was attended by his family and army mates. He was 44 years old.

Ken Burke was discharged from the army on 14 December 1945. Though he still had his sense of humour, he wasn't in great physical condition, so the days of competitive football and tennis were long gone. The dashing lifestyle he had led before the war was just a memory. Instead of mingling with his peers, now well established in Australia's commercial life, he opted for an existence with as little stress as possible. Shortly after the war he married an extremely feisty Australian Women's Army Service drill sergeant named Grace, whom he met when she was running a boatshed in Nowra on the south coast of New South Wales and he was working as a sales representative for a stock-feed company. They shared many things, including a racy vocabulary. After they married, they moved back to Sydney, eventually settling on the northern beaches. Ken golfed, surfed and kept an interest in horse racing and rugby union, but he enjoyed these interests either on his own or occasionally with his wife. His involvement in Anzac Day services was marked by both brevity and sobriety.

By the late 1950s his health had deteriorated even further. The occasional bouts of malaria were becoming more frequent, other illnesses were taking their toll, and his regular 18 holes of golf at the Long Reef course was down to an occasional nine, if he was lucky. By the 1960s he was spending a chunk of his time in the Concord Repatriation Hospital. He finally gave up the long battle on 5 October 1966 at the age of 60.

Allan Brown reached the rank of major and was also awarded an Order of the British Empire for his 'outstanding leadership and devotion to duty' and 'organising ability and personal courage of the highest order' in Wewak. When he was discharged from the army on 17 May 1946, he resumed his career with the Commonwealth Bank. While recovering from some injuries at the Lady Davidson Home in Sydney, he met a visitor, Audrey, and they were soon married and began a family. Allan also resumed his accountancy studies and later joined the Australian Taxation office, retiring in May 1977.

While Allan Brown, Ted Body and the very ill Ken Burke thought their exploits in Ethiopia had been all but forgotten, they were wrong. In March 1966, Allan Brown, then living a genteel existence with his family in Mosman, found a surprise waiting for him in the mail. Though the British military hierarchy had chosen to ignore the Australians' work in Ethiopia, Haile Selassie had never forgotten the debt he owed. To celebrate the 25th anniversary of the 'triumphal entry in 1941 of His Imperial Majesty Haile Selassie I, Emperor of Ethiopia, to His capital', Allan Brown was invited to Addis Ababa to 'commemorate and honour the men who participated in the campaign to drive out the Fascist invader'. Brown would join a selection of the other British and South African officers who had fought with Mission 101 and Gideon Force. The only other men from an operational centre who were invited were two NCOs from the No 3.

Allan Brown was delighted to accept the invitation. When not participating in the formal parts of the trip, he dined with Haile Selassie, took a tour of the stables and the obligatory lion enclosure, and was chauffeured around some of the countryside on newly sealed roads – a dramatic change from the mud and scrub he had slogged about on foot during his last visit.

Haile Selassie also made sure that Australians knew about the involvement of their countrymen in freeing Ethiopia. In 1968, at the age of 78, he made a state visit to Australia, the only continent the wandering head of state hadn't visited in his long career. At a dinner in his honour, he spoke of 'the aid given by these Australians who fought a hard war in the then feudal kingdom'.

Though the Emperor was getting on in years, his reign did not end with death from natural causes. In 1974, Ethiopia was devastated by famine, one of the numerous natural disasters that afflict the nation. Outside the country he was respected as the world's longest-serving head of state. Inside the country, the people were not happy with the old Emperor and his rule, and as is common in Africa, a Communist military junta known as the Derg seized power. Haile Selassie died on 27 August 1975, reportedly from respiratory failure. His doctors, however, reckoned his death was a little premature, and rumours swirled around Addis Ababa suggesting that the respiratory failure was caused by a pillow placed firmly over his head by Mengistu Haile Mariam, who would become leader of the ruling regime. As is common practice with Communist dictators, Mengistu moved into the Emperor's palace, and was reported to have had Haile Selassie's body concreted under the toilet to make a point a few times per day.

Allan Brown kept an active interest in, and great love for, Ethiopia even during these dark years. Unfortunately he did not live to see Ethiopia freed once again. The quietly spoken and dignified grandfather, Allan Brown, died on 14 December 1988 at the age of 74.

The last man standing was Ted Body. He returned to the family property, Bundemar, and when in Sydney was a debonair addition to the social scene. His sense of humour and mischief were very much intact. One unsuspecting doorman at Ted's hotel of choice – and not by coincidence the hub of Sydney's nightlife, the Chevron in Potts Point – got the Body treatment. When the dashing but rather under-the-weather Mr Body asked the young man to drive him home, he readily agreed. Mr Body was, after all, a well-known and well-liked patron. Ted slipped into the backseat of the Oldsmobile and off they set, Ted giving directions in between dozing off. As they climbed the Blue Mountains, the penny finally dropped: home for Mr Body was not a local apartment, but near Trangie, around 400 kilometres from Potts Point. Ted arranged to have the unsuspecting young man taken back to Sydney, with a decent tip.

In 1953 he took over as studmaster at Bundemar, following in his father's footsteps as one of the 'best sheepmen in the west'. Bundemar was noted not only for the quality of its sheep but as a magnet for young men entering the pastoral industry. Ted 'instilled in all of them a great feeling of achievement and superiority, and was recognised as one of the generals in the industry'. In 1964 he married Joan and they remained at Bundemar until it was sold in the early 1970s. Ted and Joan then moved to the northern beaches of Sydney. The last Australian member of Brown's No 1 Operational Centre died on 28 April 1994 at the age of 78.

The work of the patriots is celebrated each year in Ethiopia with a public holiday on 5 May, the day that Haile Selassie returned to Addis Ababa. Shortly after the war, Selassie rewarded each of the patriots with a small plot of land to farm. During the Derg regime, these lands were confiscated and many patriots died destitute. Some patriots, usually those who fought as children or young teens, survived the war, poverty and the Derg, and now receive a small government pension of around sixty birr (about AU$3.60 per week).

The British role in the liberation of the country is remembered by streets in Addis Ababa named after some of the prominent players including Churchill, Wavell, Cunningham and Wingate. The Sandford International School, established by Dan and Christine Sandford after the war, remains one of the country's best schools.

ACKNOWLEDGEMENTS

Researching a slice of history that wasn't well reported at the time was a fascinating challenge, and I am deeply in debt to the terrific people who gave me a hand. My apologies to anyone I have inadvertently omitted, and I can only blame my fading memory and perhaps an excess of wine and the odd martini (for medicinal purposes) on my recent travels.

Coming to grips with Ethiopia and the logistics of getting about were made much easier by Jason Andean and his merry band – they also did a fine line in hospitality too. The Land Cruiser is infinitely preferable to camels and mules.

John Mellors of the Anglo Ethiopian Society in London for pointing me to the various experts on Ethiopia.

Andrew and Martha Chadwick for their guidance and advice on the patriots.

Steve Kippax for his insight on the Public Record Office in Kew and Craig Brown for his expertise on the SOE.

Allan Miles for knowing who to call and giving me an introduction.

Richard Pankhurst for his entertaining emails and advice on matters Ethiopian.

Martin Hislop and the Melba Suite in Kingston upon Thames – always a fine place for peace, good conversation and one of those glasses of wine I mentioned earlier. The terrific staff at the Imperial War Museum in London and the Australian War Memorial in Canberra – they make research a dream.

The staff at the Fryer Library at the University of Queensland for access to their treasure trove of information on Arnold Wienholt. The staff at Sydney's Mitchell Library and the State Library of NSW – national treasures.

Diane Irving of the Trangie Historical Society.

Neil and Pam Body for their help with Ted.

Audrey Brown, Allan Brown's wife.

Sarah Wynn for Bill Howell's letters and memorabilia – a pot of gold for a researcher.

David Burke (no relation to Ken) – Bill Howell's nephew for some anecdotes.

Adrian Burke and Lance Stewart for their help with our mutual uncle, Ken Burke.

Tom Miller for his advice on the scent of Sri Lanka when approached by ship.

Jenny Pearce of The King's School for snippets on the former students.

To my aunt, the late Grace Burke, for wonderful storytelling up until her departure at 96.

As ever, my great thanks to my agent Lyn Tranter, and to everyone at Pan Macmillan for their simple brilliance in turning my meanderings into a book – they help make writing the pleasure it is.

AUTHOR'S NOTE

Ken Burke was my uncle, and though I was only very young when he died, he did give me a few snippets of his adventures both in Ethiopia and in New Guinea. Like most of his colleagues, these weren't subjects that were regularly aired. I think he shared some of the stories simply to put an end to a child's relentless questioning. Many of his stories were later passed on to me by his wife Grace, who died in 2009 at the age of 96. She was a terrific source of information, and a great asset to the distillers of Scotland right up until her final days.

Tracking down the relatives of the five men required me to dust off some old detective skills, and it was well worth it. My deep gratitude goes to Audrey Brown, Allan's widow; to Neil and Pam Body, the Body family biographers and source of a few entertaining yarns about the bon vivant that was Ted Body; to Sarah Wynn, who had kept many of Bill Howell's letters and photos sent to her mother from 'beloved uncle Billy'. My detective skills, however, failed me with Ron Wood. With the death of his brother and sister-in-law many years ago, chances of tracing any surviving family members became remote.

While there have been a few books written about the Ethiopian campaign, the involvement of Arnold Wienholt, Allan Brown, Ken Burke, Ron Wood, Ted Body and Bill Howell received scant mention, and as is often the case in war, accounts of the actions tend to vary. Fortunately contemporary articles and the letters and accounts of the Australians themselves have helped me to tell the real story. Where variations between accounts have occurred, I've tried to dig down to the correct or most likely information, and any errors are mine. When talking about towns in Ethiopia, I've used the most common modern spelling, as I found they tend to be a moveable feast.

SELECT BIBLIOGRAPHY

Australia in the War 1939–1945, Australian War Memorial, 1952

The First at War, The Story of the 2/1st Infantry Battalion 1939–1945, EC Giveny Association of First Infantry Battalions Editorial, c1987

Guerrilla War in Abyssinia, WED Allen, Penguin, 1943

Fire in the Night, John Bierman and Colin Smith, Macmillan, 2000

The Ethiopian War 1935–1941, Angelo Del Boca, University of Chicago Press, 1969

The Wind of the Morning, Hugh Boustead, Chatto & Windus, 1971

Wingate's Phantom Army, Wilfred Burchett, Muller, 1946

The Second World War, Winston Churchill, Cassell & Co, 1959

One Man in His Time, Xan Fielding, Macmillan, 1990

An Australian and a Hero, Cyril G Grabs, Darling Downs Institute Press, 1987

Kokoda, Paul Ham, ABC Books, 2004

Six Years in Support, EV Haywood, Angus & Robertson, 1959

Chapman-Andrews and the Emperor, Peter Leslie, Pen & Sword Books, 2005

To Benghazi, Gavin Long, Australian War Memorial, 1952

The Secret History of the S.O.E Special Operations Executive 1940–1945, William Mackenzie, St Ermin's Press, 2000

Orde Wingate: Irregular Soldier, Trevor Royle, Weidenfeld & Nicolson, 1995

Ethiopia under Haile Selassie, Christine Sandford, JM Dent & Sons, 1946

Bare Feet and Bandoliers, David Shirreff, The Radcliffe Press, 1995

The Eccentric Mr Wienholt, Rosamond Siemon, University of Queensland Press, 2005

Bardia: Myth, Reality and the Heirs of Anzac, Craig Stockings, UNSW Press, 2009

The Life of My Choice, Wilfred Thesiger, WW Norton & Company, 1987

The Work of a Scout, Arnold Wienholt, Andrew Melrose, 1923

The Africans' Last Stronghold, Arnold Wienholt, London, 1938

Visit our website and discover thousands of other
History Press books.

www.thehistorypress.co.uk